Cease Fire! Cease Fire!
COUNCILMAN CHUCK, A HERO(IN) ADDICTION

Chuck Richardson
WITH
Monte Richardson

Cease Fire! Cease Fire!
COUNCILMAN CHUCK, A HERO(IN) ADDICTION

Copyright © 2021 Henry Wallace "Chuck" Richardson

Cover Composition by Visual Appeal, LLC, www.visualappealllc.com

Book Formatting by Liona Design Co., www.lionadesignco.com

All rights reserved.

ISBN 978-0-9981672-1-3

Library of Congress Control Number: 2021909096

First Edition. All rights reserved. No portion of this book may be reproduced, stored in a retrieval system, or transmitted in any form or by any means — including by not limited to electronic, mechanical, digital, photocopy, recording, scanning, blogging or other — except for brief quotations in critical reviews, blogs, or articles, without the prior written permission of the authors.

1. BIOGRAPHY & AUTOBIOGRAPHY / Political
2. HISTORY / Military / Vietnam War
3. SELF-HELP / Substance Abuse & Addictions / Drugs

Acknowledgments

My sincere appreciation to Dr. Raymond P. Hylton, professor of History at Virginia Union University. In addition to his insightful Foreword, Dr. Hylton's encouragement and guidance provided impetus for this book.

I'm deeply grateful to my sister, Valerie R. Jackson, for her valuable editorial input. To my daughter, Nichole R. Armstead, who persevered through so much to help her dad get this done.

And to the following people who, at various stages, helped a senior citizen who was not exactly a computer expert: Jonathan 'Jon' Vazquez, Eric King, Chandra Wilkins, Thomasine Stroble, Gary Black and Latika Lee. Thank you all so much.

Special Acknowledgment

To my younger brother, Monte, who helped me take fifty unbelievable years, spread over dozens of legal pads, and make one unbelievable story from it. More importantly, however, is the enhancement it has contributed to our relationship and the increased perspective we gained of each other. I am fortunate to have him, and six other siblings, in my life.

It is rare that in today's world of self-centered, jealous, and competitive spirits that a family of eight siblings can be blessed with maintaining unconditional love and honest respect for one another. Charles, Valerie, Ruth, Monte, Vicki, Robert, and Rick, all have stood by me and tolerated the faults and frailties that many would have long forsaken. Their steadfast loyalty sustained my spirit and hope in times of trouble, difficulty, and wariness.

I would, therefore, be remiss not to acknowledge their special individual support—and significance in my life. It is comforting to note that while fortunes may take flight or fate brings pernicious challenges, when so many friendships release their bond, there remains, still, my seven brothers and sisters.

Dedication

re·cov·er·y /rəˈkəv(ə)rē/

1. a return to a normal state of health, mind, or strength.

Easier said than done. I've dedicated a hundred-thousand words to say it. It seems that life itself is a series of recoveries, from minor falls to major collapses, each instructive and evolutionary. This work is dedicated to those in a *life* of recovery, the chronic demand to struggle for a "normal" state again. Those for whom there is a constant form of echo in the body, or mind, that splits a life apart; recovery must be reached each and every day.

It is dedicated to those who are recovering from the myriad wounds of an insidious war, like my brothers from Vietnam. From the primal scream of substance addiction, like those who shared my battle as an addicted veteran for over two decades—and like those who fight it today. To those recovering from the vile wounds of racist bigotry, deprivation, and an unjust justice system, like my people as a whole. I dedicate this to the millions who have faced pernicious battles with gambling, alcohol or drugs, PTSD, and other emotional and physical traumas, and still fight each day. And, to those *unable to recover* from the loss of a child or spouse.

As a society, the expression of empathy toward each other, one might think, would be expected. But our notion of "exceptionalism" and "rugged individualism" inhibits that response. We generally dismiss as weak the inability to overcome injuries of the mind, whether chemical or emotional, viewing the need as somehow selfish, and often dealt with punitively. I know recovery, I know the battles, the pain, the fear—and self-loathing. And I am thankful for the dedication others have shown me.

"There but for the grace of God go I," my mother would say. A grace seemingly without rhyme or reason, unless perhaps, to test *our* grace. Yes, easier said than done, but I am doing it, too. Believe me, trust your struggle, your fortitude—and the sincerity of those who love you. To those in the battle, this is for you.

~ Chuck

Table of Contents

FOREWORD	**8**
CHAPTER 1: ONE MAN'S TREASURE	**15**
CHAPTER 2: IS IT WORTH IT?	**29**
The Draft	44
CHAPTER 3: THE THOUSAND YARD STARE	**54**
Que Son Valley	59
Mortar Attacks	68
CHAPTER 4: FEAR'S FOOTPRINT	**70**
Instinct	72
Heroin	75
Texas Pete	81
Sometimes It's Just "F-It, Let's Eat!"	83
CHAPTER 5: PLAYING WAR	**88**
The Strength in Peaceful Voices	92
Black Vets	96
CHAPTER 6: AS THE WORLD RETURNED	**104**
Accountable Representation	118
Power	129
Wainwright	132
Project One	136
CHAPTER 7: ZORRO	**144**
Getting Credit: The City Stadium	149
One Swimming Pool	152
The Uprush and Downfalls of Heroin	157

CHAPTER 8: DON'T BLINK, JUST ACT   **164**
   MLK Holiday   *167*
   Henry, Doug and Maynard   *172*
   ...and Uncle Roy   *177*
   C-SPAN   *178*
   Catching a Purse Snatcher   *183*

CHAPTER 9: AN INFINITE DEBT   **188**
   If You Think It Hurts Now, Wait Until Tonight   *191*

CHAPTER 10: THE FOG OF MORE   **196**
   Undercoated   *204*
   Busted   *208*
   Raw, Honest, and In Front of Hurting People   *229*

CHAPTER 11: WHO WAS I FOOLING   **235**
   Drawing the Line   *237*

CHAPTER 12: THE LONG CAUSE: MONUMENT AVENUE   **263**
   Shallow Excuses for Symbols of Oppression   *265*
   Arthur Ashe   *271*
   And Now, An N-word from Our Sponsor   *275*

CHAPTER 13: NOW IT'S HISTORY   **278**
   Grand Jury   *286*

CHAPTER 14: FORTITUDE   **302**
   Rightful Pain   *309*
   Dirty Red   *313*
   Politics: Fighting the Landfill   *317*
   What Matters Now   *327*

Foreword

Raymond Pierre Hylton
Professor of History, Virginia Union University

It is often a measure of a person's uniqueness when his/her supporters and detractors alike consistently refer to them in superlatives. Chuck Richardson is just such a rare individual. He is one of the most colorful and controversial Richmond political figures of recent decades, and one factor that even his most bitter adversaries would not deny was the dash, verve, dynamism, and commitment he displayed while serving on Richmond City Council from 1977-1995.

Councilman Chuck (as he likes to be referred to) was the youngest of the five Black candidates in Richmond, Virginia, who were elected to the first Black majority Council in Richmond's history and who then picked the first Black man (Henry L. Marsh, III) to be mayor of the former Capital of the Confederacy. The impact of someone as articulate, outspoken, and well dressed as Chuck who took an unpopular political position favoring Black people, poor people, gay people, Muslims, and other minority groups was bound to ruffle the feathers of Richmond's White conservative population. He kept them irate, and his constituents thrilled as they reelected him time and again.

But there was a rub to this dashing, heroic figure that he displayed, a secret life that he kept hidden for ten years. He had brought home with him from Vietnam an on-and-off heroin addiction that he publicly admitted to. In 1987, Richardson was on trial in a possession of narcotics (heroin) case that would turn the Richmond, Virginia, judiciary and political world, so to speak, on its heels. To understand the case, in fact to understand anything about the entire Chuck Richardson story, one must understand the man, the city, and how much race has played, and continues to play, in our lives as Americans. Not to equate them, but before Marion Barry, there was Chuck Richardson. Before the O.J. Simpson trial and others, as race demonstrated itself, even in the late 20th Century, as still the key piece of evidence for defense—or—prosecution, Richardson's case foretold the impact of the evolving power of Black citizens in America.

The contours of Chuck Richardson's life were carved by the realities of the 1950's-1960's Virginia society within which he and other young African Americans had to cope as second-class citizens, or lower. This was the Virginia dominated politically by Senator Harry F. Byrd, Sr., who had re-forged a powerful Conservative Democratic machine that had monopolized power since the turn of the 20th Century. Byrd served as Governor of Virginia from 1926-1930, and in the U. S. Senate from 1933-1965. Nearly every office holder at the State and local level depended on his support, followed his every whim, and almost religiously enforced his ideas on racial segregation and disfranchisement of minority voters. The young Chuck Richardson felt some of the sting of the racist system and was often bullied and subjected to racial epithets by White classmates at formerly all-White Henrico High School, which he had been among the first to desegregate. But he also had the chance to witness the Byrd Machine begin to fall apart, and a new era to begin to take shape.

There was the 1951 student boycott in Prince Edward County, Virginia. African American students and their parents had for years been robbed with inadequate, even decrepit, school facilities while the blatantly racist Byrd Machine Board of Supervisors lavished funding on the White schools. When crowding at the Black high school, R. R. Moton, in Farmville, went beyond unacceptable levels and the only response by the supervisors was to prop up some flimsy tar-paper shacks, the students went out in protest and filed a lawsuit.

In 1956, the Richmond Crusade for Voters was organized to challenge the White establishment's stranglehold on municipal government, and on January 1, 1959, Dr. Wyatt Tee Walker held the First Pilgrimage of Prayer at what was then called The Mosque (now the Altria Theater), which resulted in Richmond's first mass protest Civil Rights demonstration. And, of course, on the national stage, there was the May 17, 1954 Brown vs. the Board ruling against racial segregation (one of the cases included in the decision was the one filed by the student protestors in Prince Edward County: Dorothy Davis vs. The Prince Edward County Board of Supervisors.) This was followed by the Montgomery Bus Boycott in 1955-1956 and the Little Rock Desegregation Crisis in 1957.

On February 22, 1960, 34 students from Virginia Union University—including Chuck Richardson's future sister and brother-in-law—were incarcerated in the first mass arrest of the Civil Rights Movement while participating in a sit-in protesting segregated facilities in downtown Richmond. Richardson later attended that same university and met his future wife there. The Freedom Rides, Albany Movement, Birmingham Movement, March on Washington, John F. Kennedy Assassination, Mississippi Freedom Summer, escalation of the Vietnam War, and Black Power Movements followed during the tumultuous 1960's.

Chuck Richardson was then drafted into the Marines and went on a tour of duty in Vietnam that—for him as well as others—would prove to be a harrowing, nightmarish, and life-altering experience. For Chuck Richardson, Vietnam would not only encompass horrific memories, but also the heroin addiction, which he had to battle in secret for years to come and which would threaten to destroy him completely.

Despite the obstacles, African Americans started to make inroads into the political realm; in 1968, Dr. William Ferguson Reid was the first African American elected to the Virginia House of Delegates since 1891, and the following year, L. Douglas Wilder was elected to the Virginia State Senate as the first African American to serve there since 1890. In 1970, Dr. Miles Jerome Jones became Chair of the Richmond School Board; and in 1977, Dr. Franklin Gayles became the first Black Richmond City Treasurer—a post to which Chuck Richardson's daughter, Nichole Richardson Armstead, would later be elected in 2017. And, as mentioned above, that same year saw Chuck Richardson's political debut as City Councilman.

For years, the White conservative clique that ran affairs

in Richmond kept defying the city's changing demographics and locking out African Americans and others opposed to them through an at-large city council election system and annexing predominately White sections of neighboring Henrico and Chesterfield Counties. Under such high-sounding titles as "Richmond Forward" and "The Team of Progress," this clique perpetuated its racist policies until the courts suspended their right to annex county land and ordered the implementation of a district representation system for city council seats. Now, at last, the city's African American population achieved its fair share of representation, and talented individuals like Chuck Richardson were accorded the opportunity to contribute.

Like his childhood—and present—hero, Zorro ("the Fox"), Chuck Richardson combined audacity to a strong sense of social justice. Similarly, he has made his share of friends and enemies, and has certainly been cast down on more than one occasion. But like very many of his generation, he is resilient and has always persevered and come back in strength.

>Raymond Pierre Hylton
>*Professor of History, Virginia Union University*

Cease Fire! Cease Fire!
COUNCILMAN CHUCK, A HERO(IN) ADDICTION

CHAPTER 1

One Man's Treasure

Was it really Hell? It had to be! I was looking right into it. I was barely six or seven years old and I was seeing Hell, burning and flaring deep under the earth with a sickening smell. I was on my knees, bent with my head twisting to see if I could see it all—all of Hell! I called my brother, Butch, to look and see if maybe the Devil and his demons were stirring down there. As a child, my concept of "Hell" was simply what I had been told it was: a burning netherworld of eternal suffering and pain where bad people went; purgatory. I was scared but fascinated, hesitant and wondering to myself—if I yelled, would someone answer and beg for help—and if I should if they did?

If it was not Hell, well, then, my mother was wrong, and she was never wrong. My mother was not only wrong that day... she was joking. I had run home to tell her that the earth was burning underground and that we had seen the glowing walls of a fire without flame in some places. It was so unbelievable she didn't believe me. She dismissed it and brushed me off saying it was, "Hell, and you'd better stay away."

I learned later that I had not seen Hell, and I learned even later in life that Hell can look like, or be, anything at all, just like heaven; that they are places: by fate or by fault, reaped not from the depths of the earth but the core of the mind and the heart. No, I had not seen Hell, but dangerous burning methane gas. The fusion of everything from

Cease Fire! Cease Fire!

My mother, Ruth holding me, a new baby boy in 1948.

old food to clothes to bottles and tires compressed upon itself over and over, day after day, fermenting and releasing a gas that would literally catch fire at times deep in the earth. I had stumbled by a large crack that allowed me to see 'the Devil's workplace.' When I was a child, we lived next to a landfill... a dump.

All kinds of stuff were left at the dump about fifty to sixty yards from our house; in the late forties the area became ground zero for putting things out of sight. I was, at the most, about six-years old when I first remember seeing the trucks and bulldozers pouring smoke and moving the trash and dirt. We were not allowed to go to the dump, but by seven, boys will be boys. Some businesses would make routine trips to the dump and, in many instances, some valuable things were left there. Furniture, clothing, broken toys—everything you could think of. I recall the "Snyders" man would leave fruit, groceries, candy, and other perishables, much of which had not yet spoiled.

Each day would also reveal a rush of human bodies from the 17th Street bottom where impoverished Black people came up over the Ford Avenue hill from behind a tree line and onto the area looking for anything of value. One thing that we found a couple times was cash... Confederate cash. Butch, Valerie, and I once found whole stacks of it. I thought it was so pretty: pink and purple and gray with fancy writing and pictures of the Richmond capitol building that adorned it. It was rumored that a large load of it had been dumped there early on. I have no idea what happened to the stuff we found; it's likely there must have been a huge amount, though, given Richmond probably had more cash than any other place in the South at that time. But, most likely, it all burned, appropriately, in the pits of Hell and methane.

We lived on Ford Avenue in the section of Richmond known as Church Hill. The dump was located in a poor Black area, of course, and much of Richmond's White trash (no pun) was dumped there. After the city officially closed the landfill and stopped activity, Butch and I would walk across it to a store on the other side, Eugene's, up on the hillside at Mecklenburg and Wood Streets. It was during those walks we could sometimes see underground fires actually burning, gaseous methane fires beneath the ground. It was an amazing sight to witness beneath the eroded areas where small openings revealed them.

My mother, Ruth, raised her four young children there while

she and my dad weren't much more than kids themselves; they were in their twenties, and four additional siblings would come later in life. Mama was always teaching us her strong faith in Jesus and the Bible, telling us Bible stories almost every night. We, nor anybody I knew, had a television, so Butch, Valerie, Ruthie and I were painted scenes of Bible "miracles." My favorite story didn't really have a miracle, but more skill and courage than anything: 'David and Goliath.' Many nights I fell asleep bewildered by the thought of 'walking on water' or living in the 'belly of a fish' or a blind man seeing again with 'spit and mud.' But I had no doubt it was true; my mother's faith gave her children belief.

I attended school at Whitcomb Court Elementary, and I remember in the fifth grade we got a television! On that TV, we watched the trial of Adolf Eichmann and I learned of the horrific Holocaust during World War II. I couldn't believe that God would allow the deaths of six million Jews, maybe a million children, that way, and I began to question the concept of God. One day after school, I mustered the courage to ask my mother why God would not intervene in the deaths of so many innocent children. I was afraid because I thought maybe she would punish me or something for questioning God. Her response was, to me, less than an answer, but she simply said as she looked at the basket of clothes she continued to fold, "God works in mysterious ways, His wonders to behold." I was a little confused by her response because it was not given with the certainty and conviction in her voice that she usually had when telling us about Jesus Christ and God. Before long, our bible stories were often replaced by other stories of good vs evil: TV Cowboy Westerns, "Maverick," "Cheyanne," "Paladin," "The Rifleman" and others riding 'white horses'. They came into our home in black and white and started the narrative that we all would believe about America: that Americans, always, were the good guys of the world, no shades of gray. Everybody had their favorite 'Western', and mine was "Zorro!" No other fictional character influenced my thoughts, dreams and aspirations as did the dashing defender of the poor, Zorro. There was nothing more impressive to me than this enchanted figure attired in all black who would appear out of the dark of night to disrupt and defeat the diabolical plans of the powerful wealthy men who would exploit and oppress the poor.

Not quite 'Zorro' yet, but ready to be a hero.

Cease Fire! Cease Fire!

I'm really unable to measure the influence that fictional character had on me then—and even now. The parallels were too poignant in my life on City Council many years later. The 'Zorro' imagery seems to have followed me long after the childhood fantasies; maybe the sub-conscious effects of role models stay at work with some of us beyond our awareness. My record as a Councilman was characterized primarily as a defender of the poor and oppressed, fighting with a sword of tongue and wit. And, in ways, like Zorro, because my life during the day was in stark contrast to the night: relieving the burdens or unjust treatment of poor citizens in daylight, then, a nightly appearance fighting an addiction to heroin in a world much more dangerous. And it is, perhaps, pure coincidence that I drove a beautiful black Lincoln Continental and dressed sharply in heeled boots.

And like Zorro, I was resented by those who had, loved by those who had-not. Interestingly, many years after my close call with Hell in the landfill methane, I fought hard to save an area of poor housing that had been built on just such a place. I fought H.U.D to get help for the people whose homes were literally falling into the earth where pockets of methane burned away at foundations. I remember recalling my first-hand experience with those underground gases thirty years earlier.

The notion of race, and things seen in a 'Black and White people' world, was still unrealized for an eight-year-old like me. It was a grown-up item of discussion; so many answers to unasked questions were just "understood" without explanation. Why was there an imaginary line that I dare not cross? Why were all the men working on the dump that drove the large powerful bulldozers White? Why didn't any of them live in our neighborhood? Why didn't they have children, and if they did, where did they keep them? Why couldn't we visit and play with them? Hell, we looked alike! Our family was a very light-skinned Black family, what some called 'high-yellow.' We, as children, weren't aware yet of what defined 'Blackness' in America back then.

But of all the unanswered questions, these bothered me the most:

Why did my daddy act so differently around those White men?

Why was he so eager to talk and joke with them, while otherwise fairly aloof?

His demeanor became less than the usual confident, controlling man he was at home or around his peers. He almost changed back

*Young happy kids living next to a landfill (dump).
From left: Charles (Butch), Valerie, Ruth and me.*

to a boy around those White rednecks. For this, deep down inside of me, was a shame and a placid resentment. But Daddy was my hero and I acted like it never happened. I just kept it to myself.

My dad, Charles H. Richardson, though light-skinned, was the most apparently Black-looking person in the family and never stayed long at the dump. It seemed to be a strategic plan for him, slow steps to build relationships with those White men. This one guy, Ray, a bulldozer operator, became friends with Daddy. I remember, in vivid color, his jet-black hair combed perfectly to the side or back with a part on the left, a downward nose, and upper teeth that protruded like a chipmunk. He always smelled a little of alcohol with his flushed, red skin and tiny veins appearing across his nose and cheeks. It was unusual for us to be around White people in those days, and thus, I was filled with curiosity about their differences.

Those visits to the dump shack, where Daddy and Ray would talk, did leave an impression on my ears if not my eyes. The background music was often "Hillbilly" Hank Williams, and even at home, Daddy played country music, filling my childhood with country music as much as any other kind of music. Years later, my political mind always told me it was incorrect to be attracted to such music, but like the heart or the eyes, you can tell the ear anything you want; it will like what it likes. So, over the years as I became an adult, I have had to sneak off quietly in a corner of my own home or ride alone in my car to listen to it. I have never let people on to this somewhat embarrassing, almost politically suicidal divulgence of liking country music...(Shhh! Don't tell anyone...)

We lived next to that landfill on Ford Avenue until the City forced daddy to sell it to them, the old "eminent domain" routine. My father had worked hard for a dozen years making it a true diamond in the rough with a beautiful lawn and graveled circle driveway, but "progress" for a White developer meant housing projects that stand today. In the early Sixties, we would eventually live on the north side in a neighborhood called Providence Park and, in a matter of months after moving, my exposure to White people would go off the chart.

I started realizing so much more than what I had seen with Ray and a few others. I realized the vast majority were not used to Black people like Ray; that they not only liked country music but, more passionately, they held a very deep reverence for that Confederate money that was buried next to my old home. Maybe Mama was right. Maybe *I was* looking at Hell.

In 1962, the Cuban Missile Crisis brought the world to the brink of a nuclear catastrophe. As a Black family in the segregated school system of Richmond, Virginia, we were all scheduled to attend V.A. Randolph, an all-Black high school. Randolph was about fifteen miles from our home, and my mother, Ruth, decided that if nuclear war was a real possibility, her children would not be fifteen miles away from

Even as a kid I was front and center with my Mom looking like a movie star for a run to the grocery store.

her, especially when a new all-White high school was only two miles down the road. For the love of her children, she thought one thing: *Where will my children be if something like war were to break out?* That was it, and as a result, the Henrico County High School was integrated by three Black siblings and one other Negro on September 3, 1963, without incident. This was an example, out of thousands, when people act out of pure necessity that precipitates a change. My mother was not motivated by any grand design to integrate a racist school system; her decision had everything to do with a love for her children. But I was so naïve, I didn't understand what the kids meant when they asked me if the NAACP had asked us to integrate the school. Necessity is both the mother of invention and the father of change. An average person, with no great unusual talent, just decides he or she has had enough and, by their single action, changes the course of history!

Gabriel Prosser and Nat Turner were Virginians like Patrick Henry, but liberty *was* death—necessarily for them! Unless something changes because of your personal struggle, then your best efforts have gone for naught. Your struggle cannot be a carefully designed plan to simply attract attention; genuine change grows out of a genuine need to improve the living conditions of the oppressed poor. Rosa Parks was just tired, and so are we! "Events are in the saddle and ride mankind," said Ralph Waldo Emerson, and it seems indeed that I would bear events through life.

In as honest terms as possible, this book generally is about the motives and real circumstances behind the difficult efforts to bring about change. Specifically, it touches upon aspects and behind the scenes facts, involving racism, humanism, and Man's egotism in the latter half of the twentieth century. Experiences in high school, Vietnam, Richmond politics, courtrooms, law enforcement, and our outdated prison system carry this. The situations are real and truthful. Only the flaw of memory is responsible for any error or inaccuracy.

As we all do, I often ponder how or what determines the balances in life or what constitutes justice…or if there is justice at all?! It is an imponderable question unanswered, but to conclude that everything is simply left to chance is unacceptable. With the wife I received, good children, the fortune of public office, and a great degree of undeserved blessings, sometimes I feel maybe it is reward for my suffering in Vietnam. In particular, my wife, Phyllis Antionette Johnson, was more than I could ever wish for! She was the single biggest reason for my success and for my happiness, and I only regret not having sufficiently expressed that to her during her life. But if there is a God, and I pray there is, my lasting message is that she knows that no one could have made me happier.

We met in the eighth grade at Benjamin A. Graves Jr. Middle School, dated through high school and college, and were married before Vietnam. And, I can truly say, that despite my inexcusable, indiscreet, dog-like behavior, she was a faithful, loving, and devoted mate. I am convinced that it was her memories of our becoming acquainted as children that she carried with her that enabled her to endure my adult stages of life. I was always good and faithful to her until I returned home from Vietnam. I am not certain whether it was the experiences and guilt-ridden atrocities or drugs that caused my indifference when I returned, but she always used to say, "My Chuckie that went to Vietnam never came home!"

I think I took it for granted and never realized how deeply affected she was by *my* change. My ego-driven, self-centered, dumb interpretation of her complaint was not hearing the cry for her previous friend! I only heard some bullshit about a mean, hard man returning, instead of the soft, sensitive boy she once knew and loved beyond my worth. She would say it more than a few times, and even now I experience a welling up and painful remorse as I recall her saying, "My Chuckie never came home." I recall responding to her once saying, "Yes, baby, here I am, right here with you. I made it back."

She replied, "That Tarzan body is here, but that sweet guy that would once stoop to tie my shoestrings is still over there, walking the jungles in Vietnam."

I had lost touch with that fundamental viewpoint I still had when

I stopped Private Stephens from raping a young Vietnamese girl—a basic sense of moral decency… and the defense of it! There was no excuse for my behavior: not war, not drugs, not the pressures of political stress or the way women were throwing themselves at me. I had simply changed in a way—necessarily or not.

It's not to say I wasn't a good guy when I started standing up for the little man while on City Council. I was sympathetic towards those who were down and out, defending Black people, gays, the homeless, and disabled. But still, on a personal level, because I had access to an abundance of sexual encounters, I threw caution to the wind, disregarded the moral or emotional consequences—and that was wrong! Only in retrospect am I able to evaluate how irresponsibly selfish and cruel it was to my kind and devoted wife who was always there waiting, taking care of home and children, and often, my financial responsibilities. I felt that indiscretions and outside affairs were, without question, wrong, but also I was deeply committed to the belief that it was a matter between my wife and me. Whatever explanation or debt of amends, they were duly owed to Phyllis!

It is no small task to acknowledge these truths that pain me greatly, but I am comforted in a small way in the knowledge that she shared with me the reasons she felt duty-bound to stand by me despite the faults and frailties of my character. I tried to describe the relationship between the nights she had seen me in a cold sweat, scrambling to gather my wits as she held me, whispering, "It's a dream, baby! Just a dream. It's going to be alright," and my avid support for those poor who suffer other ways. On a very emotional night when we cried together, she explained to me how she had witnessed my genuine care, concern, and patience for those suffering people with problems—the times I had taken up for them in ways that few would have done. She explained how she had heard me on the phone making promises and getting out of bed at 3 a.m. on that winter night to help the Wilkins family, allowing the young mother with three children to stay in our basement bedroom when the City had turned off her gas.

She told me, "Rich (what Phyllis used to call me), all the love and tenderness I used to get, I now see it's going to your constituents. Although I do get jealous and feel neglected, I can't get but so angry when I hear you talk to those people. Rich, you take care of those people as if they are your own children and I want you to love me the same way, but I understand your care for them is real and goes so far beyond doing it just to get a vote."

The connection to those like the Wilkins was, perhaps, from guilt. My country had beguiled me, along with thousands of other young naïve American boys, to go off and fight a people who were much like us, by and large poor, struggling everyday people, sent to war. Those people were very much equivalent to the many constituents for whom I fought and represented most vigorously on the City Council. Perhaps as compensation for having been betrayed by my own country to carry out the nefarious military actions against those poor people, I was inclined to consciously, and subconsciously, fight as rigorously and powerfully as I could to oppose forces that, symbolically, represented those forces that exploited my misinformed youth—and potentially my life. I suspect also, as a Black man, I had some guilt for having been used to participate in a war to, ostensibly, secure for poor people halfway around the world the rights and freedom we didn't even have in our own country. I believe, in retrospect, it was a form of compensation; that my incessant opposition to authority was a behavior that reflected my lingering resentment for what my government had done to me.

One of my counselors analyzed me and said that I used my daily council platform to 'return fire' upon authority symbols. Dr. Shotwell, a psychiatrist and follow-up consultant for my post-traumatic stress disorder, theorized that my anti-status quo posture reflected my continued resentment. He compared my often, rapid-fire criticism of the city's administration with my machine gun in Vietnam. I would target the American government as the culprit of my sorrows and used the City Council's microphone as the "M60 machine gun"—my words as bullets.

It sounded creative and cute, but I didn't necessarily agree with his analysis. I was just an angry man who talked fast with aimed, unrelenting attacks on my opposition or those who disagreed with my point of view. Any government rule, project, or policy I thought to be ill-conceived or wrong, I shot down; those I favored, I attempted to protect with the same weapon. You win some, you lose some, but you never stop fighting for those in the battle with you.

Although I harbored deep feelings of resentment and animosities towards the U.S. government, I had no illusions of entitlement. I understood that along with thousands of other young Americans who had made sacrifices and endured the unfair insufferable pains of Vietnam, I had no special privileges and deserved no more than they! But what did encourage or give me cause to fight on, prove that our cause was just? The limitations of a man's existence on earth are usually set by his resources. Sadly, the resources of too many could not fill a thimble, but necessity can afford a boundless resource of courage and commitment. We are our brother's keeper—and shall afford them these resources.

CHAPTER 2

Is It Worth It?

In 1963, when I was one of three African American students in an otherwise all-White school, some of the students criticized and harassed me one day for not placing my hand over my heart during the morning pledge of allegiance to the flag. They accosted me for being disrespectful, for not seeing something that was, in their eyes and hearts, an obvious obligation. I admit my mind was not on the flag or much else at that moment because my mood was just a continuation of a mood I had carried from the previous day. My mood was resentful and weary of my environment at this all-White school. I didn't raise my hand to my heart because my head was still spinning, still bemused about where I was and why.

Those kids might have had, perhaps, some understanding of my 'disrespect to the flag' had they been in class with me the day before when Lynn Ford asked the teacher a question: "Didn't you tell us to back up and kill them? Oh, that was if it was a nigger." The whole class burst into eager laughter with the grinning adult in the class. It was an exchange between student and teacher in my driver's education class. The teacher, 'Coach' Lowery, was talking about the various circumstances and consequences of automobile accidents. Coach, as he was called, was talking about how weird it is that sometimes bad accidents can be as costly as fatal ones when insurance cost are looked at. Lynn Ford, the student, reminded him that earlier he had said, "You should back up and roll over him."

And that's when the coach responded, "That's if it was a nigger." Coach said it very matter-of-factly; he was in a way 'dead' serious.

It was a set-up by Lynn, hoping Coach would repeat himself in front of me, in front of the class, a humiliating laugh at my expense. Coach Lowery probably failed to recognize the "nigger" in the class. I was light-skinned, and he probably looked right past me—used to an all-White classroom—and was probably used to delivering the "nigger" line every year. I was stunned and couldn't move, virtually paralyzed, maybe thinking any movement would draw their eyes. Slowly, a deep sense of humiliation and sadness hung over me like a cloud of disbelief. That cloud remained with me the next day as I allowed my arm to rest at my side when all others touched their hearts during the pledge.

"You should be thankful to be allowed to live in a country like America!" one female student shouted at me, telling me that I should demonstrate my loyalty and gratitude every opportunity, and never fail to pledge allegiance to the flag! I looked at her, but I was unsure how respond to a girl, a pretty girl, instead of some form of chest pounding I would have confronted one of the boys with. I calmly asked if she was finished and began to calmly tell her about the insults and laughter at my expense the day before. She was quiet for a moment, with that look of mild shame yet determined to stay proud. "Well, I wasn't there, I don't know," she said.

"Maybe if you talk to the others and you all go to the office and tell them about it, I might feel different," I replied. She turned and looked at the group of mostly boys, and they looked away in all directions as they dispersed quicker than a fire drill.

She walked away at that point too, showing her peer allegiance. I just stood there, hearing the echo of hate around me and the words and laughter of Coach Lowery's class clearly as I hear them today. I can still remember staring at the shiny waxed floors while the class roared with laughter, and Coach, grinning in front of the green chalkboard with his crooked, protruding front teeth and his tight crew-cut hair style.

As a sixteen-year-old, I had lived in segregated neighborhoods and was largely naïve to the ways of America's White society. My mother had a strong Christian faith and believed all people were basically good no matter their skin color and had raised us to believe so.

I was stunned by the overt racism I experienced at my new school. There were so many incidents of daily bigotry, but the day I saw an entire class laugh uproariously at the suggestion to kill a Black person, that Black lives did not matter, it left me numb in a way about things. I didn't speak about that day for years. At the time, when I refused to cover my heart for the pledge, the gesture was rooted in a psychological numbness, having no feeling of community, of national allegiance. Only years later did I come to appreciate it as an act of protest, a reflexive need to act, that might make a change.

Racism was very often reflexive as well, given the broad and normal demonstrations of it in the sixties. Our school, Henrico, had an open campus, kind of college-like, so fall mornings were chilly going from class to class. The look of warm breath streaming from the mouth of dozens of kids as we went about was typical, disappearing the moment we entered a classroom. So, it was a real shock to see the warm smoke pushing its way out the vents of my locker one morning when I entered homeroom.

I rushed to open it to see what the heck was happening, but it was obviously fire—and intentional. The metal door and steel combination lock were hot, and I gingerly entered the three numbers to get in. Meanwhile, half the class was chuckling, or worse, laughing enthusiastically. But some, indeed some, had somber looks of sympathy that gave me hope, hope that all the kids at Henrico were not mean and did not agree with prejudice and undeserved hatred. It was subtle, not overwhelming at all, but there was enough goodness and sympathy around those walls to build hope. But there he was, almost as soon as I opened the hot, smoking locker, the proud culprit, Jimmy Atkinson, who stood over me laughing. I looked up at Jimmy and asked, "Why did you do it?"

He responded loudly with a vicious and venomous yell, "Because you're a nigger, and you don't belong here!!"

My hope was that more faces of sympathy were in that classroom, more people like Kenny Chaplin, who I remember telling me, "Henry, you don't have to take that shit." Kenny had walked in at the end of the fire. He was a buddy of mine who had grown up in Oregon Hill and was new at Henrico. Sitting alone during lunch was a miserable ordeal each day. After three weeks of eating alone while all the other

The teenager who integrated Henrico High School.

students talked, laughed, and joked, one day Kenny walked over and just plopped his tray down in front of me, joining me for lunch. He never realized the role he played, a kind of hero, in helping me to get through a time in my life when I was close to giving up. Kenny would quit school and join the Army, and eighteen months later, be killed in Vietnam. Henrico would later rename its stadium after him: Kenny Chapel Stadium, Henrico's hero.

My brother, Butch, also quit Henrico as well, for different reasons, including an incident in the stadium—at another school. Butch was on the Henrico football team and they were playing Manchester High. After Butch had had several big plays as running back, the players really went after him and, after one big hit, his helmet popped off. Just seconds later, "There he is, there he is! That's the nigger," shouted one of them, and the whole defensive squad started toward him. Butch said he felt the swirl of air around his bare head and, without a second thought, took off away from the field down into a wooded area while the coaches and referees calmed the boys... he assumes, because he didn't look back. Later, one of the opposing coaches picked him up with his car.

Butch was also in a couple of fights that required my mother to bring him back twice and apologize, even though the White kids started them. When the third fight happened, he told my mother not to bother, "To hell with these crackers," he said, and within a few weeks, he went off and joined the Navy. It was a damn shame; little things, big things, but it was happening to us.

I was angry about my burned-up tennis shoes, and tired of getting called "nigger" every day. I was angry and humiliated to have had fifteen to twenty White guys hear Jimmy Atkinson yell, "because you're a nigger and you don't belong here!" I was outnumbered, so a physical confrontation was out of the question. When I told my mother about this incident with the fire, I had hoped she would have sought more help for me, but no, it was the same solution:

"Chuck, you have got to put your faith in God. Jesus tells us to love thy enemy."

I told her that I believed that with all my heart, but if she would allow me to transfer to Virginia Randolph, the Black school, I could manage to love my Black enemies easier, 'cause Jesus didn't have to deal with those kids (I was thinking 'crackers') at Henrico. Her response was an absolute "no!" She said that God had given me special gifts, how I could make people laugh, how kind I was, and how I never held grudges.

"People like your artistic talents too, and you're a good-looking boy," she said. "Chuck honey, these burdens are yours to bear and if you react badly, you will prove their point—that you do not belong there. You have to ignore their insults, even the teachers', and show that your goodness is greater than their evils!"

She went on to explain that we couldn't complain to the NAACP or others, that it would just alarm other Negroes of their behavior. And the greater damage was that it would frighten other students and discourage their interest in attending that school next year. When I think back, I realize my mother wasn't smart—she was brilliant.

Between Mama and Jesus, my high school diploma should be split into at least three different shares and sections of credits. I didn't always buy into Mother's deeply held faith and religious convictions, but I always bought into her advice, so whenever she was done, whenever she said, "Believe me, Chuck, if you love those who would do you harm, forgive them and hold no grudges, if you do unto others as you would want them to do unto you," I at least felt better about myself!

After Mama and Jesus completed our talk around the kitchen table that afternoon following school, the second half of my Black/White life began. This half was safe, secure, comfortable, and socially well-grounded in a Black neighborhood known as Providence Park, just one street away from a White neighborhood. However, I would never, ever cross Meadowbridge Road to play with the kids I attended school with. My eagerness was to get to the Providence Park playground, rather than dwell on revenge or retribution. I was where the Black guys all warmly greeted me with "White boy," Chuck or Elvis. These were welcomed changes and let me know that I was truly accepted somewhere for the rest of the day.

The one thing my mother's faith did was to absolve me of the anger, resentment, and animosities that I might have carried towards White people. I realized that the act of forgiveness could benefit me as much as those to whom I had extended it. My mother's attitude had been critical guidance in my survival of challenging events and episodes where I was in the right but could not win. Because of the kitchen talk with Mama, as obsessed as I was, I accepted that Jimmy Atkinson was probably a nice guy who had been raised on a diet of daily prejudice and was just showing off in front of his buddies. So, I forgave him, grabbed my basketball, and happily trotted off to the playground. Keeping Jesus around was my mother's way of saying, "Don't worry, be happy," long before the song came out. The fire incident might even be seen as terroristic in today's world, a hate crime or something, but in 1963 Richmond, it was hardly shocking.

"Well Henry, is it time? Or is it worth it?" That was the question the kindly, large, stocky, White pilgrim-looking school principal, Mr. Tubbs, asked me. I distinctly recall the softly lit lawyer-like quality of his office, with its oak-paneled walls and maroon high-backed chairs befitting a judge's chambers. The atmosphere was stoically poised, so much so that it intimidated me into feeling guilty about a rightful complaint—my damn locker had been set on fire!

So, when he asked the question, "Is it time, or do you think it's worth it?" I had no immediate response. I thought to myself, "What does he mean!?" He had a genuine look of concern on his face and I believe he thought he cared about me and that he wanted to do the right thing. But he obviously wanted to fascinate me into believing that my role of integrating an all-White high school was an ominous task requiring strength, sacrifice, and poise, and that these acts of violence and destruction should be expected, taken in stride, and tolerated if we, as a Black people, were to succeed. That it was my duty as a young Black student, to suffer, for my people, the slings and arrows of the Civil Rights movement.

After a few moments trying to read his intention, I concluded that he didn't know how, or if, to punish Jimmy Atkinson, a top-ranking White student, for squirting lighter fluid into my locker vents and dropping a match into it, setting my books, lunch, gym shoes and clothes ablaze. Was it worth it? Was Mr. Tubbs suggesting to me that this might be a small price to pay for breaking a racial barrier that could have resulted in far more devastating consequences than burned clothes and lunches? Though he was well justified in making the point, how many instances of unjust treatment should I have been made to endure before it would have been the right time, worth it? How many more burnt lockers, how many more instances of laughing White boys standing around a humiliated Black man fiddling with his combination lock while his fingers burned? How many more times should I ask Jimmy Atkinson, *why did you do this?* How many more times should I hear, "'Cause you're a nigger and you don't belong here!'"?

Young, politically naïve, articulate though with a limited vocabulary, my vernacular was oriented more toward the jargon of the street rather than college. So suffice to say, at 16, I didn't get his point. I had no idea what he meant by his question. Shocked, surprised, but not wanting to appear uncool, I took a shot in the dark and with swagger and aplomb, I said, "I think it's time, Mr. Tubbs."

He cleared his throat and sat back straight as though I had hit him. I was befuddled at his actions because I thought I had said or done something wrong, but I didn't know what! And he simply said, "Okay, Henry, we'll get on it. We'll get you some new books, a free tray lunch, and some tennis shoes for your cross country meet this afternoon against.... is it John Marshall High?"

My eyes widened and I replied, "Yes, sir."

In retrospect, I realize I had given the proper answer that he had not expected, and that I, at the time, did not know how right it was. I stood up proud that I had said 'it was time.' Mr. Tubbs was asking whether it was time to do something regarding the racist kids who wanted to express their opposition to me at Henrico, and maybe even in society, as a whole. Yes, Mr. Principal, it was worth all the pain and suffering that I was forced to endure, but it did not mean that you—

persons in positions of responsibility and authority—should turn their heads to cruel acts of racism and allow it to go unpunished in the name of 'timely' progress and cooperation.

This principal, Nathan G. Tubbs, was in an awkward position of dispensing justice during the cutting-edge period of school integration—in an area where segregation was an accepted way of life. Integration had no paradigm in public education, had never been experienced before, and was as experimental to those of us who were the integrators as it was for the integrated. What Mr. Tubbs seemed to fail to appreciate, however, was that the wrongful deed committed by Jimmy Atkinson was a violation and had everything to do with whether my struggle to integrate an all-White high school was worth it! His act had to be recognized as wrong, or he and his peers would not have understood that there were consequences to their acts. The school principal, in all his wisdom and strategic tact to teach me the virtues of patience and sacrifices, had been indoctrinated into a culture so biased that he failed to recognize that, in instances of justice, the right time is always now!

During that era, it was not a certainty how such an act would be perceived by the parents of a student like Jimmy. Would they treat him as a misguided delinquent, or would they defend his actions as upholding the conservative, prejudiced, anti-integration sentiments of most Southern Whites? When I left his office, all the staff's eyes followed me. They had all heard about what had happened that morning, but nobody ever said a word to me about what Mr. Tubbs did or said to Jimmy Atkinson. Perhaps he was stern with a punishment, maybe he called his parents, maybe he called other parents? Or maybe, he thought the time was not right… that it was not worth it. I suppose I'll never know. And never know how many other Kenny Chapels there really were at Henrico who lived there at the wrong time.

It is so interesting the impact things have on you when you're sixteen or seventeen, an impact that can shape concepts and narratives for the rest of your life. Some are cumulative, like a repetitive wave that might knock you down by surprise, and some are barely noticed

Cease Fire! Cease Fire!

at other times. Henrico was that way, memories of heavy waves that became less and less surprising as the years there passed. And that is the thing that shapes you through life: certain waves and realizing that waves of all manner can and will happen.

I remember once my biology class took a field trip to collect leaves, acorns, moss, and other furniture of the forest, so to speak. Mrs. Forrester, our teacher, even had the name for it. The wooded area was on the far side of our football stadium, and it sloped down to a stream that was not too large, but we had to hop over it to keep our feet dry. Just before the stream, there was an old half-fallen fence that may have been there eighty years. It, too, had to be navigated, requiring us to "high-step" over it. The boys easily jumped or stepped on the fence and crossed; the girls had to carefully step over it.

As we boys crossed and moved further down the slope, we couldn't help but be boys, and some would turn back inconspicuously to sneak a look at the girls as they lifted their dresses and raised their legs to cross the fence. Several did so, and me being innocent and dumb as a brick, tried to thrill seek as well. Just as I paused, two voices hit me, soft and hard at once: "Henry, don't you dare look! Boy, you're crazy." The other grabbed my arm and said, "C'mon, Henry, *you* can't look. Keep going." It was Kenny Chapel and a friend of mine, Vernon; they were trying act like it wasn't urgent so as not to attract attention, but I picked up my pace. Kenny said they would hurt a colored boy "bad" for looking up a girl's dress and he pulled at me again. We didn't look back, but Kenny told me to ask Vernon about it.

After a few more minutes, Vernon and I started picking up leaves, leaning over pretending we were selecting special ones while he talked to me. Vernon explained to me that a colored man up near Bowling Green was beat up and hung for supposedly looking at a White girl. "Man, they beat him bad and hung him dead in a tree," Vernon said. He was serious, I could tell, and he was nervously looking around as he grabbed leaves. Vernon told me that his uncle had bragged about how he and a group of others "hung this nigger up" in Bowling Green. He kept looking at the ground, but he said to me, "Henry, you're not a bad boy, but I can't let nobody say you were looking up a White girl's dress." He said if his uncle would do it, anybody would. Anybody would because—Vernon's uncle was a policeman! I was perplexed (a word I didn't know then) and wondered if it was true. *Did somebody really get killed for looking at a White girl?*

This was about eight years after Emmett Till had been murdered but I had forgotten about that...or maybe believed it was not true. I definitely remember that day and the realness of that world.

Those three years at Henrico did have some normality, for lack of a better word. I ran cross-country track and was actually a regional standout, something rather unusual for a Black runner at the time, as most Blacks excelled in the sprints. I was also a very good art student and sculptor. I had made some really nice sculptures of a hand with its palm up and a foot as if running. One day early in my senior year, the same principal, Mr. Tubbs, walked through my art class and noted how talented I was. He asked if I thought I could make a warrior head. Henrico's mascot was a Native American warrior; we were "The Warriors." I told him I could, and about a week later had a small, maybe foot-tall, sculpture done. He was utterly impressed and asked that I make a large version we could present to the school as our graduating class gift in 1966. The next thing I knew, they had over a hundred pounds of clay delivered and I got to work.

It turned out beautifully. This one about three feet tall. It was of a strong-jawed, high cheekboned Native American, hair parted in the middle and pulled down to each side with bands wrapping it just below the ear, and a single feather flowing down from the hair on one side. A cast was made by the art department at Virginia Commonwealth University (at the time Richmond Professional Institute) and was then sent to Ohio where Reynolds Aluminum created the final product. When it came back, I was blown away like everyone else; it was even more majestic. It looked like a million dollars! There was even a news article in the Richmond newspaper. When it was unveiled at graduation, I received a standing ovation!

When I entered Henrico, like my brother and sister, I was the

Cease Fire! Cease Fire!

Following the unveiling of the Warrior Head and being congratulated by the Principal, Nathan G. Tubbs, 1966.

center of attacks, taunts, and jokes, and shown little to no respect from students or some teachers. Even Mr. Tubbs had challenged my resentment and complaints after my locker was set on fire. Now, all were standing to honor me. The next year, my sister, Valerie, won the very first 'Miss Warrior' pageant in 1967. When she entered Henrico with me, she received the 'welcome', too: taunts of "Ruby lips" and "Sapphire"—kids not wanting to sit next to her—"I'm not sitting next to the nigger." Some even refused to play the role of her relative in a school play. Amazingly, by sheer talent and effort, two of the first Black students among an all-White student body of over a thousand, some of whom would not even sit next to them when they arrived, would now stand for them as they left.

When I attended Henrico High School, I did not acquire the benefits of all the educational opportunities that that facility offered me, but I did learn something about racial matters: whether you're a pilot, a doctor, an architect or lawyer, if you're a teacher or scientist trying to solve the problem of cancer or a mathematician calculating the trip to Mars, or the utility analyst who keeps our drinking water clean and safe, the only time color matters is when it's measuring the amount of gray matter in your head. It's about doing the best possible job in serving the rest of a society—that happens to be made up of all different skin colors. We, as a nation, have always—on the surface—extolled the sentiment of Thomas Jefferson that "all men are created equal," with certain unalienable rights. However, we also know some of us are more equal than others. The need for us to balance that disparity has taken shape in all manner and form over the centuries, from slaves spitting, or worse, in the master's food to the subtlest micro-aggressions when opportune; it is a natural reaction.

There is something I've never told anyone about in over fifty years now, a favorable moment for me at Henrico—NO, I did not spit in someone's food. So many acts of prejudice and racism were heaped upon me, my brother and sister and one other Black student, and I could never get back at people, so I was forced to restrain myself. The humiliation by racist teachers and coaches laughing about Black men being lazy while my father labored two jobs all his life to raise eight children! "Hey, Henry! Speaking of Black loafers (shoes), how's your father?" Bruce, a loud-mouth redneck, would yell such things across the entire cafeteria at me. This kind of thing was a daily ritual and I eventually learned to raise my head to acknowledge as though I enjoyed the attention and smile. Many of the students were only doing what their parents taught them was right, and they were blind to the pain and hurt they caused. They were blind to the notion I was "equal," and so could not realize any empathy.

My need for balance was a part of my gift to Henrico, the 1966 High School Class gift that I sculpted. As I worked on the Warrior bust that senior year, I was proud of how strong and realistic it appeared, commanding attention. When I got to the final touches, I had indented markings for the eyes and began working on his gaze, but as I worked on them, I thought of that Native American I had rendered and what he must have seen. It occurred to me that the many students at that school were blind to the racism and bigoted behavior they portrayed. After several minutes I decided. I smeared clay smoothly over the iris and pupils. It left the effect of a sightless oracle, that was probably considered unintentional or maybe the result of an uncorrectable error by most because I don't remember a single person mentioning it to me, ever.

Only I would know it was an intentional symbol, a message in silent clay, that reflected the character of the school during the time I was there, and the lost time for Native Americans. Only God and I would know that this was my revenge for the blind racism that I suffered during three years at Henrico High School. Even though the original statue was destroyed by a bomb in the early nineties, photographs remain to remind the person of that era that those Henrico Warriors were blind. The image of 'Lady Justice' blindfolded with scales is iconic in our national narrative, but unfortunately, the injustices have been in full view too long, yet unperceived by too many. Whenever I gaze upon my well-kept secret from many years ago, I recall their blindness and still wonder: *Why did no one ever ask me, 'where are the eyes?' so that I might reveal to them my long-held secret?* However, the Warrior oracle saw beyond those years. He envisioned the role of his Black graduates in Richmond, Atlanta,

The class gift, the Warrior Head, Henrico High School 1966.

the NFL, and today the top-ranking Black woman in television news, Ms. Rashida Jones, president of MSNBC. It reminds me of the poem

'Justice' by the great Langston Hughes:

> That Justice is a blind goddess
> Is a thing to which we Black are wise:
> Her bandage hides two festering sores
> That once perhaps were eyes.

The Draft

In 1968, at the height of national opposition to the Vietnam war, I was caught between Muhammad Ali and my father. Martin Luther King, Jr., had announced his opposition to the war the year before, and now was dead. Men across America were burning their draft cards, huge protest and marches occurred weekly, and by April, my predicament was tenuous at best. I had no money to return to Virginia Union University in the fall, and Muhammad Ali was doing his spring college tour. He came to Barco Steven Hall Gymnasium to speak and then walked, legions in tow, up Lombardy Street to Maggie L. Walker High School. Hundreds of students filled the street, closing down traffic with throngs of worshiping followers, a spectacle only Ali could have created. Phyllis and I moved with the crowd, getting as close to him as the sea of young Black people would permit.

It was the height of the Civil Rights movement, and his speech was moving and convincing. I had just joined the Richmond chapter of the Black Panther Party, which was somewhat of a joke compared to the men and women in Oakland, Philadelphia, and Detroit, where the F.B.I and local police were killing young Black people on a whim. I was twenty years old, an impressionable, idealistic Black American who was just beginning to read Frantz Fanon, Malcolm X, and James Baldwin: radical things only remotely understood by my parents at the time.

My father, Charles Hoover Richardson, was a Republican.

Named after President Herbert Hoover, he was born the night he was elected: November 6, 1928. A well-kept secret, and source of some embarrassment, was his White Italian grandfather who went unnamed and virtually unknown as it was prior to the twentieth century. Although seldom if ever discussed, my father never seemed ashamed of the supposed hereditary fact, even given the thought that the Italian had not felt the same of him. Charles was the only male sibling in a lot of six, and had never served in the military, but maintained strong patriotic beliefs that all men should be willing to serve their 'duty' in defense of the nation. He frowned upon Muhammad Ali's action as a conscientious objector, seeing it as a deceitful ploy to avoid service in Vietnam.

My father was a complicated man, and we were miles apart politically. He was not particularly astute about the Civil Rights Movement, though he was a member of the NAACP. When I even thought about ducking the draft or avoiding my 'duty', it was a subject best kept to myself. It was an almost impossible emotional subject to address. In our small bungalow style home in Providence Park on the northern rim of the city limits, nothing was out of sight and nothing went unheard. It was an open space from the back door to the front door, perhaps twenty-five feet apart. A front room, a makeshift bedroom, and the kitchen made up one side, and two small bedrooms and a bath took the other.

In that small bungalow, we all interacted yet managed to avoid immense feelings about some things; it seems almost inconceivable. The entrance was always through the kitchen, and it was where one emotional climax did occur. Late one evening, Valerie fell to her knees when she entered, learning that her fiancé, Theodore, had died in Vietnam, only a week before his tour was up in November 1966. My mother and I tried with inept futile attempts to console her painful wallowing, while my younger siblings sat, bewildered, feet away. My father was at his second job that night, and I don't recall his immediate reaction. In 1966, I was eighteen, and after high school graduation, my father deeply resented my presence at home, all but saying, "It's time you got a job and get out, man!"

Although my parents were not able to contribute anything toward my college finances, I had managed to secure a federal loan to attend Virginia Union University to avoid the draft. The Vietnam War was a daily source of death notices about classmates, friends and kids from our neighborhood. Theodore's death was a vivid reminder of how utterly near I might be to the same fate. However, my father would have been ashamed and embarrassed if I had taken any step to avoid, in his mind, my obligation and duty to serve in the military.

Some friends went to Canada or elsewhere to avoid the draft, to avoid the boxes we would see returning on the evening news, images we would try to ignore or quietly talk about in that small space. If Muhammad Ali was on, or draft dodgers or protesters, everything got eerily quiet. With such deep-seated feelings floating between such small spaces, where we were hardly ever more than an arm's reach from each other, how in God's name did a conflagration of emotions not occur? And, in the end, when I received my draft notice to depart the Broad Street Union Station on December 8, 1968, they all took it as inevitable destiny or something that might come with honor.

As much as my mother loved me, and as much as I recognized that she preferred that I not go to Vietnam, not once did she speak in defense of my position to resist the draft. She realized how much it meant to her husband, Hoover, that he could live vicariously through one of his sons as the war hero he was not. Even at the price of my death. We were worlds apart on this. My mother and father only had the American version of the story: 'Freedom Ain't Free', 'With Liberty and Justice for All', and 'When Duty Calls You Must Go'. The difference was I had had a taste of something different.

After attending Henrico High and experiencing the words of Muhammad Ali and others at Virginia Union, and after being at Black Panther meetings, I had a starkly different perspective. I was learning what we were *not* learning from the television and newspapers, developing a perspective which forced a tortured decision about my life's fight. Do I fight for a country that is not dedicated to the proposition that had been taught to me, a centuries-old false narrative?

My parents were, politically, largely unaware of the reality of things, the deception past or present, yet I could not hold them responsible. To do as Ali had done, or many for that matter, and refuse to serve would have destroyed my father. My mother was more intuitive, or maybe faithful, and convinced me that God had given me the strength to survive and this was just a challenge that I was strong enough to endure as a Marine.

My amazing mother and father Cora "Ruth" and Charles "Hoover" Richardson sometime in the late 60's.

Many of us bought into those inauthentic, empty promises, simply accepting them to survive. So, when my father and I prepared to leave for the trip to the airport to take me to war—that we had rarely spoken of—we passed each other through our little tight kitchen as we had a thousand times, and I thought of so much: regret, bravado, his vicarious pride, sadness, and fear. Still, nothing was said. All the closeness that a whisper could suffice, yet a distance too great to reach, was between us. As we walked out to the steps, we teetered between a handshake or a hug, and it occurred to me it may be the final time ever for us, but there was no embrace. He looked up and down but not at me as he searched for words. I thought to myself, *He looks guilty. He thinks he's the reason I am on my way to Vietnam*...that had he not made me feel so obligated to accommodate the family's honor, I would have opted for jail rather than an M60 machine gun.

There we were, unable to hug because, I believe, of one of the horrible legacies of slavery: the need for Black mothers to teach sons that physical affection among men, even father and son, was wrong. The misleading device by Black slave mothers to protect young Black boys from the deviant behavior of overseers and masters, instructing them that men should not be touching, an orientation the mothers would recall from the Bible. It was a form of culture that carried over and may be the reason today many Black fathers and sons have difficulty embracing or expressing genuine love for each other in a healthy normal way! I almost cry when I recall the moment.

He shook my hand and turned quickly before I could see the tear in his eye. It was moving because, for a moment, I thought he might express something I had never heard him say. That my father, Charles Hoover Richardson, the man whom I admired or loved more than any other, might possess the power at that moment to evolve and tell his son he loves him. Instead, he asked, "Got everything?" The two of us loaded my single duffle bag in the car and we both left for the airport—to serve.

Many, many years later, when my father was very near death, he was kept at home. Family members would come to visit on a daily basis. Dad was slowly leaving us, lapsing in and out of consciousness. Our lives are statements of our roles. That afternoon, at my father's bedside, it was about to happen again when I unconsciously touched my father's hand. He did not move, so I reached again. As I held my dying father's hand, I noticed how large his thumb was, and I took his large hand into my grasp. I was startled by the size of his hand. I embraced it into both of mine and held it, determining if they were really that large.

I was caught in a moment of disbelief because, with hands this size, I should have noticed them after a half-century of being his son. As this all dawned on me, I quietly began to weep and gently pull away. I realized why I never knew how really large daddy's hands actually were: we had virtually never intentionally touched. After over fifty years of rarely, if ever, touching in a loving way, I felt deeply remorseful that I had missed something too late to find.

Marine Corps training at Parris Island was legendary for its harsh conditions and tough punishment. The second you step off the bus, your world is transformed into something shocking and alien to even the toughest of men. Any level of comfort is shattered and shocked from moment to moment. At breakneck pace, drill instructors kick and punch and threaten groups of forty to fifty recruits from one building to another. After being stripped of all possessions, clothes, and every hair on our heads in a matter of minutes, we were hustled off to chow.

"Quick, quick, hurry up you maggot! Eat, eat, eat!!" The drill instructors (DIs) yelled as they walked on our tables, stomping at our metal trays of horrible half-cooked 'food,' and bitter drinks. Within eight minutes of starting our meal, we were up and on our way to the barracks, carrying a sense of dread and hopelessness and fear, that would mark the next 120 days.

The physical training was brutal, but the mental stress was worse. Things have changed since then, but in 1968, it was humiliating. They would strike you in front of the whole platoon, insulting your mother and father and telling you how many men were back home screwing your wife or girlfriend. The DIs were mostly big, mean White guys who held no compunction about insulting anybody or anything in your life. My DI, Staff Sergeant Willis, believed in mass punishment; when one recruit screwed up, all recruits paid. Therefore, it was imperative we police ourselves. I asked the instructor how far we could go in 'policing' each other. "Whatever is necessary, faggot!" he yelled.

In training, platoons are comprised of four 20-man squads. Each has a squad leader and a platoon leader called the 'guide', who reports to the DI. The next day, while selecting the guide and squad leaders, DI Willis

Cease Fire! Cease Fire!

asked, "Where's the guy who asked about policing other recruits?"

The guys called me out. "Richardson, they asking for you!"

I went to the front and Willis asked if I liked "kickin' ass," and I told him, "Only when necessary."

He looked at me like he was questioning himself, but then he said, "You're the guide."

I thought the leadership was an advantage until about three days later, when he called me and the four squad leaders into his office and had us line up against the wall. It was mid-morning and nothing of consequence had happened so I assumed it would be a casual talk. He lectured us on how sloppy of a job we were doing in not pulling the platoon together any better. The five of us were standing at attention against the wall and he approached us. "At ease, men," he said as he slowly moved toward me…and Wham! A dead straight shot to my chest with his fist knocked the wind out of me, and I collapsed to the floor. I had to struggle to regain my senses and get on my feet. I'm sure

Front and center, the troop leader that was known as the "guide."

Staff Sergeant Willis didn't have any idea he would knock me down, but it played well into his game of intimidation and the fact that the other guides would spread the word of how tough he was.

I could tell Willis was concerned he may have seriously injured me, but he tried to maintain his poise when I hit the floor. "What's the matter, guide? You got a posture problem?!" he yelled. He didn't want to appear concerned; it might have revealed a sentimental softness that's forbidden in the Marines.

I managed my footing and answered, "No, sir! Sir, no sir!" I was proud as shit to have gotten that out as the others were about to piss in their pants thinking they were next. He told us to get out, and as the other four squad leaders exited the doorway, I paused only for a second and looked back at the Staff Sergeant with an undetectable smile. My eyes were asking, sarcastically, if *he* was alright.

He realized I sensed his concern, and knew that I knew he had a heart. He hadn't expected the possibility of seriously injuring someone he was responsible for. He had subtly exposed himself to me as a human being, not just a Marine, something which is supposed to remain two different things. He looked up with an angry surprise and said sternly, "Guide, get the hell outta here!" I remained one bad-ass platoon leader for the duration of training at Parris Island.

There were a couple weeks of break after Parris Island, and then it would be off to the war by late May. I was only a day or so from leaving when I received word from the Commandant of the Marine Corps: "You're going home for a few days!" I knew what it must have been: my girlfriend, Phyllis was pregnant. We thought it was possible, but when her father, Dr. Ford T. Johnson, a prominent Black dentist in Richmond, found out, he wrote a letter to the Commandant. He basically said, "Look, my daughter is pregnant, and she needs to marry the father before he goes. God forbid anything happens to Chuck; my daughter and that child would need support." He wanted to ensure there would be a spouse benefit to her.

It must have been an impressive letter because they snatched me from Camp Pendleton outside San Diego and I was quickly getting

Cease Fire! Cease Fire!

married in Rockville, Maryland, just outside of D.C. My new brother-in-law, Ford Jr., paid for a three-day honeymoon in Nassau, Bahamas. By the fifth day, I was back in California and headed to 'Nam on the sixth. It was surreal to grasp what had happened in just over a week. But needless to say, within a couple more weeks, my idea of surreal would change dramatically.

Before I left for Vietnam, I put a ring on it and married Phyllis Johnson, my one true love from junior high to the end (deceased—2006)

Chuck Richardson with Monte Richardson

Our first official photo as Mr. & Mrs., Rockville, Maryland, 1969.

Prepared for a weekend honeymoon before I left for Vietnam.

CHAPTER 3

The Thousand Yard Stare

"Pull yourself together, Marine! He's gone...he will feel pain no more, but you, you must go on, so get a bag, help pick up those parts."

Words from a tall, dark-skinned Gunnery Sargent, who stepped with a prompt certainty as he bent to snatch up body parts that were still steaming from the chilling morning air. The artillery round had just landed on our command post and destroyed everything within a twenty-five-yard radius, including six marines. Less than three minutes before, I had walked away from these six, telling them to "find Charlie" before we pulled out.

"Charlie" was Charlie Welch, my close buddy from Philadelphia; we completed Infantry Training Regiment (ITR) machine gun training together. That artillery round was from a fire mission we had just called in. Our own artillery had hit us. I had heard him cry, "Cease fire, cease fire!" He was yelling into the radio hand-mic and I heard the rounds going off in the distance. Our radio man had just returned from R&R in Hawaii where he had spent time with his wife and their three-month-old daughter.

The explosions were getting louder: Boom! Boom! Boom! Still, I could hear the yells: "Cease fire! Cease fire! Cease ..." and a white flash appeared overhead like the Devil's lightning. The horrific noise of a thousand truckloads of dynamite went off. Our radio man, a new father, instantly left us, literally. The very man calling so aggressively for the cease fire was sadly rendered the target. The artillery round landed less than forty yards from where I was standing, but thank God, we were on an island, Barrier Island. The island was a body of sand more than anything, which somewhat cushioned the impact of the explosion. Our circumstances would have been much worse had we settled in on hard ground where rocks and stones existed, but the sandy earth was an ally, an island we ironically called "the rock." There were trees and bushes, but the ground itself probably saved many.

Death came from many forces in Vietnam, a madness many of us have carried all our lives. It almost found me just a month earlier after only being in 'Nam a few weeks. We were crossing a heavily flooded stream on a make-shift narrow bridge, which was just a series of concrete pylons. They were maybe two-foot square, submerged a couple of feet in the swift waters. We were moving slowly, one step at a time, unable to see where we stepped, just following each other. Suddenly, I was falling underwater from the slippery footing and pulled down under the weight of weapons and rations in the swift current. I believed it was over. I was going to fucking *drown* in 'Nam. I strained to keep my mouth above water and reached for anything I could but slipped under. Then, like a scene in a movie, a hand grabbed mine and my head was almost instantly out the water. I saw the face of the marine behind me, "Big Bill" Davis.

Bill was a tall lanky, red-headed White dude from Alabama who could bend over on that "bridge" and not hardly touch the water. He looked at me without saying anything, just a smile as if to say, "I got you, Marine." Bill pulled me up as I gagged with a panic you can imagine, grateful to that White boy that smiled with a gratitude of his own that he had saved his fellow Marine. It was really only a matter of seconds, the whole event, but the fact that race was not relevant in the act was a poignant altruism; reaching to help each other should be a reflex, instinctual. I must add—very sadly that—William Francis

Cease Fire! Cease Fire!

"Big Bill" Davis, was killed later that summer in the Que Son Valley.

Barrier Island, which was fairly large, was used as a staging point for the Vietnamese Army. It was about thirty to forty miles south of Da Nang, a key asset to getting the enemy troops south. The Marines would be tasked with taking the small island, a task taken too lightly. It was a mostly rural farming area with a sand base, so it was primarily used for raising livestock such as pigs, chickens, etc. The Vietnamese were every bit at home in this terrain and place that very few others knew.

We initially experienced snipers, booby traps, and small arms but no significant confrontation. With all our superior firepower, communications, and training, though, we were often unable to locate any significant number of them. Yet they would appear briefly to ambush a few of us at time. There would be occasional firefights, but we could not rout them and begin any real control of the island. That, and the many primitive booby-traps would take its toll on the Marines; headquarters was frustrated, losing men one or two at a time consistently. One Marine, fully equipped with protective gear and arms, can be quite a formidable force alone, but a battalion would be considered invincible. It was unacceptable that such a force could continue to have their asses whipped after a week on such a small island by small groups of men running around in black pajamas with little things called AK-47s.

Men in Washington, and even in the Marines, were learning on the job about this relatively new art of guerrilla warfare. The Viet Cong had kept abreast of our every move, every man by the inch virtually, yet we could barely find footprints or indications of any of their presence. Thus, it was decided we would evacuate after barely a week. So, the Colonel, in all his wisdom, came up with a brilliant plan to relocate an entire battalion of Marines under the cover of darkness. It was crazy, we thought; all the things that could go awry gathering 600 men, supplies, food, and gear—and then try to steal away from a man's backyard—was a monumental task.

After a grueling all-night six-mile march, the plan was to have large Sea Horse 53 choppers swoop down at first light to pick us up. As the early faint light gave the sky color, word scattered desperately that a man was missing! Private First Class (PFC) Chard, a young Mexican recruit, had been left. Private Nelms, a friend of mine and Chard's, had seen him the evening before, even when we had taken a headcount. Chard was sitting with his head down appearing to be just resting, Nelms said. He was very upset at the thought that he may have fallen asleep while everyone was gearing up for the march. It's a true saying: "Marines don't leave anyone behind," and Chard was not an exception.

The entire battalion would return immediately to our departure site. But first, it was determined that we should call in artillery fire between our current location and the previous location the night before. The idea was to hit any enemy troops that might be in our path. There was the possibility, as well, of killing Chard during this fire mission because he most certainly would be in the strike zone. Nevertheless, it was the risk they decided to take. The risk was ubiquitous, including with us.

It was during the artillery attack we had called in that 'friendly fire' landed in our lap, killing six, including the decimated radio operator. Following a short period in which I heard nothing but the sound of my beating heart, I rose to my feet in a stupor. That's when I heard the gunnery sergeant. "Pull yourself together, goddammit! He's gone!"

How strange, after all this time, that I can still see, in my mind's eye, the steam rising from a backbone, sheared of everything, that just minutes ago was a man. I recall the M16 rifle laying in the sand with its barrel curled like a twisted string of black spaghetti. I was astonished at the power and destructive forces that could do such damage. When I raised my head, there in the distance was Charlie Welsh, standing in his characteristic bow-legged stance. His hands were near his ears and he looked bewildered as he stared across the smoking remains of the explosion.

The aftermath of any combat experience such as this is bittersweet. Despite the painful loss of someone so close and the anguish it causes, your own survival is appreciated, if not celebrated, with such an intense rush. Of all the emotions such as sadness, sympathy, remorse, and fear, nothing overrides the exhilaration of being alive! The gratitude of surviving is overwhelming, considering the dead and mangled bodies that could have included yours. Yet, the fear of facing the uncertain future renders the mourning of a lost comrade short-lived. We had to go on.

Even though the Vietnamese knew virtually all our movements, we made it back to our original location, finding Chard where they had left him—in the middle of the path as if to say, 'here's where we left him.' PFC Chard had been executed with a single bullet to the back of the head. The thing that has always haunted me was how Chard came to meet his fate. To awaken in the middle of the night all alone in the jungles of enemy territory and find that you have been left is more horrifying than I could imagine.

On the fifth day of the operation, the battalion leadership, disgusted, frustrated, and in despair, decided to evacuate the battalion on the same spot from which we had marched the night before. The general decided to evacuate in broad daylight, and to risk this evacuation from a "hot LZ" (landing zone) vulnerable to snipers. The 3rd Battalion 7th Marines, arranged in parade deck formation, called in more than eight Sea Horse 53 helicopters. One by one, each large chopper came from the distant skies like majestic gladiators to sweep in from the heavens.

When the enormous aircraft sat down in the middle of the large rice paddies, like clockwork, approximately sixty Marines at a time formed a running semi-circle around the magnificent birds. They were quickly loaded up and into the drop-down rear plank, disappearing into its belly. The large choppers methodically left the area until all that remained over Barrier Island were the blue skies of Vietnam, receiving the souls of sixteen Americans that would never see the world again.

It was early in my tour of Vietnam, the start of my year there. Barrier Island, in hindsight, was a snapshot of the whole conflict. The whole ordeal was one massive conglomeration of poor decisions that ultimately demoralized the troops. We had invaded an island with no understanding or respect for the enemy. A battalion of Marines, we were seeking yet seeing very little to no evidence of enemy troops. We were losing many to snipers and traps, called artillery onto ourselves, lost an abandoned Marine, and many of us were wounded as well. And then, we ended up back in the same combat site in which we had been … and we had left Chard. What was all the tragedy for? What was the suffering for? Why? The North Vietnamese, as we know, would take the South after all, and today Americans visit there for beautiful, popular vacations: hundreds of thousands of lives later, billions of tears later, a cease fire.

On LZ Baldy, before our descent into Que Son Valley Troop

Que Son Valley

It was a beautiful, sunlit morning with a gentle breeze bending the tips of the tall jungle grass that covered most of the mountain tops in the area. It was like a floral scene of a picturesque resort or vacation spot.

Cease Fire! Cease Fire!

But it was 1969, and no spot within eyesight was without the suffering of warfare and the sounds that belied the gentle waves of grass. Our place on the mountain top was peaceful—on that morning—but the stresses were not. The tension was distinct, breaking our brows and corrupting the easy movements we made as we off-loaded artillery, supplies, and ammunition from the large green CH-53 helicopter we called the 'Jolly Green Giant.' We knew there was something big ahead and the fear would seemingly inch up our spines while we prepared.

Abruptly told to pack our gear for bivouac and to lock and load all weapons, everybody was afraid. We spent most of the day preparing supplies, checking gear, and planning for our foot descent down to the valley: Que Son Valley. U.S. Army troops were being relieved after enduring heavy casualties and defeats in the valley. The word was there were North Vietnamese Army (NVA) regulars down there, not the Viet Cong (VC). The VC were mostly groups of guerrilla fighters, but the NVA were well-trained soldiers and were better equipped.

The Que Son valley was about two miles from the Laotian-Cambodian border where some of the heaviest concentration of enemy troops existed. At the time, we (the troops) never really knew exactly where we were; we could have been in Laos, Vietnam, or Cambodia. My official orders had us at Quang Nam Province in Vietnam.

After a day of getting ready, we started out about 6:30 that evening down the mountain. Two things stand out in my memory about that evening, besides everyone being scared shitless! One, a new Black Marine told some of the guys that he would shoot himself before he went down to that valley. That new Marine was scared, but calm, and, sure enough a few minutes later—BAM! The clear sound of an M16 vibrated through the air. He exited from some tall grass with his finger dangling half-on and off his hand. A man cannot shoot his weapon without a trigger finger. Our lieutenant knew it was self-inflicted but could not prove it in an area like that, so a medevac was called in. That brother left the rest of us showing no sign of pain, remorse, or anything; he just boarded that chopper with a sheepish, blank look on his face.

Only idiots and those who had a few snorts of dope appeared

to be calm while the minutes ticked by. Narcotics and heroin, Benoctol 7.5s—the kind of stuff that calms and deadens the senses of pain—were not unusual. I never saw anyone use marijuana in the fight zones because it created paranoia, and the ultimate paranoia is death, so it could be a quick way to an ass-kicking!

The other memory was about halfway down the mountain when a young corporal began having dry heaves. We were held up treating him as his pain seemed to overwhelm him. And the painful heaving didn't end. He struggled on, but I learned when we got to the bottom that he didn't survive. It's odd how we never realize the many ways of death under the circumstances of war, and while it is likely the story of how he died is known to his family, it seems kinder to say that he died in combat. No mother should know through her life that her son died a slow and painful death such as that, another added torture.

When we reached the foothills of the mountain, we came to a dirt road and soon saw the U.S. Army troops we were replacing marching up the mountain. I was shocked to see the number of Black soldiers in that unit. They were all walking away from combat and wore on their faces a look as if all feeling were gone. I wanted so badly to ask one of them what happened. *Is it bad?* I could tell by the very look on their faces, passing in a single file as if they were dead already, that it was very bad. They had the "thousand-yard stare" in their eyes, looking past us, around us, through us, and deep into us. It was a foreshadowing for those of us marching down the road they were leaving.

I had a powerful impulse to turn and go back, to join them, no matter the consequences; every impulse told me to stop marching, to save myself. It was like having the very fate of my life in my hands in those moments. But it was impossible. How could I? How could I turn and walk away—even if it meant saving my life? Sometimes, no matter what the consequences might be, you have to do what is expected, what is counted on by others, even if it means dying. I must admit it was the most frightened I've ever been. I could not help thinking as we plodded down into that valley, that maybe that brother who shot himself back up top was smarter than the rest of us.

I'm certain every Marine on the trail that night must have had the same thought but we all continued to walk down that road.

On August 23rd, 1969, my company, Mike Company, 3rd Battalion, 7th Marine Division, marched into the hellhole called the Que Son Valley. It would come to be the most horrid and devastating week of human loss I experienced during my tour of duty in Vietnam. Even after fifty years, I am unable to write of things that occurred during that sad and shameful time in 1969. I may begin to write but, for some reason, I cannot put to paper the pain I feel, and I fight back tears of anger, guilt, and remorse. As young Americans, we did inhumane things to the people of Vietnam. Yes, it was war, and yes, at times inhumane things were done to us; but NO, it was not right for many thousands of civilians.

We walked through a shocking scene of families: young women, little girls, babies clinging to breasts as they lay horribly burned to death by the gasoline jelly Napalm. The day before we arrived in the valley, the villages and forest had been relentlessly bombed. We had watched the bombing from the mountainside as it rained total annihilation. The Phantom jets swept in releasing 'precision' strikes to clear our way. We watched with great pride—almost gleeful as the explosions rose up in dark gray bursts, instant glows of bright orange and blue from their center. It held us in awe, breathless at the fact that we were so close on that mountain top as we watched, as we killed the 'enemy.'

At the time, it did not impact us as deeply as it does today. As an M60 machine gunner in the U.S. Marines, they had inculcated a sense of purpose in us, and that I was an effective part of a meaningful cause: fighting back Communism and its "evil" forces. But I remember, I remember walking down to the village to see largely only women, children, and babies. There was no justification for what we did, and it is only now, after years of contemplation, that I consider, and believe, *we* were the evil force—I was the evil force. Those poor village peasants probably didn't care about Communism, Democracy, or who or what was in charge. They were struggling in their rice paddies to grow crops, raise animals, to simply sustain themselves.

They possessed little more than their clothes, animals, and the huts they slept in.

The NVA were hidden deep in the thick, low hills, long gone from the areas the jets had unleashed hell on the evening before. After we passed through the devastation and carnage, we headed to the tree line at the other side of the valley where the true enemy was. When we reached the edge of the tree line, 'the bush', all hell was unleashed: snipers, mortars, automatic, and even small arms were brought to bear on the 7th Marines. We fought with ferocious intensity through the morning as platoon leaders yelled unrelenting commands to forge ahead. We were held down at an embankment on the edge of an irrigation wall, maybe a hundred yards or so from the enemy. Tree roots protruded from the battered earth which gave us footing to fire, often wildly, over the top. The embankment was not like the horrible trenches of World War I at Verdun, but it was hard to imagine going over, and yet there was no choice. We all continued to fire over the top, waiting for air or artillery support as the dirt and sweat and hot shells flew, and the yells of panic, bravado and direction held together the chaos.

At one point, one of my best buddies, Marco Aurelio Fregoso, stood up and jumped over to advance and protect his Marine brothers. Marco got about twenty feet. He went down, and a couple of us almost immediately went up after him. Myself and two others grabbed Fregoso as another Marine was hit in the eye coming to assist us, not a fatal wound for him, but it made everything so intense I seemed to go deaf, as if my mind were shutting down the sounds.

The Marine who helped me drag Fregoso back was crying and shaking as we pulled him back below the embankment. Marco, my new friend, was dead, but we yelled for medics frantically, hoping there was hope. I looked down at his bloody flak jacket and saw a small wrench which we used on some of our weapons, laying on the ground next to him. Even in those split seconds of hell, a memory flashed in my mind from the evening before.

Fregoso and I were chatting while he smoked his 'Tareyton' cigarettes; nobody smoked that brand but Fregoso. They had a nasty taste with their charcoal filter. He told me he only did it because Tareyton was the brand his wife smoked, and he smoked them while thinking of her. He offered me one and I took it and said, "Sure, damn right, here's to your wife." That's when I loaned him that wrench I later saw on the ground next to his body. Marco and I had been friends since the early days on 'the rock' (Barrier Island), before our descent into the Que Son. Fregoso and many others did not make it that morning. His loss has always been one that I remember, and feel, when I think of Vietnam.

After several hours of combat, with only short lulls of almost constant fire, my M60 machine gun began to jam. The dirt and dust and the capacity of my weapon to fire over 500 rounds per minute left the barrel of the gun red-hot. It required us to wear asbestos gloves to switch the barrels amid the fight! At one point, I flipped the gun over to shake loose the jammed cartridges and the barrel burned my wrist. To this day, I still have the mark of that burn, occasionally reminding me of that day but also of the Marines and soldiers. From that mark I recall the self-inflicted wound to escape that valley to the loss of life to a stomach bacterium to the Marines who displayed incredible bravery and valor, but it mostly reminds me of human character. We all have images of ourselves and the character we carry—even in war—and some of us never flinch from it.

When my gun jammed in that battle, I knew I had to be 'cool' even as my wrist was branded with the mark of that chaos. It was like a movie scene, with the yelling for gloves and support to regain the firepower of the M60. There were many Marines that day who remained cool, some almost as if it were their job, almost like a John Wayne or Audie Murphy. But in reality, combat includes mishaps, humor, embarrassment, and a whole range of feelings.

Brother Brooks was the kind of guy who talked, and mostly rhymed, all the time. He was quick to lie about an illness or injury, assaulting an officer, even mental disorders, to get out of the bush but not this time. Brooks was a tall, square-jawed, handsome guy from Detroit with sparkling white teeth that chattered constantly, even in battle at Que Son. We usually didn't know if he was saying something to us or just himself. Brooks didn't wear a helmet most times, just a blue baseball cap with a big white 'B' in the front. Standing next to my a-gunner, Brooks yelled for the gloves I needed as he looked at my M60 smoking, and said with the same chattering confidence, "Brother Chuck! Your 60 is like me... red hot!"

I can see him clearly, with a string of M16 clips around his neck, standing with one foot bracing himself against the embankment, releasing a cartridge and quickly slapping another into place with his weapon on full-automatic. Then, at one point, he put it down and when the butt of his weapon hit the ground...ba-ba-Bang!...and it fired straight up! The round took off his baseball cap, going right through the brim, flying up, causing everyone to look. Brooks was scared shitless; the shock in his eyes seemed to scream, but seeing that everyone had seen it, he broke a broad confident grin and shouted, "I'm so bad my gun shoots by itself!"

Que Son was, with all else, a maddening display of irony and ignorance. During one of our few breaks from the dangers and hazard of "the bush," two friends got into a heated argument. A Black fellow, I think his name was, well ... we called him Detroit, and a White guy called "Big Red." These two guys were best buddies as it goes in the combat zone: a machine gunner and his ammo humper, the A-gunner. One day, Detroit and Big Red had heated words over the Confederate flag painted on Red's helmet. We had never seen the two of them disagree like that. In combat, when lives depend on the trust between each other, the bonds can be deep and meaningful, but the Confederate flag is a symbol with profound racial overtones and, even among the best of friends, can create some intense differences.

Detroit and Big Red trusted each other with their lives, but before one night's end, they were hollering and cursing about that "goddamn redneck symbol of hatred." They said everything short of the N-word before hitting the 'rock' (bed) without resolving their conflict. It was an altercation that had ramifications beyond the two of them. It was racial, and other Marines shared the same feelings, including my buddy Thomas Nelms, a White guy from north Georgia. Nelms was as good a man as I would have next to me in combat. But still he was raised, like Big Red, on that Georgian mythical bullshit about the Civil War and the South's heroic, noble heritage.

The next morning, we were quickly engaged in a firefight well before any chance to argue about the Confederate flag again. Now, we were all under the 'Stars 'n Stripes' defending ourselves. But midway through combat, Detroit, who had been moving with Big Red to better cover us, received a fatal shot. Big Red and three others dragged Detroit to safety, but he was hardly breathing. Despite our desperate efforts and Big Red pleading with the corpsman, Detroit stopped breathing. We lost him. We continued fighting into the afternoon, then a chopper medevacked Detroit back to first med. After things settled, and we were safely below the embankment, we all saw Big Red weeping. He was cussing and pacing with intense anger and disbelief when he threw the helmet from his head forcefully to the ground, then dropped to it himself, and sat with his hands over his face. When he looked from his hands, he happened to look straight at his helmet that had landed right side up and showed the clear image of the confederate battle flag with the deep red 'Stars and Bars' looking directly at him. Big Red, a strapping 240-pound man, suddenly released a torrent of tears, crying and cussing softly as tears and snot poured from him.

"Why, why, why goddamn it!? He was a good man, Brother Chuck! Why did he have to die? And why did that flag, that stupid flag upset him so fucking much!!? Why?!"

My buddy, Thomas Helms added, "Yeah, Richardson, why did he hate that flag so much, I wanna know?"

"Yea, we gotta know," Big Red said.

It was early evening and we had all gathered into a small group. I paused for a moment wanting to say the right thing. I could tell how much Big Red was hurting because he never got a chance to make amends with Detroit. He wanted to understand how his flag could be the reason. I said to Big Red and Helms that sometimes we can't know things because we don't take time to listen to each other. I said, "It's nobody's fault. We just don't listen because we don't realize how much people mean to us until they're not around anymore." I told them that the Confederate flag means something totally different to them than us! That Black people define that flag in a gravely different way.

"When you guys from the South see it, you think about brave men on horseback, pistols firing, and swords flying as cannons roar. You imagine romantic versions of them, courageous and noble, fighting for a way of life you have rarely thought a lot about. You don't see what we see! When Detroit saw the Confederate flag, he was insulted by what it defended: men who owned Black slaves, his forefathers. A flag that reminded us of ancestors who awakened every morning with nothing to look forward to but long rows of cotton as far as the eye could see, the 100-degree sun, and the rawhide sting of the master. A flag that represented men who raped eleven-, twelve- and thirteen-year-old little girls because they owned them: property—with the right to sell children three, four and five-years-old from their mother to the highest bidder, never to be seen again in life. We are reminded of 250 years of these atrocities … that's why Detroit resented that flag on your helmet."

"Why in the hell didn't you say something before now, Brother Chuck?" asked Big Red softly.

"Detroit was trying to tell you that the other night, but it seems like somebody always got to die before people listen to them or when it's too late," I said. When I finally raised my head up, other Marines were there listening and Big Red's eyes were closed, tears falling intensely.

My buddy Helms asked me again, "Richardson, why didn't you say something?"

I said, "I guess I thought you might have been able to figure it out on your own."

Helms responded quietly, "How do you expect a redneck like me to think with your mind when I can hardly get a good clear thought out of my own?" Big Red had no words, but I've never seen a man so big cry so long and so quietly.

The next morning, the NVA had all cleared out; they were gone—

and so was the flag on Big Red's helmet. I don't know what he did with it, but it was just a regular Marine Corp helmet now—without the camouflage covering—without the flag.

Nelms approached me a few minutes later with a mouth full of chewing tobacco, drooling, and peering through his half-inch thick glasses. He started stammering and said, "Brother Chuck, if getting along with you guys in the future means letting go a part of my past, I 'spect it'll be worth it, you reckon?"

I reckoned. Then, I looked at that redneck and gave him a big Black bear hug. I turned quickly away to pick up my machine gun before he could notice the tears welling up in *my* eyes.

Mortar Attacks

Sometimes, I awaken in the middle of the night thinking about one particular horror of war fifty years ago: the sound of stones ripping apart and trees splitting at their bases that breaks everybody's sleep. North Vietnamese mortars were raining down on us from a nearby mountain range. There was nowhere to run because there was nowhere to seek cover, and no way to know where they could land! If you ran for cover behind nearby boulders, a mortar round could hit the stone, exploding into even more pieces of deadly shrapnel. You might grab your helmet, flak jacket, and hold onto your gun and, yes, even your balls, but never is life so vulnerable and dependent on chance than under a mortar attack in open rocks and trees.

I remember in Que Son, a new guy in the company, a young, good-looking White boy had just arrived three days earlier on his second tour of duty in 'Nam. A direct blow left almost literally nothing of him. He never knew what happened.

The attack lasted several series of mortars before we could

determine their location and coordinates. The best I could do was estimate the direction from which the mortar was coming, get on the opposite side of a large boulder....then pray. We would endure five or six casualties that morning. Our forward observers could call in artillery fire from miles away with pin-point accuracy, but we were always fearful of what was known as a "short round," fired from our forces from the hills, or maybe from a long gun on a ship, miles off the coast. You could hear the deep whistling cut through the air as our large artillery came overhead before hitting the target—just a few hundred yards in front of us.

The rounds would hit the targets with such loud ferocity and destructive force. The thought of a "short round" was nightmarish, the rare but deadly "friendly fire." I often wondered how the NVA troops maintained their sanity with that kind of destruction raining down upon them, daily. B-52 aircraft unloading 1000-pound bombs, fifty at a time, must have been a hell unknown to mankind. I cannot begin to imagine what it must have been like for those enemy troops. Even when we were camped two miles away, laying on the ground as a blocking force, we could look up in the sky and see the B-52s five miles up. We would stand, watching the deadly tubes drift downward toward the enemy. Seconds later, we would watch the concussion force roll across the valley brush and feel it hit us in the chest like a horse kick. The thunderous sound would follow momentarily, one of the few "safe" thrills we could return to speak about.

It did not occur to me the real danger we were in until I returned home and learned just how technically accurate every aspect of the B-52 Arc Light bombing had to be to hit the right target and not us. With thirty bombers cruising at 250 miles away from the target point, Marine company leaders who didn't know where our exact position was most of the time, a changing wind, and the broad killing radius of those bombs, I'd say we were a pretty lucky bunch. That mortar attack in the Que Son Valley was bad, but we were mostly lucky. On August 16th, on Barrier Island, we were not!

CHAPTER 4

Fear's Footprint

—

It all depends on who was there to tell the story and if they told it right or told it in or against your favor. All too often, the truth is undiscovered, an account of what someone thought happened, and not necessarily what occurred in reality. Therefore, "his-story," or whoever tells it, becomes our account of what we call "history".

The hundreds of war medals—Bronze Star, Silver Star, Cross of Gallantry, and Medal of Honor—must be reported and authenticated by officers and substantiated by military personnel to be awarded. In many instances, there are heroic deeds of outstanding performance involving courage, sacrifice, and stunning bravado, but because no officer could, or would, attest to the event, they went without notice or recognition. In other instances, they may be small acts of little merit but are reported by an officer of standing who exaggerated and lied about the actions that would earn great honors—undeserved.

Most war medals are indeed honorably earned and should not be questioned, but like everything else, there is dishonesty and fraud by some that are authorized to record combat honors. Colonels, generals, and majors are not exempt from fraudulent portrayals. Thank goodness it is not widespread, but it happens.

Sometimes the story doesn't matter at all; it is simply opportunity. One night while on guard, Corporal Prim and I killed a teenage boy.

Our company commander was about two clicks away and heard of the "kill" over the radio. We had not seen any action in almost two weeks and the commander was overjoyed. "I'm going to recommend Richardson for a Silver Star!"

When the squad leader came back and told me this, I was upset. I had been feeling bad about killing the boy and responded, "I don't want no medal for killing no kid and will not accept a medal for no shit like that!"

The squad leader returned around noon and said the company officer (C.O.) was pissed that I would not accept a medal. He had told the battalion commander that I had apprehended the Viet Cong, taken his weapon, and killed him in a hand-to-hand battle—and deserved the Silver Star. I said, "That was bullshit! Why would he do that?!"

He said, "Look, Richardson, you don't understand how shit works over here. You killed a Gook; we all see a dead body. The company officer was not here. He can make up any shit he wants because he is a major and it makes him look good when his men earn medals killing enemy troops! They won't question it because we all saw the man you killed, so just drop it!"

I overheard the major on the radio afterward: "What kind of pussies you got over there won't take credit for confirms?!"

I told the squad leader, "The kind that ain't proud of shootin' kids!"

The version the C.O. told was "his-story," to make him, and me, look good. But it was not the truth, not near it. The difference between the major's story and mine was clear: I was there when the boy was killed. I saw his eyes open wide when the flash from our weapons lit up his face and he looked at us in the dead of night. My A-gunner, Corporal Prim, and I were on watch when we heard someone coming down the path. I called quietly to him, "Prim, someone's out there!" We waited for a second and saw the figure walk toward us. I yelled at him to halt in Vietnamese: "Dung lai, dung lai!...dung lai!"

The figure was no more than a silhouette in the darkness, and he continued as if he heard nothing. He seemed to be carrying something on his back and moments later, Prim yelled, "Halt motherfucker!!"

Blam! We fired and I saw the face of the young boy, perhaps fifteen at most, drop instantly.

When we saw him on the ground, we were shocked... so young. Why didn't he stop, where was he going, what was he carrying? We carefully searched him: no weapons. We opened the heavy backpack he wore. It was full of rice. The kid possibly was taking it to the Viet Cong up the hill or maybe not. At that point, it didn't matter; it was over. He would never see his mother, father, or siblings again, and they would never know his fate. I shot him down like a dog. No hand-to-hand combat, no fight at all. And I should receive a medal? For what?

Instinct

I'll start with a question: Did you ever kill anybody? Did you ever kill anybody? Think about it. It might sound like a fair question—for a typical citizen. Years after I returned from Vietnam, I was asked that very question.

How can I go through all the shit I went through and come back here to an asshole question like that? What kind of question is that? What kind of bullshit are they filling your heads with out here? You would expect such a question from a kid maybe, or from an inquisitive thirteen-year-old youngster. But, when such a question comes from an adult, who claims to be really interested in the war, then the question is totally inappropriate. And you want to grab the guy by the neck, choke the livin' shit out him, and ask, "What in the hell do you think?" But using the better part of judgment, you realize that some people just don't know any better! As I held my composure and considered how to answer such a dumb-ass question, my mind flooded, again, with a memory from Barrier Island.

There was only one real firefight for us on that island the week or so we were there, but it was intense. We were outside the perimeter of a listening post when all hell broke out. It was nighttime and I was in a small group ahead of most of our men, but a small group of Viet Cong snipers were firing from a tree line in front of us. But it was too close to tell whether the rounds were coming from them or us. The tree line was close, and all the tracer rounds coming from both sides had stopped. I couldn't tell where the V.C. were or where my Marine buddies were, but I heard two guys moaning over in the brush about ten or fifteen yards away. It was a jet-black night, and I couldn't see my hand in front of my face. I knew the guys on the upper side of the hill were Marines, close enough to hear one of them crying for his mama. In the fighting and scramblin' in the dark, my machine gun was out of M60 cartridges and all I had was my .45 caliber pistol in my side holster.

In the confusion and the dark, the only thing I had to go by was the sound of our command post (C.P.) about two hundred yards behind us—or the V.C. in front of me—but I couldn't tell how far. There was the distant noise of the Marines running back and forth between the C.P. and a downed helicopter, a dual-blade 46 that had gone down in the darkness. Every now and then, the shooting would start and stop. Then I kept hearing the Marine calling to his mama. I wanted to help him, but I had fallen into another foxhole or bunker while going for more ammo. My '60 was back over across a mound, covered in thick, wet grass.

I was virtually blind, seeing with my ears when I slid into that hole. And unbelievably, within a minute or so, a Viet Cong fighter fell right in behind me! I had instinctual reaction when he jumped, or fell, in the hole, and started cussing, and he instantly started yelling something in Vietnamese. I started kicking and kicking till I was out of breath. I could not stop, as if my body were thinking for itself, reflexively stomping, leaving him knocked out or dead. I couldn't tell in the pitch black. It was horrifying, the desperation of kicking so hard, that I pissed on myself. The Viet Cong fighter became motionless, and I could smell that he must have shit on himself in the fight while I had pissed on myself as well.

It was starting to smell so bad and I knew for sure, after a few minutes or so, that he was dead because his arms were getting cold and stiff. I felt around for my .45 millimeter to see if it was still in the holster. There, still in my holster, was my pistol. Yet when that V.C. stumbled into the hole on top of me, I had instinctively begun kicking until he didn't move anymore. I did not reach for the .45 and shoot him. I kicked the man (boy) to death! My Marine Corps-issued jungle boots were the weapons and fear was the fuel. Desperation is a strange thing.

I came home from the jungles of Vietnam to a place where the television news and Hollywood had filled people's heads with the glorified romantic images of war and John Wayne. And some asshole asks me a question like that! All I could think of was kicking a man to death and a buddy calling for his mother: "Mama… somebody—help me!"

There were no glorified scenes of the elimination of the enemy by the rapid fire of a one-handed M60, as perhaps that clown imagined when he asked me that question. But rather images and scents of shitty boots, the stench of urine, and exhaustion, scenes far removed from television glory.

It's not the kind of thing Marines brag about, but these kinds of killings occur more often than you might believe. They are times that soldiers don't talk about: the quiet deaths when you hear men call for their mamas and pray for Jesus and cuss in the same breath, and when they weep and admit they're afraid and know that death is near. There is nothing glorious about war, except when you're home watching it on television. But more deceiving are the subliminal messages we absorb from TV that draw impressionable young men to war. These TV images do not underscore the fact that there is no rerun. Once you are dead, you are dead. Once it's over, it's over, and yet when you are asked twenty years later if you have ever killed anyone, you know it is never over for you.

Chuck Richardson with Monte Richardson

Heroin

Unbelievably, I was a notorious "square Jones" while attending Virginia Union University, spending most of my time running and staying in good physical condition. Of course, in 1968, I was aware of the growing culture of drug use, from marijuana to acid, but I stayed away from the opportunity whenever it may have crossed my path. So, when confronted with the question of drug use in Vietnam, I had hardly even begun to experiment with cigarettes, much less marijuana or heroin. But the opportunity and conditions in Vietnam were a long way from the dorms or frat houses at VUU. There was a helluva lot more than peer pressure that soon caught up with my innocent, protected Christian background and the wholesome American narrative, not to mention the image of a needle going in my arm, that slowly eroded the idea that doing heroin was far from possible.

The cultural divide in Vietnam was as sharp as it was anywhere else. The White boys drank, Jack Daniels Black Label preferably, and the Black guys smoked marijuana—by the pitchfork loads. But increasingly, the intermingling became more prominent, and the commonalities would reveal themselves beyond the skin color assumptions. Although my skin complexion was not typical Negroid, and my grain of hair far closer to Caucasian than Black, mannerisms and cultural habits readily placed me in the African American camp. But there were many instances of doubt when men did not know for certain and would guess. Sometimes, Hispanic guys would walk up to me and start speaking some dialect of Spanish.

In September of 1969, I returned from the field exhausted, living through the nightmares of Que Son and Barrier Island, confused and frightened. All the Marines were beat, and many were hurt. I noticed two of the Black guys were snorting some sort of powder; it was heroin, and they seemed to be in another place where fear and confusion was non-existent. A couple other brothers joined them and within a minute

Cease Fire! Cease Fire!

or two they were insisting I find that place of relief.

"Richardson, we just left hell. Now we're in heaven. Come join us, brother," one said. I could only think of the heroin addicts in a TV show I had watched with my dad about seven or eight years earlier: the strung out, dazed, and dirty junkies in Harlem, and those fucked up needles!

I asked them what could be so good, and another brother said, "Hey, man! It's the King, the big horse."

I said, "That shit's heroin?!"

He said, "Yeah, man! Didn't you know?"

"Look, my father warned me about that stuff and said the addiction is too strong for any man to handle."

They rolled their eyes at me and smirked, "Man, you in Vietnam. Da fuck do you have to worry about with this shit?"

I told them, "Getting addicted to that shit, that's what."

Maurice, one the brothers doing the "big horse," stood up and looked at me sympathetically and said, "Richardson, what's that weapon at your feet you just sat on the deck?"

"It's an M60 machine gun, so, you know that," I said.

Maurice replied, "You carrying that in the bush?"

"Yeah, man, why? Whatcha saying?"

Maurice glanced at the other guys and looked at me, and said, "You just got in country, didn't you?"

I said, "June...so," as he looked at his buddies again and then back at me.

"The life expectancy of a Marine machine gunner in a bad firefight is nineteen seconds. You got eight more months of this shit and you go' see at least ten or fifteen more terrible firefights, some worse than any shit you saw in that valley, and them V.C.s go' be zeroing in on yo ass, nine-teen-seconds..." He said it like he was teaching something.

Then another added, "Yeah, bro, and all of 'em ain't go' miss, you dig?"

"Eight more months of almost certain death and you worried about getting addicted. Shiiiid, brother you worried about the wrong

76

shot!" Maurice went on. "Dig it, man, you worried 'bout something that might happen—if you survive."

They all broke into a harmonious round of giggles and glances at me while Maurice sat back down. They didn't mean any harm. They were trying to convince me that using heroin would ease the fears of going out into the bush, like an impervious shield. They had lost all but three of their company machine gunners, but the heroin would make them feel so good that they somehow had got accustomed to the idea of men dying. It seemed what bothered them as much as those deaths was them losing the heroin—and that bothered me.

I did not submit to the idea of using heroin right away. Despite seeing the euphoric ease and constant spell of pleasure that group appeared to be under, I remained aloof and at a distance for a while. I felt somewhat White-boyish, not joining my peers, my brothers… you dig? The memory of my father's words hung heavy in my mind and, although they were snorting the stuff, the constant thought of a needle and heroin addiction was the primary mitigating factor for my avoidance.

However, fear pressure can give in to peer pressure, especially between the miseries of the monsoon rains and malaria, body parts and faces that would never return. With prolonged suffering, you eventually give in to a much-needed relief. That first short white hit of opiate powder would not worry me about the other war I would fight for over two decades; it simply took me from the horror of that one. No needle, just a quick deep breath through the nose, and Voila!—my whole world changed. I would never fear combat, feel remorse, imagine disappointment, or worry about the coming of death again. They were right; heroin was all they said it would be. The dangers were as real as ever, but the perception had changed the mood of entering combat from nerve-rocking anguish and paralyzing fear to a confident ease.

Sometimes, you were just lucky, or had God on your side, because the night I walked point (in the very front) with my M60 and survived is beyond just chance. An M60 machine gun is a "crew-served weapon," usually strategically positioned between the mid-section and back of the squad. The A-gunner (assistant) carries the ammunition and has to stay close, near with the tripod, extra barrels, and asbestos gloves for changing the barrel. Sometimes, at 550 rounds a minute, the barrel will become red hot from continuous firing and jam up, requiring a change. Therefore, a machine gun is never carried at point. On this night, however, we were with some new Marines in the country and the squad leader had been wounded. I was the lucky guy who was most familiar with the area, so having been there about six months, I took point.

One bad weapon...plus, my M60 machine gun in Vietnam, 1969.

Although some of the other Marines thought it was crazy, it's really no worse on point than most other locations in the squad formation because the Viet Cong usually allowed half the squad to pass through the kill zone before they would initiate the ambush. Plus, the way I felt, it didn't really matter where I was; it would have been wasting good worry.

Two nights following that, we set an ambush. Since we had not made contact in over two weeks, we didn't expect anything that night. For most of the night, we didn't see a thing. Brother Brown and I, couched behind a large fallen tree, talked that night, more than I had ever spoken with him before. Brown was a short, very dark-complexioned Black man with two small protruding front teeth, with a chipmunk appearance, possessing a look of fear on his face all the time. Brown was easy moving and told all of us he was from Trenton, New Jersey, but one day while at the medical office, I saw his dental records and it said Pottsville, Georgia. I realized that the way he looked, he could never say Pottsville, Georgia and live it down. He was so obviously a poor Black country boy that he had to say something, so he said Trenton, New Jersey. But Brown was a good man and spent more time in the "bush" than anybody else I had been with in Vietnam.

We didn't get much sleep that night and only talked at a whisper about how bad the White people treated Black people where he was from. It sure didn't sound like Trenton, but I didn't let on that I knew where he was from. Nothing had happened all night until about 4:30 that morning. Something stirred Brown and he hit me; we heard them coming. We couldn't tell how many or even if they were Viet Cong at first, but then the smell and the ambience that was not American walked right down the middle of our ambush site. I couldn't believe it!

I could see the whites of Brother Brown's eyes and could feel the vibrations of their footsteps hitting the flat, hard pathway of the jungle trail. I couldn't believe they were actually on the trail, right in our kill zone and then—BA-LAM BA-BOOM! There were two big horrific explosions of Claymore mines that our guys had set up. All hell broke loose! Everybody was now awake and firing their weapons; red tracer rounds exposed lines of bullets into the ambush site and then bounced all over the place. I had just started firing my machine gun because I couldn't slap down my gun belt when I first saw them; they would have heard it clamp down. So, by the time I started shooting, it was thirty-five to forty seconds and it was all over.

The muzzles flash from the fourteen to eighteen weapons firing simultaneously lit up the ambush site like fireworks on the Fourth of July. I could see the silhouettes flashing, jumping, and running, and it was all over. In barely a minute, everything became deathly quiet. I could see the thick gun smoke still hanging in the kill zone and we could sense the dead and hear the wounded dragging themselves.

Brother Brown and I remained still, guns alert, ready for any counterattack. As the men began to ease themselves forward nearer the ambush site, Brown and I remained still. The sun rays had begun to bounce over the mountain and the smoke was still heavy. The only sound was the thick dew drops plunging onto the large elephant leaves, but we had some new guys in our platoon and a few gung-ho rednecks who were anxious to get souvenirs. The crazy shit that you do at the beach for seashells, it seems, will pull you even in the shadow of death. One of the Marines said, "I'm go' get me something." Just then I felt Brown's hand on my shoulder pressing down signaling me not to move as a few of the Marines lunged forward and down to the ambush kill zone.

Brother Brown's experience in the bush had taught him to remain calm until certain of safety. It was too soon to move! We heard them run down towards the dead bodies and then a muffled sound and gun fire: blam, blam…blam…blam …

"Get down!" the squad leader yelled, but it was too late. Two of our guys had been shot. The Viet Cong were not all dead and had returned fire as they lay dying on the ground. We rushed down to retrieve our dead or wounded, then sprayed the area with machine gun fire and followed up with a fire mission of artillery. The squad leader had given the order to get down too late.

Brother Brown may have always had a look of fear on his face and been a poor country Black boy, but he had a survival savvy that was amazing… a helluva Marine.

Survival could be instinctual or smart; it sometimes takes no real thinking at all. For many Marines and soldiers, the idea of dying for what many believed a waste was not ambiguous. It was clearly idiotic.

There was no question that virtually all of us would give the ultimate to protect and save a fellow Marine, but meaningless orders, whether from the Pentagon or an asshole lieutenant, were a very common battle before the battles. It is well known the regrettable fate of more than a few commanding officers who were "fragged," as they put it then: the murder of commanders who would, in reality or perception, steadily waste the lives of their men.

The manner would usually be by grenade, the "fragments" as dedicated reprisal. A far more common way of avoiding a danger was to simply pretend to carry out a task then and say you had. That was called "sandbagging." If the order was to go to the bottom of the hill and patrol the two-mile base around it, most would just walk to the bottom and sit out the night. Even squad leaders would understand what was happening but knew damned well they would probably do the same damn thing. It was that kind of fucked-up war.

I remember when one Marine paid another to shatter his ankle with a baseball bat. Two- hundred dollars on the dirt and he placed his ankle across the end of one of the wood cots we slept on… WHAMMMM!! and the crack of that bat, that almost shattered the cot as well. It sent that boy home. There were, of course, gung-ho, Rambo-types that hyped themselves and, too often, fell into the dark side, killing with reckless abandon. I must charitably suppose it was their desperate, deplorable, and desolate way of getting out, too.

Texas Pete

"Let's go, Richardson! You're outta here," the corpsman said.

The Naval officer recently attached to our unit was a tall, dark-haired, unkempt White fella, unassuming but conscientious about his medical duties. He only looked once and recognized without a doubt the blood in my feces. Leonard was his name, and he had been aware of my condition from earlier complaints, watching me puke and stumble. He suspected I could have been ill, but there was no real evidence or proof sufficient to justify a medical evacuation. The only memory of that morning prior to Leonard is that of a bright glistening sun's reflection on a small bottle of Texas Pete hot sauce. Malaria can make you delirious and dizzy, stumbling about unable to remember little things. So, it's like a dream mixed with reality, mixed with the surreal, that I recall anything about the bright flash of morning sunlight on that little red bottle.

I do remember the green knapsack laying on the ground, partially opened, and the clean new bottle and label of Texas Pete hot sauce sitting at an angle that caught the morning sun. At that moment, while I defecated on the jungle floor, it did not dawn on me to use that hot sauce as a ploy to escape "the bush," but sitting there in a dream-like trance, it seems some power overtook my awareness of things and my movements. That Texas Pete, and the consistency of my stool, gave the perfect appearance of blood from the bowels. For a second, I almost fell back into my staged setting of intestinal hemorrhaging, missing my shit by inches. I called for the corpsman and tried to grasp what I had apparently done, but barely remembered just moments later. The absence of a clear recollection of planning that action or my ability to remember the circumstances of that lone bottle of hot sauce in my knapsack that morning, and the enormous consequences of that bright, hypnotic reflection of light on my life, has occupied many hours of thought for fifty years.

For some reason, a bottle of hot sauce allowed me to walk past my captain who asked, "Where the hell you going?"

"Blood in the stool," replied the Navy corpsman while I stumbled with him to a medevac. The captain was rubbing the feet of a fellow marine, Sanchez, by a fire. Sanchez was suffering from a thing called "trench-foot," a condition the result of being wet for too long, leading to the loss of skin. I felt somewhat guilty, but little did I, or the corpsman or captain, know that only a few more days of my progressing case of malaria might have been too late.

When the dual-blade 46 Sea Knight lifted off and the Marines shrunk away, I looked to the sky and said, "Free at last, free at last, thank God almighty, I'm free at last," thinking I would never allow anything to bring me back. When we reached the ship, they discovered I had been suffering from malaria and a form of yellow fever. They immediately plunged me into a tub of alcohol and ice to reduce my fever, fed me intravenously, and found I had contracted several worms that even today they have been unable to identify or remove.

There are three types of malaria in Southeast Asia: P. ovale, P. vivax, and P. falciparum. I had all three and they have yet to conclude the disposition of my relationship to each accurately, but that's the Veteran's Administration for you! Another couple of days, and it would have been curtains. Thank God for good old American Texas Pete!

Although the ploy was simply an excuse at the time, it was a legitimate reason that resulted in the much-needed relief that may have saved my life or at the very least extracted me from the life-threatening circumstances I faced. The thought of that day always triggers another: two days later, "Recon," a Mexican brother that had walked directly behind me for thirty-six days, stepped on a land mine, killing several and injuring seventeen. I would have been just a few yards ahead of him but for a bottle of hot sauce. Recon died in the chopper before even reaching first med in Da Nang.

Sometimes It's Just "F-It, Let's Eat!"

When I got back to the bush after treatment, I had concluded over half of my tour without any rest and recreation (R&R). I was pretty much convinced that the war was all wrong, as did most of the guys in Vietnam, and there was no "Esprit de Corp." Morale was at an all-

Cease Fire! Cease Fire!

time low and protests back home were making us feel like we were the enemy. The draft was in full swing, and young brothers were rolling in everyday, scared, mad, or just plain young without a clue about life outside "the world." We referred to home or the States as "the world." It was, "When I get back to the world," or "They going crazy back in the world."

The situation was impossible, to be there as a soldier fighting for reasons your country did not believe in. We felt as if we were all on our own fighting to save ourselves or each other as Marines, but no real cause for our country, so to speak. Back in the previous summer, "the world" was all proud and hyped up about just three men who had left the world, Earth. Those Apollo 11 astronauts were probably not in much more danger than we were, shit, maybe less. We could have cared less that day in July when they took "one small step." The small steps we were taking could have damn sure sent your ass on a "giant leap".

I heard the news on a small radio while I was walking through a wide mosquito-swarming stream up to my knees; none of us could have given a rat's ass. I remember the thing we talked about was the song that had just played: "McArthur Park," and what the fuck was a "cake left out in the rain"? Another bizarre thing they considered back in "the world."

Some of the Marines, low information-level guys who just did what they were told without question, created a conflict with the Marines who questioned the war. It divided the troops, and the environment was hostile at best. Squads would "sandbag" patrols and fake operations. Some Marines would argue, and the war became a war within the war. The circumstances were awful; it was useless to attribute fault or blame. It was just getting impossible.

But outside the world, it didn't matter. All that mattered was to endure, survive, not to give up, and learn a great lesson. When the perils of life offer no rational explanations as to why, accept the moment as unearned suffering, and do not waste good worry. Get on with life, keep living, and solve the problem, then and there in the minute.

Too many Marines wasted too much time on matters they had

no control over, could do nothing about, and could not change; anything said would be superfluous and meaningless. Moreover, it would likely evolve into a fight or conflict that would only make matters worse. So, before it got too far, I used to say, "Fuck it, let's eat! Fuck it, let's play cards," or just, "Fuck it," real loud. If they needed a long loud narrative, I'd give them a monologue on the dumb politicians in Washington D.C. who didn't know a damn thing about Vietnam, Southeast Asia, or Communism, the cocksuckers who got us in this shit and "it's all their fault, so fuck 'em!! Let's eat!!" I was always pretty good at talking shit, making friends, and bridging racial issues, and before I was done, everyone was against going back out in the "bush" to fight.

What I did not know, and to my delight, was that while I was in the 1st Med (medical) Unit, my good buddy Thomas Nelms had put my name down for R&R, and I was next in line to leave for Hawaii at the end of January! When I found out Nelms had picked Hawaii, I went off. "Why in the hell would you pick that tired, boring, no free pussy-getting country, Nelms!?"

He said, "Well, fuck you then, Richardson! At least I was thinking of you, you goddamn ingrate." All the Black guys would go to Bangkok, Taiwan, Philippines, Japan, or Singapore. In those countries, women might be waiting at the airports in groups for the soldiers, and guys would return with stories of carnal bliss and sexual fantasies beyond our lustful expectations. In fact, some guys never returned from those R&R trips, probably living today, retired, in a culture and environment with grandkids in a whole other "world". But the die had been cast, and Hawaii it was. As I considered how I might control the roll, I went to work.

By the time that large Continental Airlines jet lifted off from Da Nang Air Base in Vietnam, my plans were intact and laid solid: to hit Hawaii, fly stand-by to California, get home to Richmond, and be with my wife for the birth of my first-born child due in the second week of February. That was my stealthy plan.

My friend Nelms had unwittingly made a God-sent decision

to select Hawaii, I believed. But as my plan evolved, and realization of that plan took on reality, my return to Richmond was fraught with a thousand "ifs" that haunted me the whole time I was in Hawaii. It delayed my impetus to make the final move to get home, back to the world. Do I risk returning home and getting caught, charged with AWOL? Will I have the resilience to return and face death after having tasted home again? Will I lapse into my old Chuck Richardson "Fuck it" mindset and never return to the Corps? Is it my ultimate fate to be one of the Vietnam statistics on the nightly news? These questions stifled my plan and, for some reason, prevented me from purchasing a direct flight to Richmond. Maybe I should have considered the relatively low risk of just shooting my finger off like that brother at Que Son. Damn!

A new plan took shape on Oahu. Three "Army dogs" and I had rented a green Chevrolet when we arrived, and to avoid returning to 'Nam, we decide to wreck the vehicle and turn it over. It was risky, pretty perilous, actually, but we had seen terrors that made those thoughts look like a nine-year-old jumping from a swing set. Bracing ourselves, with me driving, we built speed as we approached the guilty curve with the three of them yelling, "Faster, no slower, hit it now—hold on!" We hit the curve and I pulled the wheel hard to the left but—we hit sand! And instead of rolling over, we just turned onto the right side and slid like butter in a hot pan. That Chevy hit a fire hydrant, knocking it from its base, but the impact was not sufficient to cause the vehicle to roll, doing little damage to anything... other than my driving record. A reckless-driving record trying to survive a reckless war.

Our plan to avoid returning to "the bush" did not work out, but we did not sit around commiserating our possible fate. We didn't waste time attempting to figure out what went wrong or why we had to go back, asking ourselves if using heroin was right or wrong—if we would ever see the world again. Sometimes, it makes no difference contemplating your predicament because it doesn't change anything. Sometimes, you have to just say, "Fuck it, let's go eat!"

We went to a burger shop and had this big new sandwich called a Big Mac, happy to be alive in that moment. Maybe that's the reason there are so many overweight people in the world today. When there are no answers, we seek a temporary solution, and food is one reliable temporary relief that is not immediately fatal. I'm not proud of it, but sometimes I still say, "Fuck it! Let's just eat!"

The three of them made the return trip to 'Nam at 2200 the next night. I got lucky, though, not from a wreck but from a relapse of malaria! I was back in the hospital—ironically delaying my return. I did return to 'Nam about six weeks later, however, but before I was released from first med in early February 1970, I got the news I was a dad! A simple telegram was handed to me informing me I had a son, "little Chuckie". I was very happy but now even more afraid; I had a son to think about, too.

CHAPTER 5

Playing War

———

By the end of February, I was back in the fight —away from "the world." Much of our time in 'Nam was spent walking: through rice paddies, thick jungle overgrowth, up and down mountainsides, and between the villages. We would sometimes run short of food and other supplies, and the resources of the village people became fair game to the Marine troops. Once, while on patrol, we entered a village for supplies. The corn, rice, pigs, or chickens were available for our taking and we would not hesitate to shoot, stab, or kill a chicken to eat when our food supplies ran out. On one occasion, this old mama-san (respected elder woman) was going into a grief-stricken fit, following the killing of one of her chickens. She was crying bitterly, and all the other villagers were attempting to console her grief, but nothing would help.

Reincarnation is a strong element of Vietnamese religious beliefs, something many of us were clueless about. The chicken we had killed was not just a chicken. We had killed, in her belief, the old woman's sister; even eating her, consuming her spiritual parts for lunch! Nothing would console this elderly woman from screaming and clawing desperately towards the heavens each time one of those Marines would take a healthy bite of her "sister." But the Marines, not having eaten for two days and with no serious concept of reincarnation, saw matters in a totally different light. We were a thousand miles apart in our understanding and nowhere near a resolution with this mid-day luncheon dilemma. It can appear to be insignificant and vastly unimportant on the scale of war, but in a much larger context, it represented the essence of not only Vietnam but almost all wars.

As the elderly mama-san cried and grieved for her sister, and the Marines consumed the limited bits of a morsel to assuage the pain of hunger, we were all functioning under beliefs that were equally as alien to the other. The United States government had become involved in a conflict where we did not understand the people, their culture, their habits, language, and religion. We had no idea of what motivated the Vietnamese: their goals, desires, and *their* cause. As much as I regret admitting it, my/our ignorance and often disregard for others in the world is shameful; the witness of suffering civilians in war truly impacted me. In Vietnam, the American soldiers viewed the Vietnamese people with little respect, a subconscious perspective similar to that given to a pet. It was not some triggered cruelty, disdain, or resentment, but rather a feeling that only Americans should be viewed with full accord as human begins. It was only after returning to "the world" and a long contemplative evaluation of my own behavior that I recognized the prevalence of such attitudes among Americans. For whatever the reasons, we were indoctrinated to interpret only Americans and American beliefs to be compelling, suitable, and valid.

The lack of concern or desire to understand other peoples is certainly nothing new for us, and probably the reason for many wars, How could a small country with primitive weapons and antiquated means be effectively resisting the best technologically advanced military in the world. Why?!

So, we go on fighting wars, not over food, land, or other natural resources, but rather ideas. We ridiculed, laughed, and demeaned the idea that her sister was being eaten by Marines. And yet, we believed they should respect our beliefs: that a man could walk on water, live in a fish's belly, hear a mule speak, or that a virgin could give birth. To them, all our ideas were equally ludicrous. Each conflict, struggle, or political fight that has evolved into a war is primarily over beliefs:

"I believe a religious, cultural, or historical evidence entitles me to one thing—and you believe in something different." Unable or unwilling to compromise, we cast each other as less than "us", eventually losing all empathy, and strike at our brothers. The tragedy of it all is that there are no material differences in what it would require for us to live together with the same amount of land, food, or natural resources, and survive with those resources, but for the differences in our beliefs.

While incarcerated at Deep Meadow Prison in Goochland County, Virginia, I encountered a man from Vietnam who had escaped his country and committed an offense in America. He spoke fluent English, understood our customs, and recognized the lifestyles and traditions of the American people. The two of us talked at length and eventually became well acquainted. However, when we discussed why nations could not agree to exist together peacefully, he said, "Americans have monstrous egos and feel sanctified in their righteousness." He laughed at me and said, "You are intelligent, you should know these things." He asserted very adamantly that Americans feel they are right on all things and unwilling to accept any other people's beliefs as being valid. He cited religion as an example!

I was deeply affected by the poised, calm, and intelligent manner he presented his reasoned position. He was so much more conversant and knowledgeable about the history of America than I was. He logically advanced the conclusions that we, as have so many in history, go to war because of religions, leaving no room for compromise. I asked him why he believed that. He said, "God." He was convinced that all our gods—Allah, Jehovah, Buddha, Jesus Christ, and others—tell their followers that "there is no God before me." I could not argue his point.

That "commandment," in a sense is a declaration of war itself against any other God or believers of that God, providing little if any tolerance of the "infidels." I can't understand why there has to be a double blade in so many religions. On one side, we have the simple understanding that promotes an empathetic "live and let live" doctrine. On the other, we have a form of hostility, physical confrontation, and violence. It is regrettable that throughout history, but for the presence of "God," man may have been less committed to the destruction of his brother.

The Vietnamese inmate went on to criticize me for having fought for this country when, as a Black man, "You don't have the rights for which you were fighting! You are all wet, my brother." Again, I could not respond to him. He was right! I felt small to hear him denigrate, almost comically, the Christian religion.

I said to him; "You are treading ground upon which you know not precisely!"

He said, "And none of us know." His point to me was that despite everything that all men profess, and despite how deeply any might possess the faith, since there is no proof, we can only assert at best. "This is what I have chosen to believe, and I leave it at that," he said. We continued to argue until it became futile. After weeks of hot debate, things evolved into intelligent, tolerant discussions. We each took turns describing the absurd beliefs that various religious groups have accepted as fact. The unlimited capacity to believe—what they want to believe.

When our nightly conversations over a ten-month period concluded, I thought about the serious dilemma we face as a society that seldom listens to the other side. It would not be such a high price to pay to just stop and listen to our fellow man once in a while, to consider that one man's belief is as sacred as another's. Until we take each other's belief with compassion and understanding, we will never take each other seriously, and the mutual atrocities will continue to go on. Put ourselves in their shoes and imagine the pain you would feel if it were your brother, father, or loved one being devoured by a group of hungry "others."

The Strength in Peaceful Voices

It is hard to understand how a young boy could be playing one day with his dog, helping his grandfather gather pails of water, or keeping an eye on a curious, running two-year-old, and the next be part of an army, hustling supplies through enemy lines. But the reality of war and fighting has become as common as feeding oxen in a rice paddy or weaving the non la hats for the village. For the Vietnamese civilians, that horrendous war brought so much death and misery that the death of a young teen at the hands of an American could be seen as part of childhood in that forsaken land.

One morning while patrolling the edge of a Vietnamese village, we heard the soft sound of little voices easing between the palm trees and elephant grass. The dew was still dripping from high trees and the rhythmic pattern of the droplets gave the gentle voices an almost crippling lure. I could feel the pace of our patrol slowing as if to allow the serene harmony its performance.

As we came closer to the source of the voices, they became more distinct and familiar. They were melodies, school songs being sung by Vietnamese children in a small village. Though very few of us understood the meaning, each of us could feel their message. Each Marine approaching the village school could discern the easy peace and innocence of precious children behind the collective sounds. Even though none of us understood the meaning of any of the words in the song, we could sense the plea of their voices. I realized at that moment how valuable, how precious, how innocent, and how equal all children are no matter what country they're from or what color they might be.

When we got close enough to see, they were fewer than they sounded, but they were no less impactful on the softening souls of war-hardened Marines. It didn't matter what the words in the song said, nor what the song was about, or whether the children were American, Vietnamese, Japanese, Buddhist, or Hindu; communication could never have been clearer, more honest and purer. In the physical midst of war, there was an epiphany of peace on that jungle's edge. While I held back the tears and fought to believe that war could even be possible, much less know that I was in one, I saw the faces of reasons we all understand. The feeling only escaped a couple, and while it was our responsibility to search and destroy (burn) every physical structure in the area, I knew this was one time when doing the right thing would be on my side. I did not have the rank, but I could see there were a number of us who would join me to stop anybody who might want to burn, beat, rape, or kill anybody there.

In this world, there are always a small number of people who just cannot see right, cannot do what is clearly the decent thing to do. In war, many can envision such men. We called them "gung-ho": always ready to take an action against anybody, to hurt, kill, or destroy something—with impunity. Two of this type of man moved toward a young girl. Before they make their intentions obvious, I raised my long, black M60 machine gun. While the children continued to sing, the two adult women stood there looking nervous as if they knew what those men had in mind.

Because so much cruel and heathenish pain was heaped upon Vietnamese children barely in their teens, the women feared the worst would happen before their eyes. But when I raised my gun and turned it on the two "gung-ho" Marines, the women cried and seemed to pray. Then four other Marines walked around and stood behind me. Reluctantly, the two backed off and the women held each other and sobbed. They glanced at me with a look of relief, and let their tears convey their emotions and gratitude.

The squad leader had now approached us and looked towards me, then turned to the rest of the squad, and signaled them to move on. As the children resumed their songs, we all slowly walked past them and out of the village back into the jungle. My heart was thumping as we stepped on through the brush, praying that that other Marine could hear them, and wished the children would sing a bit louder. But that morning, the children's voices had already carried the day with a sound that was so richly righteous that even the vilest of those there were influenced by it.

I had been confronted before with Marines who wanted to bring harm to innocent Vietnamese civilians. In many instances, sadly, they prevailed, and I often wondered how far I would have gone if those little voices of peace had not helped to soothe the beast that lives in war. I think I learned that morning, at the age of twenty-two, that when something is so clearly right, and you know it is right without any question or doubt whatsoever, it is not difficult to do right. You just must see it so clearly that nothing else, not even fear for life, should prevent you from doing the right thing.

Whenever we as Americans are so arrogant that we can drop large bombs upon others as though they're not that important because they're not Americans, we need to stop and imagine the sounds of their children singing. I think we would give much fairer consideration before dropping those bombs if we could just hear the children sing—and imagine—"Happy Birthday," "Jingle Bells," "Joy to the World," or "Jesus Loves Me." Imagine children singing—little children, three-, four-, five-years old. The whole world is full of them, from Saigon to Aleppo, from Gaza to Rio de Janeiro. When they die, whether by careful or callous hands, we should cry. I know I will cry again, but also listen for a hopeful sound.

Remembering Vietnam today, I think of my friend, Marco Aurelo Fregoso, from that summer of '69. I think of a quote from the Roman Emperor, Marcus Aurelius, whom my friend

My fellow marine, good friend and American hero, Marco Aurelio Fregoso. Lost in Que Son Valley, Vietnam 1969.

may have been named for, who said; "The best revenge is not to be like your enemy." The tough question about that year was who was the "enemy"? Was it the Viet Cong, the rednecks from Georgia, the men in Washington that sent me there? Or just another man like me—and how do I not be like me?

Taking a relief from the "bush" in this beautiful land —wishing I had been there on other terms.

Black Vets

The second greatest irony in America's string of hypocrisy is that the Black man had to fight for freedom in Vietnam that did not exist for him in America. The late '60s was an enlightening yet confusing period for Black people on many fronts. The Vietnam war was one of those moral battlegrounds, and Dr. Martin Luther King, Jr., who was ahead of his time, made the right judgment call! Looking back and calling the shot is easy but looking into the future is far more difficult.

Dr. King and Muhammad Ali, two of American's greatest patriots, opposed the war. A true patriot follows the path that protects the best interest of the nation and its individual citizens. Patriotism has nothing to do with one's eagerness to take a gun and go fight for a flag in the front of your home. These are superficial illusions that demonstrate an attitude but have no real impact on strength, righteousness, or the preservation of the ideals of America and its constitution.

During the '60s and '70s, the preponderance of young Blacks were unaware of the political nature of the war. None of us wanted to go, and we knew it was not like other previous conflicts where we were actually defending the nation. However, most of us were unaware of the linear points of doubt, question, or morality. The more enlightened element of the Black community did question the propriety rights of the government to take their sons off to this war. But even that sentiment was only slight, and it did not have sufficient influence to offset the prevailing attitude among the Black community's status quo orientation to respond to the call of "Uncle Sam."

The strongest influence at that time was the radical "Black Power" movement, but those groups were considered by some as too extreme to follow. When Muhammad Ali refused to be inducted into the military, a large percentage of the Black community frowned upon his move and even condemned him publicly. As the war grew increasingly unpopular, attitudes started to change, however. When Dr. King made his opposition public and the "Black Power" movement began to constantly condemn the government's role in the war, we, the soldiers, became the target of their criticism. The criticism was so intense that, by the time I had survived the war and safely returned home, I had to immediately disrobe that handsome, proud Marine Corps uniform with my war medals and all: two Purple Hearts, a Cross of Gallantry, a Combat Action medal, a Vietnam Campaign Medal, and others.

I could not believe, after surviving the unimaginable horrors of war, having malaria more than once, watching friends die, and the guilt over things I had done that now I would face humiliating criticism of the largely popular Black Power movement of which every proud Black person wanted to be a part. Instead of the hero's welcome I had expected, shame was my reward, "villain" was my title, and "baby killer" was my description.

The few weeks I had to wear that proud Marine Corps uniform were reduced to surviving a miserable trip through Byrd Airport when I returned. After I got home, I found some old Bermuda slacks, a Henrico High gym shirt, and a pair of shower shoes I wore almost everywhere until I went shopping at Cloverleaf Mall.

But this hypocritical mistreatment of returning Black American vets was second only to the existence of slaves in the midst of the Revolutionary war in which America fought for its own freedom while enslaving Americans. A nation's leadership had put its fighting men in a position of shame and embarrassment: young men found vulnerable simply because they wore their uniform. Can you imagine having fought and come home worrying about a brick hitting you from behind? How can those who are asked to defend the country be responsible for the errors of its leaders?

Many sons of Black families died in Vietnam, and their numbers were disproportionately higher than White soldiers. This racial tragedy was lost on White and Black leaders. It is a known fact that the poor usually make up the lion's share of America's fighting men. Since large populations of poor Americans were Black, there were systematic and intentional efforts to channel Black men into the combat categories.

While Black men were largely prevented the opportunity to fight in an honorable war (if there is such a thing) like World War II, they were *forced* into fighting in Vietnam. Racism in the military was more than obvious during the Vietnam war. The at-large Black population during the war was around seventeen to eighteen percent, but the percentage of Black men fighting was at least thirty to thirty-three percent. The closer you got to the fighting fields of 'Nam, the significantly higher number of Black faces you saw. However, in specialty designations, such as support, administrative, air wing, headquarters, supplies, artillery, and other non-combat zone specialties, you saw fewer Black faces. This was obvious, not simply me just attempting to raise the point; it was real! Anywhere in the military, you could stop and take a count of the Black faces. Invariably, the Black men were in much higher percentages in the combat zones. We used to look around, shake our heads, and say, "Man, the closer you get to the front, the darker it gets!"

When these dark faces returned home, they faced yet darker circumstances because, despite the war's unpopularity, "official" White America seemed to automatically respect their own soldiers regardless. Sadly, for Black soldiers, the war only carried an additional negative stigma for them: having abandoned the cause of your own people.

In 2017, I attended the 50th Henrico High School Reunion of my sister Valerie, and encountered a sadly sick, lying individual who had not changed a bit since high school. A now much older man who was always mired in an egocentric swamp where all those around him were drowning, he seemed never to be aware of his self-ingratiating comments that rarely strayed from the same single topic...himself. In high school, well, he was one of the very few who "tolerated" me, as we were both on the track team. Being the only Black around all the time, I had to appreciate any company that would accept my presence without being called by the "N" word. So, when others would simply walk away using the A-hole word to describe him, I could never get a full understanding of just how the White students actually felt about him.

But this night, when he began to talk about his military exploits in cool, calm braggadocio, it became very clear to me why they used to just walk away. The initial conversation was filled with backslapping, good-to-see-you memories of track, but when he began telling the group about his Vietnam experiences, I could immediately discern that truth had vacated the premises. His words became embarrassing ...inconsistent with anything close to the truth. Though in his mind, he may well have lied these lies so often they were no longer in his fanciful, imaginary narrative of himself; they were simply his history. Boasting to his former high school peers, explaining in great detail the type, style, and series number of the weapon he carried, I asked him, "What did you do?"

He said to me, "I killed people. I was on a six-member 'hunt and kill' team and I killed people." He repeated this statement with such pride and certitude as though he had done it on many occasions.

I could sense without any doubt whatsoever that he had never seen a combat zone or fired a weapon or done anything at all close to killing another human being. This high school alumnus was a fraud. No man that I know or have ever known who has killed could take the act so lightly that he would glorify in it. That he would praise himself, brag in front of a group not feeling the pain, remorse, guilt of having taken the life of another human being. "I killed people" were his words, spoken without a single scintilla of compunction. The way this man could speak of killing people in such celebrated terms convinced me he knew nothing of how it felt to kill. If he was not lying, he was a sociopath looking for attention.

Some men, unfortunately, possess an emptiness that needs fulfillment regarding their own self-perception and must, therefore, convince others that they are more than they appear to be. Since war, combat, and death are perceived by so many Americans to be the ultimate example of manhood, I have observed numerous occasions similar to this one at the high school reunion, where exaggerations of exploits in war are typical because no one can disprove their account of the event. There are, however, certain facts obvious and undeniable, that "G.I. Joe" should not have revealed in his fable that made it clear to me that he was not being truthful. I do not resent his need to be perceived an as honored war veteran; if he served at all, he deserves as much. But *his* war story version minimizes the truth too many cannot bring themselves to think about, much less boast of. What made his arrogance doubly harmful was that his attitude toward killing affects other generations of impressionable young men—other listeners, unaware of the truth, beguiled by his prevarications and taken by these romantic notions of honor and glory, and consequently, too often look forward to opportunities of war or combat for themselves to tell others they "killed people" as if they were proud to have done so.

I remembered that fool a few years later in the winter of 2020. It was a pleasant afternoon spent watching the Super Bowl pregame show. In one of the segments they highlighted Rocky Bleier, a star running back of the Pittsburgh Steelers football dynasty of the '70s. Bleier was also a Vietnam vet who actually fought in the same place at the same time as I had. In 2018, Bleier made a trip back to 'Nam, something a number of vets had done and countless others considered, hoping to perhaps gain a healing perspective. He was followed by ESPN television network to the place he was wounded in the Que Doc Valley on August 20, 1969. Que Doc ran somewhat parallel to Que Son Valley where I was, less than a mile from me. The Army in which Rocky served was positioned in the Que Doc while the 7th Marines were in the Que Son, and we basically acted as one front. Those army units we passed coming down the mountain, soldiers wearing the thousand-yard stare, had likely come from his battalion.

The TV crew followed behind him as he first entered the area he had seen combat in 1969. Bleier, dressed in all white in the August heat, took measured steps up and across the mounds and trenches where he was wounded forty-nine years earlier to the day. As I watched, I began to almost quiver, and my heart started to race seeing virtually the exact area I lived my most horrible experiences of Vietnam. Seeing the tree line and the ridges of earth we hunched below was like time travel for me. It was not literally the same of course, as the battle-beaten earth and trees were now green and lush, but it suddenly flooded me with flashback images and memories; it fucked me up.

At the same time, Rocky broke into tears and eventually collapsed. It was overwhelming for me as well. I had hardly expected to be dropped in the middle of Que Son in August of '69 on that Sunday afternoon in 2020. Rocky was taken back to a hospital and treated for heat exhaustion but was able to return two days later. Again, he cried and reflected on the utter waste of life in that war. I couldn't enjoy the game that day, I couldn't see anything but that valley and relive the day the 7th Marines battled behind irrigation walls against an enemy in the trees. A view I had not so clearly seen in fifty years! It stayed that way for me for several weeks.

When you actually see what Rocky and I saw, you don't brag forty-five years later that you "killed people… a hunt and kill team." It is not something that lives so cavalierly in the mind. Rocky Bleier probably has dozens of great memories of heroic efforts for the Steelers, but I promise, none have caused him to collapse in tears the way those memories do. It was often difficult to conceal the sudden moments when I recalled the guilt, despair, and pain of the 'Nam memories that would bring me to the brink of tears. No one would ever know or understand such episodes, and I never told them. Many Black veterans have suffered much worse fates because of their guilt and inability to cope with those experiences: drug addiction, alcoholism, permanent un-employability, divorce, loss of family, and social alienation in general have destroyed lives of good men. Doctors, counselors, and loved ones allowed them to float away without really knowing the reason why they had drifted from the world.

When I was at Virginia Union before being drafted, I knew a young man named Rennie. Rennie was an exceptionally talented and good-looking basketball player. He was always so clean, meticulously dressed, articulate, and smooth. The girls were attracted to him and showed it with unusual fervor and loyalty. We all knew he was destined to succeed at something, it was obvious, but Rennie left VUU—and was drafted.

The next time I saw Rennie was five or six years later; I was stunned. He was walking in Byrd Park on Lakeview Avenue. It was a hot June day, and he was wearing a heavy overcoat, layered dirty clothes, and large boots with no socks or shoestrings. I was unsure at first if it was *actually* him. His face was peppered with blackheads and his teeth covered with thick yellow gunk! He walked along gazing at the ground and then the sky, walking because walking was seemingly all there was. I stopped my car and went across the street to speak to him. My mind was racing about what I was seeing, certain but still unsure that I was seeing the same person from college.

His once beautiful black hair, smooth and laid down, was now dirty and stacked five or six inches on his head. I said, "Rennie!!?" He just smiled and looked at me. "Rennie!!?" I said again. He said not a word in response, but just smiled and kept walking. With my car still running, I watched him walk on down the street slowly out of sight. I returned to my car daydreaming, in total disbelief. I later found out that he had returned from 'Nam and had been living with his parents for the last two years. A mother and father would be the ones who cared, who refused to let him walk alone in a society that ignored his sacrifice.

Few people took an interest in 'Nam veterans, particularly Black vets; there was no effort to really understand them. The thousands who returned never received any special attention. It was "shell shock" and that was war. But it was a culture shock that greeted those warriors returning from 'Nam. Not many, but some, did survive unaffected ... as far as I could tell.

'Brother Brown' and me in Okinawa on the way back to the world.

CHAPTER 6

As The World Returned

Thirty days home from Vietnam, I landed a job at the Richmond Regional District Planning Commission (RRDPC). The job was perfect for me and I, in a sense, was perfect for it. RRDPC was a nonessential governmental agency comprising of Richmond and seven surrounding counties. I would be its first Black employee and they needed a special type of Negro whose criteria I apparently met. I was not too dark, not dark at all in fact, not too intimidating, not too educated. I had only two years of college at that point, and I was a decorated Marine just home from Vietnam. My father-n-law, Dr. Ford T. Johnson, a successful dentist, was well connected and was, in fact, a friend of Richmond's first Black Director of Personnel, Ted Thornton. Mr. Thornton made the referral, and I was next meeting with the assistant executive director, Ed G. Council. At my interview, he was convinced on sight. I don't even think they interviewed anyone else and I was hired within a week. They needed a Negro, and I needed the appearance of work.

It was August, and only a few weeks after I started, when I was summoned to appear before the Executive Committee—to be fired! I was never asked about my position on the issue: I was simply told that the committee was taking up "the matter of your dismissal" at 4:00 p.m. and I should be there. The executive committee was made up of just a few members from the general commission who would get together to address matters, as if with God, in some untouchable way.

There were only two Black members: Alex B. James and Clarence Townes. And I knew God wasn't Black. I also believed the issue must have something to do race. I arrived shortly before 4:00 p.m. and sat in the plush lobby of the Commission offices. I sat and thought to myself, *What the hell is this about?* I retraced all kinds of things I had done or said that would warrant my dismissal. But what was really bothering me was why nobody once came to me about it, much less got my opinion on whatever it was. After a few very pensive minutes, I remembered something ... it was that old, ugly White secretary at the 21st and Main Street Henrico County Court building. I was furious, sitting there thinking how damn unfair to have gone through the last year of pain, misery, and loss for my country, to be subjected to the racism and bigotry at the hands of many secretaries, social workers, sheriffs, and judges who were supposedly "serving the public" with equal justice. Those people never appreciated that I had risked my life for them; they would not accept it or me.

I had been on assignment to conduct a survey, interviewing government officials, judges, prosecutors, and planners. A certain Judge Hennings was on the list, one of Henrico County's notorious "good ole' boys." I entered the building looking as sharp as a tack and ascended the granite steps outside his office as I thought of what I would encounter in a few moments: not exactly tea for two. I had actually met with him once before and left with a resentment about his demeanor toward me. I said things to myself on the way up in what one might call Marine or sailor language about his honor. Having only been home less than two months, it was hard to snap out of the language of 'Nam. The F-word was so common among Marines it was virtually used in every sentence among us, understandably.

Watching the steps and talking to myself—in Marine parlance I'm sure—I raised my head at the top step and my words dropped right in the face of that secretary. In retrospect, I don't think I did anything that would be considered an affront to anyone because I was talking

Cease Fire! Cease Fire!

to myself. But she heard me and looked at me with an exaggerated expression I saw often from resentful White personnel while doing such surveys. I'm sure she must have hurried into the judge after I left and passed on what she heard me say ... at the least. The judge, then, must have called RRPC and, well, here I was outside the office waiting for my dismissal.

But you know what I thought. *I ain't going nowhere! I paid my dues and I ain't leaving, even if I'm fired!* I sat there for several minutes running through the things I knew I needed to think about: my response, possible challenge, future job prospects, my finances, and underlying it all was my internal fight with addiction. But it was all suppressed by an anger—anger about the world I had come home to. The people that I had seen so many die for sitting around acting like it was still business as usual—still only another "nigga" at home in America. I had to control the anger I felt for some who had no compunction about resenting me, though I had spent a year in hell for the maintenance of their place of exceptionalism—in a world they were clueless about.

After a few minutes, my heavy heartbeat and racing mind were interrupted by the swift opening of the meeting room door, and a large presence broke the vacuum of my thoughts. It was a Black presence, Dr. Alex B. James. Dr. James softly walked over to me with a paper in his hand and leaned down to me pointing at the paper and whispered, "This is what did it, Rich," and walked calmly away. I looked and realized what it was; my DD-214 form, my military record. I thought to myself, *damn, maybe God is Black!* Edward G. Councill, Dr. James, and Clarence L. Townes defended me in that meeting. Some of the words they passionately spoke still humble me:

"Gentleman, what are we saying here? Have you considered the context of this dismissal? This is no ordinary individual who happened to use some profanity on the job, my friends.

"Did anyone check the details? Richardson was just hired in July; he was still in a combat war zone in June! That's less than sixty days ago. He looks normal, but this man was seeing his buddies blown to pieces barely two months ago! Look at his record, look at his Marine Corps record. He was an M60 machine gunner, shot twice, with, what's this...a Cross of Gallantry and Combat Action medal.

"It says he had malaria twice! Do you know the kind of language these men use when they're sick and delirious? Jesus, just normal Marines in that situation! Barely sixty days ago and now he's here. Any reorientation to a normal world... right, the plane ride home."

"Look, he seems normal to me."

"What do you expect him to look like? Some wacked-out zombie?! Okay, he looks fine but look at this record; Twelve months of I-Corps combat in Vietnam changes the brain, gentlemen."

"What this boy did is only natural for the environment he just came from...we're lucky it's only profanity. We don't need to be discussing his dismissal; we need to thank him for the sacrifices he's made and find out if there are ways we can help and make sure he's okay from now on."

"What do we tell Judge Hennings?"

"We're not going to tell him anything."

"Well, he's gonna be expecting something. He was particularly upset about his language and Richardson's fancy clothes he was wearing... he called them 'jigga-boo duds.' Clarence, you know what he thinks of your kind? He told you as much a few months back at that dinner."

"Just tell him where this kid was two months ago and tell him if wants to make something of this, he'll have to do it on his own. Forget it! We're keeping him, let's go."

There were decent White folk around that didn't get recognized enough, now and back then. Edward Councill was one of them; he was good man. I must say, regretfully, however, that when I had the chance to be good to him, I failed. It is one of the few regrets I have with my actions as a councilman. In the very early '80s, I was the deciding vote on whether he should remain in his job. Ironically, it was on the

Richmond Planning Commission where I now sat with him. It was a petulant move on my part, and I can't recall what reasoning persuaded me, but I was wrong. I can now appreciate what it took for him to stand up for me. He believed in fairness and doing the right thing. I didn't do enough back then to express my appreciation for his decency and I'm remorseful. Ed showed great courage and integrity, and I will always appreciate his forward thinking and understanding during a naïve phase in my early career. I want his wife, Beth, and son, Corey, to know what he showed in the early '70s was remarkable. I really regret I didn't consider it when I made the choice to remove him from the Commission. Ed Councill was a good man, and I'm sorry.

I had few writing or technical skills needed for the government job, but I was not dumb. I simply had not been taught those types of skills yet. For several years, I struggled competently, learning as I went along. However, I certainly looked the part: a handsome physique in high fashion, tailored three-piece suits I had purchased in Okinawa—high-collar Edwardian styles, which were more suited for glamorous sports stars than a typical office job, and I was verbally proficient with the outward skills needed to project confidence. My wife, Phyllis, would get up each morning to help arrange my look. It was a loving ritual of hers, preparing me for something closer to a Hollywood movie. The overdressing was probably obvious to everyone and nobody at all. By that I mean, if a brother had an office job at all, it was his option to select his level of fashion, notwithstanding public taste.

It was Black culture, and my office co-workers seemed to accept it. Women, in particular, seemed to admire our proclivities regarding habits of attire. They would comment on the discipline it would take each morning to put it all together so meticulously: cuff links and highly shined shoes, with a perfect cologne ambiance. My colleagues, as perceptive as they were, would not imagine the habit I was concealing behind the appearance of a highly maintained lifestyle. I remember those mornings getting ready, each day stopping at my bedside just before walking out, kneeling and praying that God would provide a release from my addiction to heroin. It was a prayer I would not neglect—one I wore each day.

Each day, I carried a burden very few knew, but I also carried an image some found interesting—some might say. In 1971, after returning from 'Nam, I grew my hair out long and combed it back to my shoulders and grew long sideburns with my mustache. I will say, I was one handsome dog and, with Phyllis's salary and mine at the Planning Commission, was driving that beautiful, black Lincoln

Some thought I was the original 'SuperFly' (Photographed by Johnny Hewlett).

Cease Fire! Cease Fire!

Continental I mentioned in Chapter 1. About a year or so later in the fall of '72, a new film appeared in the theaters, one of many of what would become known as the "Blaxploitation" genre—a film called *Superfly*. *Superfly* was a movie about a New York drug dealer trying to get out of the business, even though he was at the top of his game. Actor Ron O'Neal played the title role, and Ron O'Neal had a striking, uncanny, almost twin appearance to me. To those who met me or saw

Not long back from Vietnam, 1972 (Photographed by Johnny Hewlett).

110

me after that movie came out, they invariably believed I was trying to mimic Superfly, while those who had known me couldn't believe Hollywood was mimicking me!

With my super-clean appearance as well, it was not hard for some to adopt the notion that I was perhaps in the drug trade, too. This could cut both ways given my habit, and the necessary trips into some tough areas like Whitcomb Court, Mosby Court, Fairfield, and others where I'd sometimes meet up with friends to receive the caress of heroin. I would stand out, not only for my light skin, but the look of someone with power and charisma—Superfly. Through the mid-seventies, I got to know those places, those people—the young, the old, disabled, proud, dirt-poor—and struggling communities with a portion of their men and women looking for their next trip on the "horse" or "weed," or whatever.

When I started serving on Council at the end of the decade, I had a genuine empathy and understanding of those environs that existed city-wide. It was, in a way, a result of my habit and the exposure to horrible conditions and circumstances that fostered my determination to serve those communities with as much passion as any issue, if not more. Public Housing, or the "Projects" as they were colloquially referred to back then, was very much the nest of despair. The structures typically were practically prison-like themselves: painted cinder block walls and lacquered concrete floors, a few small windows, perhaps a thirty-square-foot stoop at the front door, and maybe a very small area in back with two poles with a wire line between them for drying clothes.

I remember visiting friends in the "dens of inequity," as the old folks would say, to do our dope. Almost always, there was little on the walls of those units other than a picture or two of children or family. As was the case with Black homes all over the country, you would see at least one of three portraits: Jesus Christ, Martin Luther King, Jr. (MLK), or John F. Kennedy, and sometimes all three. They hung in cheap, dusty, sometimes glassless fake brass frames to serve the spirit of the oppressed. Those icons of saviors and heroes were in many a room where I and others slowly eased into a deep numbness or "nod," as it were.

Often, the mothers and grandmothers of those who were seeking the vacancy, seeking release from the painful world of deep poverty and the systemic cruelty of racist entrapments, would not condemn their children. They understand the need, just as they eagerly sought Jesus for sanctuary in their lifetime. Karl Marx said, "Religion is the opiate of the people…The sigh of the oppressed creature…the heart of the heartless." Grandmothers who may have tithed ten percent of whatever pittance they possessed for decades, understood the nature of addiction, or at least the "sigh of the oppressed creature." It is little wonder that heroin would be so prevalent among the "least of these." The Black church in America was to the slave what might be described as the opiate needed so desperately.

One day, I was with a friend, Vince, who was now occupying the bedroom of his deceased grandmother, and I remember the portraits of Jesus and MLK on the wall. It was a room like thousands, all but abandoned only for sleep: an old lawn chair and two large worn couch cushions with no couch were on a dusty, nasty floor at the end of a bed peppered with stains and the smell of urine pervading the blanket. I had been in rooms like that a few times, places that were settings of some really hellacious things with guns, heated arguments, police escapes, and egos so intense that something had to give, or something had to be learned in those little cinderblock cells. There were two other brothers with me and Vince as we slid into our "nod." I had been looking at the picture of Jesus and thinking about this when a little girl walked in.

Maybe four or five years old, she softly, but matter-of-factly, spoke to us, "My mommy said Mr. Chuck was here and she needed to get some soap powder, can you help her?" I was stunned at the sight and had no idea who she or her mother was. But it was apparent her mommy knew me, or of me, and needed money.

I looked at her, trying to read her thoughts, then slowly leaned back in the chair and straightened my leg to dig into my pants pocket. Vince quickly put his hand on mine to stop the action. "Naw, Uncle Chuck, that's Cat's little girl. She's on crack and gamin' you, man.

Be cool, don't give her anything. She sent that little girl over here so she could get enough for a rock," he said. "Go tell yo' momma Mr. Chuck ain't here," he told the child.

The little girl turned away with a palpable sadness, then stopped and turned around, looking down and up at us, she said, "But I'm hungry…"

Vince spoke up quickly, "I don't care, goddamnit, now ge—" when I stopped him mid-sentence.

"Wait a minute, Vince. Damn, look at her!" The girl looked at me and Vince, "Come here, sweetheart. Tell Mr. Chuck the truth," I said.

She looked in my eyes and said, "He at da house now, but we ain't got no money." The crack man was at the house and Cat, the little girl's mother, was desperate for a hit.

I told Vince, "This little girl is hungry. Look at her. How can you say 'no' to a precious little girl like this?" The lovable young child was terribly filthy and unkempt, with a dirty face and hands. I knew this was a beautiful child not so different from the children I had seen suffer so horribly in Vietnam, innocent victims of adult bullshit. I saw too many I could not help, that I could not save from the fighting. I had seen too many stares begging for a stop to the pain, a cease fire to the inhumanity. That day, this little girl would have a "cease fire" I *could* provide!

Vince smirked at me and said, "See, Uncle Chuck, you go for anything. S'pose another little girl and another little girl came in here beggin'. Whatchu go' do?"

"That would just be three little girls less hungry, Vince. What you go' do!?" I said to him with an accusatory attitude.

"You don't understand shit, Unc," he said.

"I gotta go, fellas." I stood up, pulled myself together, and took the girl's hand and we walked to her home two doors away.

When her mother opened the door, she looked surprised but not unpleased. I did know her; Katherine was a classmate of mine at B.A. Graves middle school. I tried not to show my surprise at her appearance. I remembered Katherine as a very attractive girl, an A-student with a figure that young teen boys were constantly lusting after. I could tell she was embarrassed as she looked as neglected as her daughter, wiping her face, and primping with her hair.

"Oh, my goodness, Chuck..." she mumbled.

"Hi, Cat. Is this your daughter?"

"Yes, it is, Chuck. I'm sorry...I been working, but they stopped my check and I'm short this week but..."

I stopped her and told her I didn't need to know why. "Your daughter, um..."

"Jewell, her name is Jewell."

"Jewell tells me she hasn't had any breakfast and she seems hungry. She said a man was here."

"Oh, that's my brother but he gone now. He just left," she replied. She backed into her apartment and allowed me in while Jewell slowly walked to the coach and sat.

"So, Cat, I was wondering if I could have five minutes and take little Jewell to the drive-thru to get her something to eat. There's a McDonalds just a couple minutes from here." Jewell's eyes opened wide.

"Oh Lord, Chuck! You just answered my prayers. I was prayin' this morning; Lord, what am I gonna do for Jewell? My money so short, I feel awful," she said. "Could you wait a second and let me get myself more presentable, right here in my bedroom? C'mon, Jewell. You, too."

She continued to move toward her bedroom mumbling that her prayers were answered. Not knowing what to expect, I casually followed her but stopped just before her bedroom door. I was able to see a part of the room, and it was the mess I had to expect. And as I leaned and looked further—there he was, as at home as they were: Jesus Christ, framed on the wall. The patron of all our hopes, dreams and wishes, sent to forgive the sins of all, particularly the least of these. I almost cried. I'm back from war, barely twenty-five, hearing about Black Power and Black pride, seeing a sweet little Black child go hungry under the gaze of Jesus. Marvin Gaye nailed it in the name of his 1971 hit, "What's Going On"!!?

Many of my colleagues at the Planning Commission were also relatively young. Perhaps intent could be honorable, but they were most often excessively uninformed about the conditions of the truly poor and the legacy of hostile neglect. College-educated and middle- to upper-class, they'd sometimes laugh among themselves at things I would only imagine. However, one day they were laughing at a pamphlet that was handed out with examples of the some of the inarticulate communication penned by poor citizens requesting financial assistance from the City. The intent was to help us better discern the needs of such cases. They showed me a part from an obviously less educated Black woman who was writing about the dire situation for her and her husband. The grammar and phrasing were so poor it depicted almost the opposite of the woman's actual condition, including a second woman trying to start a romance with the couple but only in dirty clothes. It was sad, and I did not laugh, feeling a tinge of racism under the veneer of guilt-free liberalism they sported.

I would find myself lecturing them, temperately, about the real help and changes Black people, particularly the young and the very old, needed the most. I could not let them feel good about themselves because a Black man, Flip Wilson, had his own television show, or because they laughed at the ignorance of a character like Archie Bunker; it did not make these poor people fair game. Many so-called liberal Whites would promote integration in schools and acknowledge the horrible history of slavery and 'Jim Crow" but they would not really see the ongoing systemic failure, much less ways to confront it. I suggested they volunteer, perhaps help those poor elderly people write those letters for the assistance they need.

After I had talked them into quiet reflection, one of the girls by the name of Mary Ann Heald, a conscientious young White woman, came over and asked me privately and sincerely, "Chuck, what are you doing, what do you do for them?" I had no good answer because it was such a good question. Mary Ann was always sincere in her liberal positions and had a genuine desire to understand and help, which had an impact on me during those years. Her question to me

Cease Fire! Cease Fire!

that day was poignant and resonating. The question reminded me that many "talk the talk," but few "walk the walk." After surviving Vietnam and remembering the men who fell for this country, remembering the "thousand-yard stare" that left so many petrified, I decided I would spend my life walking the walk! And that evening, I contacted Big Brothers of America.

Deborah Meade, a young Black teenager back in the early '70s, was growing up with a younger sister and three little brothers in the poor community of Fairfield Court. Her parents had had five children at a very young age and had separated when the youngest boys were only toddlers. The older boy, Walter, whom they called "Bubba," was about nine or ten when he became uncontrollable for them. "Cursing, stealing, talking back at teachers and adults, fighting, you name it, he was constantly in trouble," Deborah said. "With the exception of drugs, he did it. They said he needed an older male figure in his life, to guide him, someone he could maybe imagine himself as," she said. Without a father, the strain on their mother was more than she could endure. It was only a short while after I joined Big Brothers that I was introduced to the family, and "Bubba."

Mother's Day 1976.

He seemed reluctant at first, as if wondering if I would be just another authority figure. We would go out and spend afternoons doing things he rarely experienced, mostly just being in the company of someone like me. I thought the first thing we could do was simply go out and eat somewhere, talk, and get to trust each other. I remember how Bubba was in awe of the "Big Mac" sandwich he had never had before. I saw him two or three times a month and we eventually did lots of things: go to a baseball game at Parker Field (now called The Diamond), play basketball and meet some of the kids in Providence Park, see a movie, and even fish on the banks of the James River. We talked and talked about many things, but the one issue I was most earnest and sober about was drugs. There was no equivocation, no hedging on the seriousness of my warning. I would never let Bubba see me when I wasn't dressed well and groomed. If I was going through the slightest difficulty with my addiction, I stayed away. I knew what drugs could do, and I was committed to keeping Bubba away from that trap, a trap nobody knows better than somebody caught in it.

Bubba's two younger brothers grew jealous, understandably, when I would come by to get him. One of them, Stuart, wanted me as *his* Big Brother, too! So, I took them with us as well a couple times. I kept that "big brother" role with Bubba for over three years, but as he grew older, our visits became less frequent. It was heartening to see the change and growth the boys developed in those years. "It changed our family," Deborah said, "They turned around after Chuck. I can't tell you what he did for us. My mother was slowly able to handle them, they did better in school; it just changed things so much for the better." Walter and his siblings grew up and re-established relationships with their father and went on with respectable adult lives. Walter spent a career in the Richmond Fire Department, and Deborah Meade became the Chief Magistrate for the City of Richmond!

"What are you doing, Chuck? What are *you* doing for them?" The echo of that question helped to change a lot, especially the way I "talked" and "walked" going forward.

Cease Fire! Cease Fire!

Accountable Representation

In the years following the 1960 census, it was recognized that Richmond's Black population would soon outnumber its White residents. The only way to maintain White control of the city was to increase the number of White voters, thus, Richmond had an annexation by 1970. But Black citizens challenged the annexation, and a major dispute arose over whether to de-annex, or not. This dispute went on for some time until U.S. Circuit Judge Robert R. Merhige, Jr., who was already resented by Whites for, among other things, ordering the desegregation of Virginia schools, recommended to retain the annexed land. He instituted a district system whereby the City was divided into nine equal parts so that representatives were assured to be elected from all social-economic levels and across the political spectrum.

Prior to the district system, the top nine winners for City Council seats would represent the entire city as at-large members. And as no surprise, given the means and social connections to procure those votes, the at-large members typically were of the same social status, income levels, political persuasion and, coincidentally, were all White and lived in the same general proximity or geographic location in the City. Judge Merhige submitted that the new district system would disrupt that scheme of social, political, and economic isolation and allow for a broader spectrum of local governance. He was right!

The district system was essential in changing the makeup of local government. Areas and cities that had never been represented began to receive a voice—their voice. District lines and boundaries became a consciousness preoccupation of City Council members, so much so that friendly quarrels would occur over boundary lines. But the single member district system was not instituted for seven years! This was due to a civil action brought against the City of Richmond and the County of Chesterfield alleging they had conspired to dilute the Black vote by annexing twenty-three square miles of mostly White

Chesterfield County voting areas, effectively decreasing the overall Black voting percentage by a significant margin.

Finally, the City of Richmond was required by the United States Supreme Court to hold its first election on March 1, 1977, under the district form of elections. It would be one of the most, if not the most, historical in Richmond, and the stakes couldn't be higher. Taking into consideration the racial and economic makeup of the nine districts, it was a good bet that four districts would be won by White candidates and four by Blacks. That would leave one as the swing district that would either retain White political power, or be the catalyst for something Black folk would not even had dreamt of thirty years earlier: Black political control of Richmond and its first Black mayor.

The swing district was the Fifth. I had just lost my job at RRDPC and was looking for a job, most any job. I even applied as a weatherman at Channel 12 television station. There was a flurry of considerations around the Fifth District to see who could win the pivotal seat. The important thing was to not split the Black vote with two or even three candidates running.

One of the prominent names was that of Dr. William Randolph "Randy" Johnson, Jr., a Ph.D. chemist at Phillip Morris, Richmond's iconic cigarette maker. Johnson was the pick of the Black "bourgeoisie," so to speak, and many believed to be the safe bet. Another Johnson, of no relation and another doctor, was my father-in-law, Dr. Ford T. "Doc" Johnson, a prominent dentist in Black Richmond. I talked with Doc about his run and he was not really interested. While flattered, he did not want such a big change in his life at that point and was happy where he was.

On the evening when he told me he wasn't interested, he turned to me and said, "Chuckie, listen, you know as much about politics and governance as I do. Why don't you run?" He was serious, and I was a little taken aback but I thought about it. Doc was right about my knowledge; working at the Planning Commission I had seen how much of governance operated in Richmond and counties like Henrico and Hanover. However, I didn't see myself in such a seat at just twenty-eight years old. I had been involved with community improvements and was seen by some as a young, articulate radical who enjoyed helping where I could, but still, as much as I needed a job I was hesitant.

A few nights later, I was just around the corner from Doc's house at a meeting of the Randolph Planning Study Board, an urban renewal project in the Randolph Street area of the Fifth District. It was on Lakeside Avenue at the home of Mr. Yates. Petronius Jones, or P.S. as we knew him, was Chairman of the Board. P.S. was a short man but had a presence that stood out. We talked about the vital needs of the area around Randolph Street that the City was, obviously, not going to address. P.S. had a passion about things, and I said to him afterward that he should run for Council and I would be his manager. P.S. reacted, almost as if waiting for the moment, and leaned into me like he was making a bet. He said, "I tell you what, Mr. Richardson. You run, and I'll be *your* manager!" He wasn't joking. "Look man, you're young, good-looking, articulate, and ain't afraid of nothing," he said. I was flattered and heard his words over and over as I drove home to tell Phyllis. We talked it over and we agreed… go for it!

At the same time in Richmond, there was a "Panic," not about the elections or some dreadful event, but the dire emotions of addicts when there is no dope. When the supply dries up entirely, even when you have all the cash or sex or power in the world, "you ain't getting it cause it just ain't there," it was what we called a "Panic." A Panic can be devastating for addicts but also fortuitous as it forces a "cold turkey" halt to use that is, in some ways, less burdensome on the mind. When you are in rehab or trying to stop voluntarily, the mental struggle is almost as bad as the impending physical withdrawals, a moment-by-moment torture. When there is no opportunity or chance you can get the drug, however, it makes the psychological fight easier because there is no counterweight in the fight with yourself. There had a been a Panic for weeks before the question arose of who would run in the Fifth District. As a result, I had been clean quite a while when I began to consider running. I was fortunate because I was clean and clear for the decision and campaign—and stayed away from the dope well into the summer of 1977.

Within a week, I had older, experienced campaign hands at my side. Johnnie and Helen Brooks, Freddie Reid, and Lester Banks—people who at been in the struggle since I was a kid. Helen Brooks was, in fact, my Den Mother in the Cub Scouts, and Johnnie, as well Fred

Reid and Bill Thornton, were founding members of the Crusade for Voters in Richmond in 1956. I also contacted Doug Wilder, our Black state senator and future first Black governor in America. Doug was also an alumnus of Armstrong High School with my mother, though he attended a year later. Doug supported me behind the scenes and we became friends, probably more as political buddies than my totally trusted friend. However, I admired and respected Doug greater than any other elected official at the time.

I hit the street and went neighborhood to neighborhood, Black to White, door to door, rich and poor, spreading my ideas about improving the Fifth and Richmond courageously. Some of those early walks and talks were cold and rainy but I was like the mailman: bringing it to the Fifth!

As the election neared, it became a very close race between me and Randy Johnson, and many were anxious to know who the Crusade for Voters would endorse. At a meeting, it was decided that they would have a straw vote; whoever won would be endorsed. And guess what? I won! But guess again, the Crusade did not endorse me. I was pissed! How in the hell could they do that? It appeared the status quo was pressing its hand. Henry was supporting Randy Johnson and had apparently twisted elbows behind the scenes, pushing the Crusade to betray its decision. Within a day or so, Henry even held a press conference to introduce his "Experienced Leadership Team" for City Council, consisting of the three other Black candidates and his choice of Randy Johnson. Many middle- and upper-class Blacks wanted Dr. Johnson also, and now with the Crusade behind him, Marsh believed he stood to become mayor if a majority Black council was birthed from this election.

I, however, had the support of Maynard Jackson, the dynamic and nationally recognized first Black mayor of Atlanta…and proud to say, he would become my brother-in-law later that fall. Maynard came to Richmond to campaign for me and it was a huge boost. So, despite the Crusade's back pedaling on its endorsement, it was far from a game changer. The Crusade had made the right choice but allowed an indignant Marsh to overrule them.

On March 1, 1977, people went to the polls. I spent the evening with supporters at Doc's house in Byrd Park, a beautiful home that sat facing the iconic Boat Lake with its centerpiece fountain. It was an almost uber-rare residence for Blacks in Richmond, the country for that matter, and it seems it became the kick-off point of a new Richmond. That night, by nine votes, I defeated Randy Johnson! The City Council would be a majority Black body. We were ecstatic, almost disbelieving that we did it, and by barely a dozen people. My life changed forever. Henry Marsh, who had not supported me, made his way over to Byrd Park to congratulate me, obviously pedaling

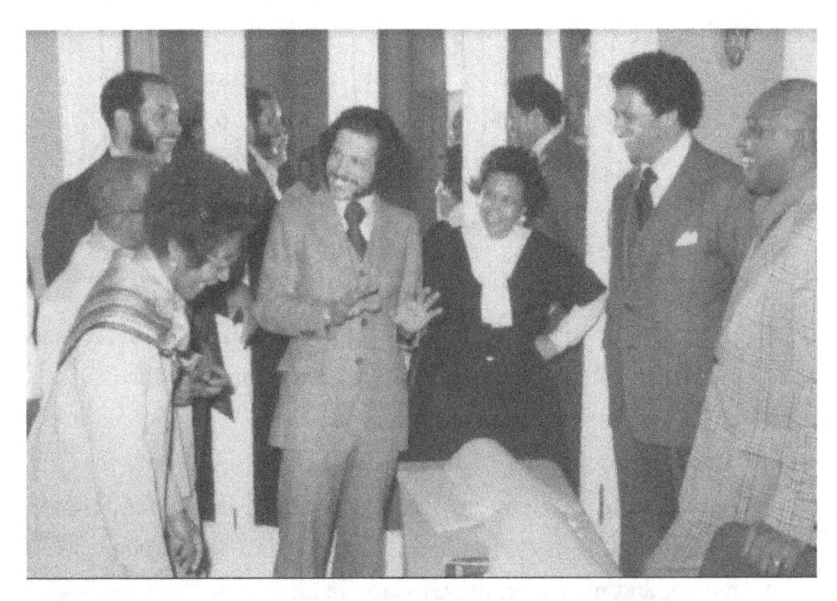

A campaign meeting with team: Audrey Burton, Petronius Jones, Richard Jones, me, my manager Nessa Johnson, my brother-in-law Mayor Maynard H. Jackson of Atlanta, GA and Joe McClenney.

again—for that vote. Henry needed my support to win the mayor's seat and he was all smiles when he arrived. I greeted him but pretty much ignored him that evening, returning my attention to those who had believed in me.

Several of my supporters gave him respectful greetings, but their "I told you so" deportment was evident, yet still joyous. I was upset at Henry, but in hindsight, understand the strategic behavior he believed was right with his endorsement, maybe; perhaps, it was nothing personal. But it was an early indication of his political character that I would be mindful of throughout my years on Council.

After the election, at the next Crusade for Voters meeting, Doug Wilder made a speech invoking us as elected officials to hold the ranks, that there "should be no further breaking of the ranks." Doug had quietly supported me, but as the Black state senator from Richmond, he gave no formal endorsement to anyone in any district. He was pissed as well with Henry for dividing the team prior to the election. Many years later, Henry wrote in his memoir a bold face lie about Maynard supposedly admonishing me to vote for him as mayor after that historic first election. Saying that, after he spoke to Maynard, Maynard then "told me to vote for him," and that I "would be a fool not to vote for him."

I had known of Henry Marsh since high school, and have known him personally now over forty years, and had respect for him. When I read what he said about my first election, I was embarrassed and somewhat ashamed of the dishonest, insignificant distortions. Maynard Jackson always maintained honest and dignified relationships. He believed the vote for Henry was the best thing but never "told me" or said I "would be a fool" not to. What Henry said simply to inflate his own appearance of grandiosity, and his influence on Maynard Jackson, was unnecessary. My sister, Valerie, was upset at that portrayal of Maynard, knowing that Maynard would not speak in such a way and certainly not misrepresent it to Marsh. Henry's "memory" was at best discourteous and thoughtless toward Maynard and belittled my early political acumen. I had always assumed that all of us would vote for Henry so, ironically, it was never even in doubt; all understood he would ascend to the mayor's office. The only person to whom it might have occurred to was Henry himself, and that was because he had endorsed my opponent and thought I would be childish and immature at my age. However, it was silly of him be so elementary in thinking, and laughable that he would write in his book that Maynard had to tell me to do so. Henry created things from a vapor of his imagination. Anyway, it was a head spinning next week or so: television, radio, newspapers, speaking appearances, and constant smiles and handshakes on the streets.

The 1977 election of the "Black" majority to the Richmond City Council by no means changed the racial attitudes overnight, but still, the whole city seemed to have a new aura of brightness. People smiled for no apparent reason, waved, and openly cheered whenever they recognized one of the new council members. The five Black faces represented a new mandate of leadership; while department heads, bureau chiefs and supervisors were still of the old order, control was now in Black hands. We were led by Henry Marsh, the conservative new Black mayor, noted for his civil rights work at his law firm. There was the tall, statuesque Walter T. Kenney, Sr., a postal carrier and union official. Then there was Mrs. Willie J. Dell sporting a sexy Afro hairstyle and Dashiki with other African tones. Also, Claudette Black McDaniel, better known as "The Lady," was always working "for the good of the Southside." And I joined them as the young, radical but dapper and unpredictable fighter from the Fifth. I had distinguished myself from the others early by not receiving Henry's support in the election. Henry never knew what I would say—or do. And not only was Henry uncertain about my position on some things, but so were the four Whites on the Council. They recognized my independence from Marsh, and as a Vietnam veteran and child of the '60s, I kept them guessing.

For the first time in Richmond's long, chronicled history of conservative, Southern genteel racism, Black people had a glimmer of hope, a possibility of fairness, and the remote sense of equality

After fighting for my country, I fought for my city. © Richmond Times Dispatch

The councilman and Richmond's first Black mayor, Henry Marsh. © Richmond Times Dispatch

at hand. As I took my seat in the marble-laden City Council chambers, I could observe the eyes of those Black people who looked to the future with hope. Alas, in the seats and around the walls there were also faces of remorse, dissatisfaction, and resentment as well. The long faces in the chamber that day foretold of a struggle for change that was only beginning, as two sides to this coin existed.

Older White faces looked down their noses at me with disdain and contempt. Some made no attempt to conceal the displeasure, rolling their eyes and turning abruptly from any appearance of respect. They suffered great pains having to submit obeisance to a young "colored" man. Nothing commendable, but I took great pleasure in prolonging those instances of agony for them. It was only fitting for these faces serving a mentality that had, at least, humiliated, belittled, and embarrassed lives of people of color for generations. For too long, history has been replete with rank injudicious miscarriages of justice based on skin color. To me, it is one of the most repugnant, vile acts of day-to-day abuses permitted by governments.

Although the laws of our City Charter give council members ultimate authority over its government, it does not require rank and file employees to like, respect, or unofficially show honor to them. Richmond, the former capital of the Confederacy, maintains the remnants and deepest sentiments of Southern heritage and the "Lost Cause" as any city in this nation. Early in my first term, I would often visit, unannounced, departments where the outward racist attitudes were legendary: the police department, fire department, and wastewater treatment plant. It was to not only to uplift and serve hope to the few Blacks in those departments, but to present a dose of reality to those who embraced an antebellum longing for a lost Richmond, a lost cause.

I would arrive and strike up a conversation with a Black employee as if we were old friends. It was quite unusual for a councilman to show up at a worksite in those days, so when I would appear and intentionally select a Black man from a crowd of employees, ask his supervisor to momentarily release him from duties to give me a tour and explanation of the department functions, it was certainly embarrassing for the White manager in front of his White underlings. Overlooking a White manager that might be in his fifties and show preference to a low-level Black employee was salt in the wound, a dynamic that was thick with shock and bewilderment for both Black and White.

I recall once when I showed up unannounced at the James River Water Filtration Plant down behind the Windsor Farms neighborhood. I walked onto the site and readily recognized Timothy Dunlap, a Black employee. While ignoring the supervisor, I approached Timothy and snubbed his boss—until I directed him to allow Mr. Dunlap to give me a tour of the facility. The White supervisor, perhaps in his late fifties, looked at me and then to Timothy with reluctance but only hesitated for a moment or so. It was a moment filled with quiet but intense conflict; the historical context of racism in public employment settings was turned on its head. There were no outward signs of animosity by the White supervisor, but the vibes were penetrating. This, of course, was a result of long-standing relationship patterns between Blacks and Whites. Even in 1977, when that shift happened in Richmond, when those learned behaviors met a paradoxical shock, the races, both Black and White, had to pinch themselves to believe it was all really happening.

Those types of visits were not a pattern, just the things one remembers when you are riding a paradigm shift. I once had the occasion to visit the fire station on Brookland Park Boulevard where Black men were finally starting to get hired. I drove up in my black Mark III Lincoln Continental, and as I left it running, I stepped out in a sharp three-piece suit with my long hair flowing back on my shoulders. That day, an old friend, Buck, from grade school was there. Buck was now a new firefighter and he, with the rest of the brothers, recognized me instantly. They all appeared to be so proud of me, as if I were more than just one of them that made good, but a kind of fighter that was putting out the fires of a long-suffered inferno of oppression. I was humbled and motivated tremendously. I walked

Cease Fire! Cease Fire!

over and we chit-chatted for a few moments when the big cheese walked up: The battalion chief. All the men froze to attention as the chief came out to command the center of the visit. I told him Buck was telling me about the station and introducing me to the firefighters.

The battalion chief, a rather short and chubby White man of about fifty, replied with a dismissive sigh and said condescendingly, "Oh, that's just Buck. He's a shitbird." Buck, as well as the others, flinched slightly and gently kicked at the ground as if it were a toll they had to accept. I just looked at him briefly. This motherfucker straight up insulted a friend of mine in front of all of us. It wasn't laughingly like one of the fellas; it was matter-of-factly, utterly rude.

I was mindful of my position but had to respond and said, "Nooo, I'm sure you're not serious. I know Buck. He's a good man, isn't he, Chief?" Before he could respond I put my arm firmly around his shoulder and pulled him away from the others. I spoke softly but firmly, chastising him for his inappropriate comment and told him he should never humiliate any of his men like that in front of the others—and that he should apologize to Buck immediately.

He stood and looked blankly at me as we both absorbed the implications of who was saying what to whom. Theoretically, I was his boss, and while he had rank and years of experience in the department, and the layers of generations of White control, he was realizing a quirk of democracy that had inexplicably placed his older, White, more experienced self in a subservient position to a younger, darker, less experienced one as I—and was duty bound to follow the rule of law!

Accordingly, like gentlemen, we turned, and he painfully walked back to the group of bewildered firemen, where, that battalion chief apologized to Buck for his awkward words. I said good-bye to the fellas and went back to my Lincoln. I sat in the still running car and waved to the guys who must have been thinking; "Damn! That was a long time coming!"

Power

Power, and projection of it, is something that governments and society should carry with integrity and modesty. All the misuses of power by the powerful ultimately lead to revolt and failure. The power that had been conferred to only wealthy White citizens prior to 1977 was now in the hands of those who understood where and how to fairly exercise it. In America, an operative power was provided to White people as a birthright, a privilege for each of them to express if only in one place and nowhere else—among Black people! At least there, for the poorest, most powerless "White trash," there was control. That dynamic transcended every experience, whether in commerce, employment, the military or even the Church; it was rare for Whites—especially in the South—to be derelict of that power.

I remember in Vietnam many White boys thought they had that little extra advantage over Black guys. That is, until the Black guy had more stripes on their sleeve. That was an acknowledged difference about military protocol versus social norms. Still, if the higher stripes or collar pins where worn by Whites, as was the case typically, that expected culture from back home was in play. In late 1969, I returned to my squad from the USS Repose hospital ship after treatment for a bout of malaria and a flesh wound. I had been in Vietnam since June and it was now December, so I had seen plenty of action. However, when I got back to my unit, there was a new staff sergeant. I don't remember the names of everyone exactly. For the sake of this memory, I will call many by fictitious monikers, except for my buddy, Primm. The new sergeant, whom I'll call "Sergeant Wilson," did not know me, but he knew my role was the machine gunner before my hospitalization.

Being from the South with a poor family background and a societal philosophy about Black men, Sergeant Wilson fulfilled his role and appointed a new and obviously inferior man to the gunner's position, Knowlton. Knowlton was a small-framed, red-headed, "peckerwood," as we would say back then, while Wilson was a large and imposing six foot, five inch White man with a big gut. Both had demeanors possessed with very similar racial proclivities; they did not favor Negros, so my role as the M60 gunner parenthetically was finished. So, instead of throwing that large, black, and beautiful M60 across my shoulder, I had to grab the canisters of M60 ammunition and carry those for Knowlton instead.

Sergeant Wilson, I am certain, made the decision based on race and skin color. In the bush, you do not argue shit, and even though I was more qualified and had more time in the country—as well as had been under fire before—he ignored the facts because Knowlton was White like he was and thus Wilson felt Knowlton should have authority over me on the machine gun team.

The squad leader, Crowder, who was also White, went along with the decision even though he knew it was not good military strategy. But, even in combat, racism is at work influencing people's decisions until action proves them right or wrong. Resentful not only because of the role of race, but of the sheer tactical error, I went along because we were returning into the Que Son Valley. Lives depended upon our mutual respect and cooperation despite race.

We got along for the first few days moving back into the dangerous valley even though bad blood existed between us. The other guys knew me well so we all got on okay together as we needed to. Then, on the fifth or sixth night, we got hit by ambush; a company of North Vietnamese Army (NVA) regulars opened up on us. The squad leader found himself pinned down in the ambush under superior fire and called for "Guns up!" as tracer rounds from the NVA were spitting off the big hard stones that many of us had braced behind. We began returning fire with M16s, small arms, shotguns, and "bloopers"—grenade launchers. One weapon, though, was unbelievably, inexplicably silent, and the leader yelled again, "Guns up!!" Knowlton, the new M60 machine gunner, was petrified. He was laying a few feet from me behind a rock, frozen but trembling, tucked into a fetal position while cradling the very weapon so urgently needed. "Guns up, goddamnit! Guns up!" The squad leader screamed as other marines returned M16 and small arms fire.

It was not *my* first rodeo, however, and I rolled over to Knowlton and grabbed the M60. I dragged the gun behind me with a belt of M60 rounds still in the locked and loaded position. I could see the red tracer rounds and the apparent area they came from as small, but lethal, shattering rocks flew everywhere. I couldn't see too far into the hilly tree line but managed to get a bead on that area where it looked like the enemy were. When I was able to get the large M60 into place, I rose slightly and prayed when I squeezed the trigger without pause. The new sound from the new weapon in the battle was game changing. My belt of 7.5 mm ammo did not last but a half minute, but it was enough to stop the incoming fire. And within minutes, the M16s, bloopers, and shotguns started going off in the direction of the NVA, followed by relative silence.

For over two hours, everything was quiet. Nobody said a word until the sun started creeping through the mountain peaks, lighting up our position in the foothills. My buddy, Primm, and I had laid there in total silence until we were certain it was all over. When morning came, it was apparent the NVA had slipped away in the dark of night. Primm looked at me and said, "Brother Chuck, you're bleeding, bro." It was not a bullet wound, but a piece of rock that had cut me next to my eye. I had felt it but thought it was perspiration.

When we all stood around after it was over talking about how lucky we were, Sergeant Wilson came over from his position about 100 yards away He commended Knowlton for the gun fire he laid down with the M60.

"Good job, Knowlton! You can always tell when that 60 is talking," he said.

Crowder, the squad leader, spoke up and said, as he glanced at Knowlton with disdain, "Gunny, it was Richardson behind the 60."

Sergeant Wilson looked at Knowlton who never raised his head, and then looked into his coffee cup in his hand. "Oh well," he begrudgingly responded, "Good job anyway." He looked back at Knowlton while he turned and walked away.

When we moved out that morning, I had the M60 on my shoulder and Knowlton carried the ammo. The sergeant passed us as we moved out and only looked down without a word. Most of us never spoke again of what had happened that night. From that point on, Knowlton carried the ammo—for me. Walking on up to the jungle trail, my man Primm said, "Did you see that, Chuck? That motherfucking gunny saw you with the M60 and did not echo a word."

"What words would have made a difference, Primm? What words?" I spoke.

The misappropriation of power is dangerous in combat, in government, in life overall. It was imperative that we, the new Black Power in Richmond, be worthy and laudable. To direct our fire (power) in the correct places, and to cease fire where it harms with triviality. Due to my off and on again struggle with addiction to heroin, coupled with my high-profile position as a Richmond city councilman, I was exposed to some unique and awkward experiences in the dark underground drug world which, eerily, were very similar to upper echelons of military and political power, events where respect of power was hardly related to the power of respect.

Wainwright

The relationship between politicians and business leaders can be a constantly morphing situation, mostly because personalities change. Business interests are almost always predictable: profit. But motives and interests of political leaders are something the business community has to grapple with on a regular electoral basis. The new majority Black City Council would require a lot more finesse and subtlety from the White business powers who were used to the "good old boy" nature of a majority White council and White supremacy.

I often observed arrogance from the wealthy magnates of commerce that believed regardless the color, or maybe in our case precisely because of color, they controlled the Council. Because after all, happy businesses mean a happy economy, which means happy constituents. At least that was the paradigm for White society in the Jim Crow economy. And the things that are friendly to business—regulations, zoning, tax rates, incentives, etc.—are still controlled by the political leaders. Historically, the age-old bribe, or some sort of "quid pro quo," was not a rarity with good old boys. With this new Council in town, however, they had to be able to persuade the members solely on merit of reason. Still, for the most powerful of the business community, the strong-arm was an early approach, using their complicit media forces to define you publicly.

Some of the larger companies would use charismatic public relations (PR) personnel: men and women with years of communication skills that develop and nurture a perceived trust. Nonetheless, the reality was that things operated under the heavy thumb of racism; bold or slight, it was displayed consciously and consistently. One morning in May of 1980, I was in the Council lounge waiting on one such operative for a meeting for which he had asked. I was chatting with a local reporter, Jim Babb, who worked the City Hall beat, when the gentleman showed up. Richard "Dick" Wainwright was vice president and head of PR for the C&P Telephone Company. He tapped on the door as he peeked in and said good morning.

"Jim, how you doing? Good to see you," he said to Jim with the familiarity of an old friend. I had seen Wainwright once or twice before at various functions but had never met him. Jim, a pleasant older White reporter, assumed the polite gesture of introduction. "Dick, this is Chuck Richardson, Fifth District Councilman. Chuck, this is Dick Wainwright with C&P."

I had not even started to say hello when "Chuckie-Boy!" jumped from Dick's jolly but offensive mouth. I was shocked, but I looked at him without the slightest indication I was ready to put my foot square up his ass. I remained calm and just looked at him without reaction.

Cease Fire! Cease Fire!

Jim stepped up quickly to engage in some small talk, but I asked him to excuse us. Wainwright looked at Jim a bit quizzically as he walked out.

The lounge was a large, plush, comfortable place with leather couches, newspapers, snacks, a television, and a coffee maker. It had a large oversized window looking atop downtown, giving the occupants a feeling of power. I asked Wainwright to have a seat and I sat across from him just a few feet.

C&P was attempting to have their tax rate reduced by 16% over a four-year span, and this "Dick" was there to lobby me. He went on for a good ten minutes about the benefits to customers and the City. Wainwright was in his fifties and had experience with the jargon of a salesman. He tried to applaud my Vietnam service and told me he had been a B17 pilot in World War II. But I didn't say anything. I sat there the whole time, poker faced, indifferent, only saying "hmmm" once. I was running ideas in my head about how to handle his "boy" remark. How should I play this?

I could tell he was getting uneasy with my silence and it was interesting to watch. Sometimes, White folk are unsure how to approach Black people with power or wealth, especially the older ones that had to reach deep for the respect they rarely had to deliver. Sometimes even today out of awkward ignorance, they say stupid things that are not necessarily meant to offend, but because of lazy, selfish considerations, they do. However, lest we be naïve, there are sometimes intentional jabs cloaked in ignorance to see how soft the dirt is where the supremacy stands. That was the situation I perceived with Wainwright, a jab to test the dirt and see how far he could push through intimidation. He certainly must have thought beforehand about how he would address me when we met. I sat there with all this running through my head while he grinned, perhaps hoping my silence was acquiescence.

When he slowed and paused for my response, I slid to the edge of my seat. Leaning in with my elbows on my knees, I looked directly at him for just a second, like I was unsure of what to say. Then, I leaned further and brought my hands together meeting my fingertips and said to him, "I know what your purpose is here today, and I understand very well your proposal. It's clear but ... but I'm wondering something. What exactly is it you want 'Chuckie-Boy' to do for you?" That man sprung to his feet like a general had walked into the room. He stuck his hand out with earnest respect, imploring a handshake from me to, hopefully, demonstrate my forgiveness.

"Councilman, I have a terrible habit of using that term so cavalierly, my wife has told me time and again to stop it. It has its place but not like that. I meant no offense if I did."

I looked askance and told him I was late for another meeting. "Let yourself out, Dick." I turned away, shaking my head, and left through a back exit for members.

Wainwright understood what he said because the way he said it was so obviously premeditated. He probably believed he could laugh it off if I had responded immediately in front of Jim Babb. But I caught him off guard after he thought he had gotten away with it. The lame guilt he showed probably did involve his wife; she may have known the times were changing and the racist supremacy in Richmond was being checked. The notion that Black people could be called "boy" and not respond was foolish. In the streets or other situations, physical conflict was typical. In a professional, particularly political setting, the contest must be fought intellectually. The battle ground for superiority is in the mind, a fight to win the truth, because a mind changed against its will is of the same opinion still.

The next time I saw Dick Wainwright was several months later in the hallway of the City Clerk's office. We had been in the same room for a function but did not encounter each other. I expected he would be cold and aloof and avoid me, but he approached me with a contrite shyness, arms behind his back until reaching me, and then earnestly reached out with his hand again. "Mr. Richardson, I want to thank you," he said. I was a bit miffed and surprised by his politeness, but I shook it. He gave a respectful nod, smiled, and walked on.

For the life of me I don't remember if we granted that tax abatement to C&P, but I'll never forget my resentment of being belittled so casually. The fact that I handled it through wit, wisdom, and fortitude in the moment was just an early example of why I would become a force to reckon with. Big business in Richmond quickly realized I was a "big boy" that knew how to "ride the bike." It also explains why a lot of things happened in the next decade or so.

Project One

The greatest mistake made in Richmond during the late 1970s when, indeed, most U.S. cities were in decline, was "Project One." It was a laudable effort steeped in a flawed theory that was designed to create a downtown center of commerce—for a non-existing market. All the best plans of exciting buildings for shopping, business, and commerce in general would not succeed if the people to use it did not exist—and, in my humble opinion, they did not in this case.

However, the planners, city policy makers, and business leaders assumed that "if you build it… they would come." Of course, we now know that was just a movie. The population base in Richmond had been gradually migrating to the suburban areas since the '50's, and it would take more than buildings to bring them back. No great cultural phenomenon ever emerged from a forest, no matter how beautiful, attractive, or convenient it was. Successful growth and change are the result of people: where they want to live, what they want to do, and how convenient it is at a given location. In Richmond, during that period of its history, the people were moving to Henrico, Chesterfield, and Hanover counties. The two major downtown shopping icons—Thalhimers and Miller & Rhoads—were in decline as a result of this migration. The prevailing thinking was that a strong anchoring element was needed for downtown to survive.

The essential unanswered question was like the chicken or the egg.

Do people draw commerce or does commerce draw people? Which comes first? I was criticized and attacked for not voting to support this project in 1977 and 1978. As a new and the youngest member of the council, some of my own supporters were outraged that I did not agree with the notion of new jobs and new business development in our distressed downtown. Henry Marsh, the senior politician, was convinced and had convinced the other Black members of the council that this project was right for Black people, and that we should join with the White members and support it.

I was somewhat new at this whole business of making major decisions; however, I was scheduled to graduate from VCU in a year with a degree in Urban Planning. The one burning question that continued to bother me stemmed from a class on population I took, which drove home a point: All urban action springs from the point where people chose to live. Location, location, location, and that's no movie. Since everyone was choosing to live outside the city, why would we invest millions in downtown? It was a fundamental question, basic and uncomplicated, and I couldn't get past it!

Well, Henry Marsh couldn't answer it; he just brushed me off saying he'd been around a long time and I should listen to the voice of experience. He wasn't condescending or arrogant, just certain that my lack of experience left me in need of his wisdom. There's a tale about the wise man who was asked: what's the secret of wisdom? The wise man said, "Good judgement." When asked the secret of good judgement, he said, "Experience." When asked the secret of experience, the wise man said, "Bad judgement." Perhaps Henry's experience, at the time, was unfinished.

Our City Manager, Bill Leidinger, was a persuasive and smart professional and, under our council/manager form of government, the highest authority in Richmond next to the council body. Leidinger had convinced the full council, other than me, to support it. It was not easy to go against the other Black members, but Henry had been wrong before on issues requiring his "experience."

Among my constituents, Audrey and Collie Burton were very

strong supporters. Both were conversant about the issue and both against the project as well. Collie was intuitive and Audrey was emotional; they were formidable and made good points not assumed at City Hall. Two other strong supporters, Richard and Bessie Jones, were like my second father and mother, so much more to me than political supporters. The mutual love we shared became stronger than any issue in politics. They were in favor of Project One and were vehement about my vote. Richard was a union representative in the Postal Service. He had a strong imposing statue and a no-bullshit demeanor. He possessed a booming voice that often might frightened people.

When the night of the Project One vote came before Council, not only did we vote on the project's approval, but along with a construction project of this magnitude, a bond ordinance approving each set of millions in capital bonds was required, and there were eight of them. That meant separate votes. I voted no on Project One and no on each bond issue... no, no, no... nine times. Our meetings were televised and of all the things I recall people saying about Project One, I remember most of all Bessie Jones describing to me how she hated hearing me say, "No, no, no!" Bessie was livid. She said, "I was so angry at you, Chuck! All you could say was 'no, no, no'... how could I explain this to our friends? You said 'no' so many times, there is no doubt where you stand on this issue!"

Not long after the plan was approved, the Council fired Bill Leidinger for unrelated reasons. Leidinger was, in his mind, the balance between the interest of the city's White oligarchy and the new Black political decision makers. But the City Manager, pursuant to the city charter, served at the council's pleasure, and this council found no pleasure in Leidinger's obviously one-sided interest. It was no secret that there was rancor between the manager and the council, but we were civil. One afternoon, very early in our new historical mandate, I received an emergency notice from the Clerk's office. Henry Marsh was asking the Black councilmembers to meet him at 8th and Main St. at the First and Merchants bank. Except for Willie Dell, we met

Henry and he proceeded to lead us to the elevator. He told us we were meeting some of the White corporate leadership downstairs.

When the elevator opened, I realized we were in the basement facing a large room with a glass front and a boatload of White men inside. Henry, Walter, Claudette, and I entered and faced what must have been fifty or more rich White men. They were all lined up behind tables against the walls, resembling an audition room, with an open space in the center of the big square. But for a hundred or so years earlier, one of us might have been in the center, on display for those men—for sale. We sat down in the few chairs left and looked around at the cast of Leidinger's constituents: corporate leaders, newspapers, banks, established old money, and new.

After a brief, token "hello, thank you for coming," one of them got to the point. A.J. Brent, the attorney for the *Richmond News Leader*, was a brash, nasty, deep-voiced spokesman for the White status quo. Brent put his hand on the arm of his chair, looked at us with an obvious sense of privilege and said, "Now, we hear the word on the street is, well, that y'all are planning on getting rid of Bill. We think Bill is doing a fine job and we think he should stay. We all want to know what your intentions are."

I really don't remember what I said but I do remember what Henry said, and I've always been proud of him for it. He stood up and put his hand in his pocket and looked at them seated around the walls and said, "Actually we are simply abiding by the city charter which says we have the sole prerogative to dismiss the manager if we wish, and we, yes, are considering it. We appreciate your concern for the city manager, but we will let you know of our decision when we inform the rest of the public."

Those old White men looked at each other as if asking, "Did you hear that nigger?" It was one of those moments that the historical message of the 1977 election, and the weight of it on Richmond's future pierced the armor of history itself. It was one thing to berate a fire chief or plant manager about their behavior, but to defy the people who had been in power for a dozen generations was a profound statement of change. They believed *they* called the shots, law or policy be damned. Even that very meeting was illegal: any city council business with two or more members must be held in public—with notice.

A.J. Brent was red with resentment but could say nothing to us. A message was being sent—on both sides. We indeed decided to fire Leidinger, and he of course protested. He demanded evidence of his dereliction. When I was first elected, Doug Wilder advised me to always keep records of communications or documents, especially with the city manager. I took that advice and when Leidinger wanted something more than our allegations, I had plenty. One case in particular was poignant. On Lombardy Avenue, between Broad Street. and Maggie L. Walker High School, there was a long, low area that passed beneath a railroad viaduct. Although there was considerable foot traffic, there was no lighting for anyone walking there at night. I had requested Mr. Leidinger to look into providing light as there had been several crimes reported under those tracks. I received no reply and sent a second request. Again, no reply. I confirmed he obtained the request and I had two separate copies of everything. After several weeks. there was another crime in the dark underpass on Lombardy; a young teenage girl was brutally raped. Leidinger was furious at the suggestion the rape was his fault, but we were indignant that he had no explanation for his neglect, though we had our assumptions. With that, and other reasons that gave cause, he was fired.

Manuel "Manny" Deese was selected to pick up the management of the project. The design, construction process, budget, and overall completion of a large bridge over Broad Street, a centerpiece of the project, was a huge undertaking. At one point, there was a grueling evaluation by a White attorney from Philadelphia. This attorney had been sent to the planning commission hearing, apparently, to embarrass Manny Deese. This fellow was quite arrogant, immaculately attired with every strand of hair in place, and using ten-dollar words to empower his vernacular.

It was obvious as to what he was attempting to do. While I could not compete with legal jargon or technical terminology, I was the city council's representative on the planning commission and maintained a broad range of authority as to what I could say. That attorney was unaware of my position as he continued to question the project. Bordering on humiliation, Manny was excoriated by "Mr. Philadelphia" as he questioned his qualifications (I suspect because Manny was Black), but when he charged Manny Deese with being over his head in numbers, I stopped him right there.

"Sir, that's quite enough from you. I don't know who you are, but the man you're talking about is our city manager, and he may not wear a lawyer's suit, but I trust his numbers as much as yours, and I don't appreciate the manner in which you demean the significance of his work on this project. You can show more respect, or I'll cut your comments short and call for the question right now," I said, rather indignantly.

That fancy lawyer began to shrink and squirm like a worm back into a hole. He immediately backed up and said he had overstated his case. Sheepishly he asked if there were any questions. And, although Manny Deese is of dark complexion, I thought I detected a glow on his face, too, as he gave Mr. Philly a look that could've cut stone. I actually did want Project One to succeed, despite my vote against it; I just didn't believe that an artificial market of that magnitude could be created. The biggest obstacle was the natural inclination of the market. White residents were migrating to the counties and even many Blacks were relocating there. Through the '60s and '70s, it became difficult to attract White citizens back to the downtown areas to shop, to do business with any banks, restaurants, or to attend sporting events, movies, entertainment, anything. The city was predominately Black ... and whenever this occurs, a stigma of fear sets in. In that case people, White people avoided the central business district.

The face of downtown became that of a Black person: scary. As far as we like to think we have come, there are still barriers to overcome. The fear of groups of Black people continues to be a real factor in our struggle to conquer our racial issues. The only successful businesses are those based in the natural market and its inclinations. With a predominately Black residential population, it was a flawed concept to expect White citizens would travel through a Black area to return downtown when all the goods and services already existed, in even greater numbers and equal quality, right where they already lived. It was an unrealistic expectation. However, today, a review of purchasing patterns will reveal that White homeowners are beginning to relocate in Richmond, and as this occurs on a significant level, then the market for other goods and services will develop. But it was 1977 and White folk were not about to come downtown.

Towards the end of Project One's first ten years and beyond, a debate emerged, a desperation to save its dwindling, slow demise. The city had attempted many different unsuccessful ventures. James Ukrop and some of his colleagues suggested we do something to change or modify the face of Broad Street to appear safer. The subject of public transportation was looked at, such as moving the bus stops on Broad Street to other less conspicuous locations. It was obvious; White folks were frightened by any gathering of Blacks and would not come ... so, move the Negroes out of sight. The problem of too many Blacks gathering on Broad Street accidentally made the newspapers and could not be adequately clarified to satisfy the headlines.

So, there we were, caught in full view. We were looking down the throat of the elephant in the room that everyone denied...as he looked down his long trunk at the rest of us. As it related to the marketing of the project, there were too many Blacks on Broad Street ... there! Now I've said it! What do we do about it? What could we do about it? The mere acknowledgement of such a thing is an indictment, evidence of the impact of racial propriety. Surely, we were beyond this is as a practical matter, weren't we? Be serious.

The restoration of Downtown Richmond—without addressing the root problem that reaches into every corner and aspect of our respectable lives—is daunting. How do we as leaders, Black and White, structure a successful downtown edifice with brick and mortar when the major problem is human beings? A successful downtown commercial area needed people who spend money. It was a hopeless conundrum with no solution in sight, which is why in the end the city eventually tore down the structures, and most of the businesses failed and relocated.

The greatest disappointment was the demolition of the bridge across Broad Street that which was to be a symbol of the two communities (Black and White) joining in a single project, built to invite the money needed to keep it above water. It seemed the White money in the suburbs was not interested. As much as I wanted to hope that commerce was possible without White investment and spending, my pragmatic approach was a simple understanding of what typically drives commerce—including human prejudice and math. Project One turned out to be one of the greatest financial busts in Richmond's history.

Years after I was the only vote against that failed and costly venture, I didn't remind those who attacked me for my vote; it was unnecessary to say, "I told you so … didn't I?" As such a young and new member in the late '70s, my position on things in the Council would still involve a learning curve, but my focus and commitment on whatever I championed in the decade after would say more about me than that first right opinion about a huge issue. And, for the sake of my constituents and the Black community of Richmond over that decade, I wish I had been wrong.

CHAPTER 7

Zorro

The one intangible quality critical to accountable representation at the local level is empathy combined with the ability to translate it into effective problem solving. It is one thing to understand a person's problem, but another thing to feel, empathize, and be motivated to do something about it. During my eighteen years of Council, I witnessed hundreds of situations where pain and suffering were at an inexcusable and intolerable level. But for some inexplicable reason, the councilperson responsible for solving the problem was not sufficiently moved to act against the circumstances and solve the problem. The councilperson had a full appreciation of the problem but did not feel the complainant's pain enough to do anything beyond the normal acknowledgement of the circumstances and express sympathy.

Accountability occurs when the council members care enough about another person's pain that he or she will expend the necessary time, energies, and resources to resolve that individual's problem. There were thousands of citizens and group complaints, large and small, where the degree of care, empathy, or concern on the part of the councilman determined the outcome of the situation. It would have taken more time, phone calls, and paperwork by the councilperson, but, again, the motivation was the depth of the pain and description of the problem coupled with the councilman's degree of empathy that would determine the results.

In most cases, each city councilperson maintains equal authority to make demands upon the administration. The extent to which the particular problem is pursued, if at all, would vary between council members. One example I am able to recall is the situation of the First Street elderly high-rise complex. An elderly housing building for low-income Black citizens in the Gilpin Court public housing area, the 300-unit high-rise was constructed without central air conditioning!

I was elected in March, installed in July, and visited the high rise in late July of 1977, where the summer heat was sweltering with temperatures north of 100 degrees, sometimes even at night. Those apartment units were intolerable and some of those elderly people lived miserable lives, sleeping outside on balconies twelve stories up. The perspiration dripped at mid-day and electric fans were insufficient, but the residents had no choice.

The force of a heat furnace hit me when I entered the 12th floor apartment units, and I could only imagine my mother or grandmother living in such insufferable conditions. I could not bear the idea of these old people suffering day after day in such heat. I summoned the Housing Authority Director to the site, away from his air-conditioned office, and waited until the hottest time of the day. I asked that he meet me at one of the apartment units on the 12th floor - and I was intentionally twenty-five minutes late in that heat.

When I arrived, he was already angered and insulted that a young Black member of the newly elected Black majority City Council would have the audacity to request his presence under such disagreeable conditions. I asked the director, Mr. Frederick A. Faye, what we could do to bring some relief to these insufferable conditions. I walked off into the cramped apartment unit as I gestured for him to follow. Mr. Faye was a stout, short, dumpy White man with a gravelly voice. He was baldheaded and always wore a French overjacket despite the heat. As we entered the bedroom of a tenant, I turned abruptly and asked him why they would allow a building of such magnitude to be constructed without central air.

"Mr. Richardson, it was just cost prohibitive," he replied.

At that point, I engaged the subject of human lives, their value in public housing, and the fact that that housing was 98% Black people. He said that he didn't set the budget and had to make do with City Council appropriations. His bottom-line response was that there was just no money in the housing authority's budget to provide central air to this building; it was not financially justifiable. I told Mr. Faye there were no buildings of 300 units without central air in the White neighborhoods in Richmond. "How do you explain that?" Mr. Faye said he did not build all the apartment buildings in Richmond: just the public ones.

Mr. Faye's explanation was not sufficient enough to excuse the empathy I felt for those older people who endured the sleepless nights of heat exhaustion and the miseries described to me by the residents of that high-rise in Gilpin Court. Some city councilpersons might have accepted his excuse, but I returned several times to listen to other residents of the building and in that next year, 1978, we had an 800-million-dollar budget with all the monies appropriated. And, with an agenda driven by empathy, I was able to convince the Council to approve over $200,000 for individual window air conditioners for every unit in that building.

I never saw a more grateful, thankful, happier, and satisfied group of citizens in all my time on City Council. It is not often that citizens are so grateful they are moved to tears, but their suffering corresponded to the measure of that appreciation. Sometimes, understanding people's problem is not sufficient; we must allow the energy of empathy to move us or it becomes no more than apathy. For some people, $200,000 is an amount too great to pay for the comfort of other people. But to overlook any cost from the outset because of the systemic disregard for Black people—like those in public housing—cannot be measured in dollars and cents. It is rather more a depth of empathy or lack thereof. Unfortunately, in this instance, the variable happened to have been skin color and that is sad. Today, that high-rise is named for the same director, the "Frederick A. Faye" elderly high-rise. Yep, think about it.

Close to twenty years later, Mrs. Mary Mann, who was a resident of that building, wrote about that summer and gave the letter to the City. I'm sure she would be happy that I share it here:

Ever since I was about fifteen years old, when somebody came round asking me to vote, I ain't seen any reason to vote, so, I didn't. I've seen people get elected from presidents to sheriffs to members of the Richmond City Council and nothing ever changed for me. I got up every day, went to work every day, and saw people come around, "Vote for me and I'll do this, I'll do that," year after year nothing ever changed, and I never seen no difference in voting or not voting—life was still hard for me! I'm sure there must've been reasons to vote, but I just never seen it; no more jobs for Black people and the housing never got better and there were still courtrooms on Monday mornings full of Black people going to jail and filling our prison's with Black faces.

And them politicians still want you to vote for 'em. But there has not been one single reason that I saw in which it would touch my life and make a difference that I could witness or feel. After eighteen years of working and I laid in my hot miserable bed with sweat rolling off my head, I would think about how wonderful it would be to sleep in a nice cool room that was not 97 degrees hot.

It was in the middle of August of 1977 and we used to go out on our balconies at night to get cool and talk. Someone said they heard this young man name "Chuck Richardson" was just elected to City Council and he said he was going to see that we didn't have to keep suffering like this at night anymore. Somebody said, "It ain't no way nobody in City Hall was gonna care enough for Black people in a high-rise building that they would spend money to put air conditioning in a building or they would have done it when they first built the place in 1970."

Well, one of the ladies said she believed Mr. Chuck was going to get it done because he loved old people and we should all keep voting for him. I told them that people been coming round all these

Cease Fire! Cease Fire!

years telling us things and why should we start believing them now? "Cause it's Mr. Chuck and he's different. He's a young Black man; he was a Marine, too," she said.

I didn't believe it, but that next spring the RRHA delivery trucks brought us large boxes of window unit air conditioners for all 250 apartments at the high-rise on First Street.

I could not believe it and the first night in July when it was too hot to sleep, I turned on my air and cried myself to sleep out of pure happiness and joy! They were right, Mr. Chuck *was* different! It seems that everyone was so happy and thrilled that Mr. Chuck had fought for us, because the Housing Authority Administration had told him it cost too much to install central-air in the building. So, Mr. Chuck gave a speech at that City Council about hot summer nights when old people suffer, that made some members of that Council cry, and sure enough, they voted to raise their budget $250,000 for window air conditioners for all us in the building!

Mr. Chuck was our hero from then on and I had a reason to go to the polls and vote on Election Day. I had never before had a real reason to vote, but for the first time in my life, I think my vote made a difference. One summer, I laid down at night in misery, the next summer I slept in cool comfort because people voted for someone who cared, and it made all the difference for us.

That was in 1979 and I was 79—20 years ago. Next year I will celebrate my 100th year birthday and Mr. Chuck will be out of prison to attend my birthday party. During the years Mr. Chuck served on City Council, he made life easier for a lot of citizens. I always wonder why good people who truly help others are made to suffer themselves so much?

Well, Mr. Chuck never complained, so I guess if it's alright by him it should be alright by us.

— Mrs. Mary Mann

That was a very touching letter. I don't recall her 100th birthday, but I am glad she was 'cool' when she reached it. And I suppose there were a few who thought they would, as well, be a 100 years old before I got out of jail. To them, Happy Birthday!

Getting Credit: The City Stadium

As a new councilman, I was anxious to be a part of a successful effort for my district and the city. The first real issue to test my will, instincts, political naivety, and everything else, was the plan to expand the Richmond City Stadium. Discussions about expanding the stadium had been made between the University of Richmond and the City's administration prior to the election of 1977 and would have been a "done deal" under the at-large system. Under the old at-large system, there would have been no representative directly accountable to the people in that area.

There would not have been a lobbying group large enough to affect a city-wide election, but the stadium was in the Carillon/Stadium civic area, which was large enough to affect the outcome of a district election. And I happened to be the Fifth District representative. As a neophyte councilman with this huge responsibility of protecting the citizens of this area, I had no idea what was coming at me. Everybody who was anybody knew someone at University of Richmond (U of R). It was one of the most powerful institutions in Richmond. It became a question of how much fight was in me, which even I didn't know until the fight was on. Some would have argued that in a larger context, it might have been in the city's greater interest to have a stadium facility to qualify for a better football league perhaps. A bigger league, better teams, players, attractions in general, some would contend would be good; but that someone was not me.

Since I represented the people whose homes would be inundated by traffic, students, noise, confusion, trash, and everything else bad associated with a big college football game, their concerns were mine. From the start, upon my election to council, I was already committed to the opposition of the expansion and there was no compromise as far as I was concerned.

Two of my early supporters, Collie and Audrey Burton, were also instrumental in this fight, along with Mary Jane Hyland of the Civic Association. It was an issue where the community was unified and in full support of my position. Whenever I spoke against it, I had a large contingent of supporters to echo my argument.

Shortly following the elections in March, the president of Virginia Union University (VUU) invited all members of the City Council to a breakfast meeting at the university. Dr. Alex B. James, speaking on behalf of the University of Richmond, was kindly requesting that we look favorably upon a proposal to grant a $250,000 parking study to determine the feasibility of expanding the existing Richmond City Stadium. It seemed somewhat odd to me that VUU was also making a request for U of R. It was also strange that Claudette Black McDaniel had a repressed giggle throughout the meeting. It was only later that I realized the breakfast meeting was a cover for Henry Marsh who had given a soft commitment of his approval and support for the expansion project. It only took me a short amount of time to realize that I had been tricked by Henry. Henry Marsh had planned to maneuver himself into a political catbird seat by convincing the White oligarchy that he could deliver the Black votes on Council, delivering to them the things they might want such as the expanded city stadium, and also convince the Black community that all would be well for them under his stewardship.

The task, however, would prove to be more than Henry could successfully pull off. Some of the things the White corporate leadership wanted went far beyond that which Willie Dell, Claudette McDaniel, or I would be willing to accept. And Walter T. Kenney, Sr., had always warned us that Henry was a very conservative person. Walter would say so in a way to give the impression that he disagreed with him, but unfortunately, was very rarely willing to publicly oppose Henry.

Each of them, however, went along with Henry initially to support the University's request to expand the stadium. The first vote on the $250,000 parking feasible study was eight to one; only my dissenting voice heard. Everyone had predicted that I did not stand a chance of turning that vote around before the next election, which would mean a serious win, or loss, for me in the Fifth District.

The expansion of the City Stadium had become the foremost issue in the district and pundits had begun to predict that I didn't have the experience, knowledge, or political wisdom to stop the expansion of the stadium. And, since I had only won the first election by eight votes, Dr. Randy Johnson could return and unseat me. I decided on a campaign of introducing a resolution each month against the expansion of the stadium. These resolutions were couched in a moral position of good quality neighborhoods and housing over a large facility for White boys to play football. Each month, I pushed the issue about poor struggling Black citizens who had been uprooted by the expressway, then again by Richmond's Urban Renewal Plan, and now, threatened by a parking lot—football parking, for the University of Richmond.

I had resolutions and arguments in Council that shamed both the Black and White members. Collie and Audrey Burton with the civic associations were getting crowds to attend the Council meetings, pushing hard against the measure, and expecting significant credit for the eventual victory. They were really helping me because the other council members were seeing all the opposition for the expansion, and the support I had for my position from the beginning. I had only one thing in mind: to get the issue in front of the Council as often as I could before the next election. The question was not even arguable. There was little debate. It was clear that it was the right thing to do to support my papers. I had to do enough until it hurt, until the members of the Council said "Uncle," and I only had eleven months to do it. I watched Henry, our Black mayor, squirm as I described in graphic terms the pain and inconvenience elderly and poor Black people would be made to endure so the rich kids could play football.

I also caught William Leidinger with his own words making my point! In my research on the issue, I found an old magazine article where he was quoted acknowledging that the expansion was largely for the benefit of U of R which, obviously, he had forgotten, or so he said. It was an early moment of victory for me when Leidinger, so surprised at the quote I read, rose from his City Manager's seat, walked down to the council's platform, and reached for the article I held like a smoking gun. I handed the magazine to him and he read it in utter disbelief, all while being televised ... BUSTED! It must have seemed like a two-year walk back to his very hot seat after that. The City Council finally cried "Uncle." They reversed the eight to one vote of support with a final nine to zero vote to abandon plans to expand the Richmond City Stadium. And this action all but ensured my re-election. My first election vote margin was only eight votes; my re-election was basically a landslide by over 500 votes!

Afterward, I gave Collie, Audrey, Mary Jane Hyland, George, Ralph, Ernest, and Brenda all the credit they needed and deserved, with the understanding that we can all get so much more accomplished if we don't worry so much about who's going get the touchdown. It's the effort of a good team…with a great quarterback.

One Swimming Pool

Shakespeare said, "Misery acquaints a man with strange bedfellows," and later Lord Lytton said so of poverty as well. Today, we know it to be true of politics. The significant thing I learned early on in my service as a councilman was that without direct involvement of your constituents, very likely you accomplish very little. However, with them, most anything is possible. Not the same can be said too often about "strange bedfellows." Constituent involvement speaks to the passion and importance of an issue and the trust in their representative. They must believe that he is listening and that he is empathetic, whether in agreement with them or not.

It was probably more a factor of my young age that I listened to my community leaders and felt no impulse of ego to believe that I knew it all at that point. Some persons, when elected to public office, begin to assume a "know it all" posture as a result of the title. Your mail is addressed to "The Honorable" and city employees may even sometimes bow to you, which can easily inflate the ego. In my case, at the age of twenty-nine, all my colleagues were ten to fifteen years older. Most of the civic leaders and people in my campaign were older than me as well, though, for me, they were like family.

Bessie and Richard Jones were my second mom and dad, and Petronius and Evelyn Jones were like my aunt and uncle. Elaine Dunn had been my sixth grade teacher; Johnnie and Helen Brooks were my den parents when I was a Cub Scout. The list of my supporters and those who made so much possible is replete with elders whom I loved and respected. For them, it wasn't necessary to further prove my mettle, so to speak; they had admiration and respect through my war record and political courage. Only Elaine Dunn couldn't stop seeing me as her "little Wallace" in the sixth grade.

Johnnie M. Brooks was a former leading spokesman for the NAACP. Fearless, with a heart of gold, Johnnie was a lion for the true causes of Black Richmond. Seeing everything with an authentic Black perspective, he was an unsung hero who imparted courage and inspiration to many who may had been disheartened by history and conditions. He was friends with all the older clan of Richmond's minority leaders like Freddie Reid, John Howlette, Lester Banks, and Bill Thornton, to name a few. Shortly after I announced my run for city council, Johnnie wanted to introduce me to William S. "Bill" Thornton. We met one evening at Johnnie's home and Bill was there waiting. At some point, the two of them spoke to each other and I overheard Johnnie telling Bill, "He's young but he's got mother wit, and he's fearless as a lion, Bill!" At the time, I was not familiar with the term "mother wit," but it had to be good if it was anything like a lion.

All those veterans of the movement made it easy for me to subject myself to their recommendations without subjugating myself to them. Certainly, Johnnie nor Bill or any of them wouldn't have expected that from me at any rate. Therefore, when they told me to do something, I could listen like an obedient son but conduct myself like an individual councilman. If I didn't agree with something they said, I could ignore them, and nothing would be made of it. That way, we shared the power, and no harm was done, no egos bruised in differences. Whenever one of my supporters suggested something to me, I would ask for some time to consider it. If after consideration I agreed, I would get it done or give them an explanation or a good reason why not. But I always made them feel a part of the process, where the power is shared, and they felt an importance to their involvement. People want to feel important—because they are.

When the constituents in Oregon Hill, a notoriously poor, rough, and segregated White neighborhood, demanded a swimming pool, it was a financial impossibility for the City. There was a public pool only blocks away in the Randolph community; but the Randolph community was Black. Oregon Hill had always maintained the stigma of an overtly racially-polarized area where Blacks were not welcome. When I first ran for office and walked Oregon Hill, my experience was "touch and go"; though my light-skinned appearance dampened the overt animosity somewhat, it was nonetheless obvious they wanted a fully White person representing them. So, the notion of those White kids joining their neighbors in their pool was quite out of the question for the typical Oregon Hill parent.

Geographically, the two communities were very close, but socially, miles apart. One was White, the other Black; one was poor, the other poorer. Today, both areas are in transition, but at the time, 1978, the White citizens of Oregon Hill wanted their own pool—and wanted no parts of treading the same water with Negroes in Randolph. The Blacks were, for the most part, indifferent, not holding such raw feelings of animosity and resentment about it. I realized that there are some instances where the best of talkers cannot match good actions, so recognizing Randolph's "foot in the water," I invoked a true community participation and hoped for the best.

My suggestion was to create an event where the Randolph Community would welcome Oregon Hill, inviting them to lunch and a swim party for both neighborhoods. I contacted the "Mother of Randolph," Mrs. Bessie Jones, and requested she arrange a party atmosphere welcoming the children of their counterparts in Oregon Hill. I told her the City would provide signs, decorations, and a large banner across Idlewood Avenue saying, "Welcome, Oregon Hill."

It was not something to assume very easily, even if the City helped promote the idea. Common swimming areas for Blacks and Whites, or rather the lack thereof, was an iconic reality in American history, probably as segregated as much, as Martin Luther King, Jr., said, as "Sunday morning in America." But I believed in the good people of Oregon Hill as well, and I went to see them. I arranged a meeting at the home of an outspoken resident by the name of Mable; she and about a dozen others there still insisted on their own pool and were not very receptive of me. Actually, they didn't seem to know what I was asking them to receive. When I announced that the children of Randolph wanted to invite the children of Oregon Hill to a swim party with lunch, their eyes grew wide as if to say, "You must be joking!" I described the positive, brave gesture of joining me for a march up Idlewood Avenue on a Saturday morning, from their neighborhood to Randolph, and being received with open arms under a beautiful banner to welcome them. Their eyes remained wide and a smirk crossed the faces of a few; others sighed and looked down and around.

One lady replied in the moment, "I ain't lettin' my children swim wif no niggers."

Quickly, another cut in and covered her mouth and said, "Stop it! You know Chuck is here."

"Well, you know he ain't one of them, not really," said another.

"Hush, hush now!" was murmured from behind them.

It was one of those times when I had to pretend I didn't hear.

Cease Fire! Cease Fire!

I didn't know what they were thinking about me; "is he Black, *real* Black?" They talked over each other trying to keep the one older woman from saying any further embarrassing quips. "Hush, hush now!" was said several times. I remained calm and let it pass as it was something I was hardly unfamiliar with as a light-skinned Black. Some of those folks may have been ambivalent about what I was, but not the image I was trying to paint for them.

I went on to explain that things would be fine. "They're looking forward to welcoming you all, free food, hotdogs, hamburgers, drinks, ice cream… and kids having fun. We can show all of Richmond how to get along," I said. Then I smiled and said, "I'll even let you throw me in the pool."

"With your suit on?" they asked.

"You know you ain't got but one pin stripe suit … your only suit," one said, laughingly. With that, a chuckle broke over them—and so did the ice.

Bringing Black and White together. Oregon Hill and Randolph pool party. © Richmond Times Dispatch

On the Saturday morning of the event, it was like a circus show for the media. Cameras bounced around the pool following smiling kids with ketchup on their mouths and pool water in their hair. It was like we were on a Hollywood set: smiles and movie stars and a make-believe setting. The big scene was, of course, me being thrown in the pool, a big splash, in every way, and not one racial glitch the whole afternoon. The City Manager, Manny Deese, jokingly described me as a social worker as much as anything; it was a tremendous success. And Blacks and Whites have been swimming together ever since! It was a community that walked in mass up Idlewood, and it was a community en masse that met them at the pool that made it work. The dynamics of those groups coming together at the same time gave the problem an energy that can make almost anything possible and virtually nothing impossible. Again, the possibilities are so broad when constituents get involved and feel empowered. One might believe that when the happiness of your children is at stake, it can make for strange bedfellows.

The Uprush and Downfalls of Heroin

How does one start the story of heroin? Not how one starts heroin, but how is one seized by heroin? How does one explain what it is that makes an addict *an addict?* Today, in America, there is a better understanding of the physical and psychological command of the need for the relief, the grant of painless life. I don't in any way wish that anyone find themselves in that position of choosing between a life they know, and, therefore, might understand and change, and the life which demands escape that can only end in a permanent void of what makes life *life*.

When I fought in Vietnam, my fight was for simple survival:

to live. When I fought to survive the world of heroin addiction, it was a fight to survive life, to persist in a life that danced on a razor's edge. In Vietnam, it was a matter of death and the ability to confront it; here at home, for me, it was a matter of now paying for that successful confrontation daily. As I look back fifty years later from those jungles with the understanding that so many there were denied their next fifty years, I only feel one thing: whether good or bad, those who did not make it back would probably gladly accept the course life granted me. From them, I ask forgiveness.

From 1970 to 1988, my intermittent struggle with heroin addiction was something I find almost unbelievable to conceive today, a weird fairy tale. The uplifting illusion of power, respect, and influence only dreamed of by many was a rare and unusual life of a Black man in his late 20's, a constant rush under which I was lucky to maintain any balance. Yet, the dark hours of the evening brought on the struggling terrors of meeting the financial obligation of a $100 a day addiction. Unmet meant the horrors of dope sickness, but once achieved, it resulted in receipt of the drug and the feeling that changed the world. At the risk of developing an even deeper addiction and being discovered, I negotiated my exchanges through some of the most shadowy characters in the city. As an elected official who shouldered the obligation of attending early morning breakfast meetings and formal evening affairs, I maintained a public persona that masked the secret, daily struggle in which I was involved.

At times, my life was divided into distinctly different worlds separated only by the hours that transformed the daylight into the nighttime. In the evening hours, when traveling to D.C., Charlottesville, or Virginia Beach, with a beautiful female in a fine automobile, listening to Grover Washington or Marvin Gaye in a Pierre Cardin three-piece European-cut suit, and the scent of Gucci in the air, it was like a dream floating up Interstate 95 North at 75 miles per hour. The contrast of such distinctly different life behaviors that might switch within a matter of minutes was sometimes unimaginable. I had to make a successful transition or risk being caught in a Councilman's world as a dope addict, or risk being caught as a dope addict in a Councilman's world. In either case, I would be caught.

Sometimes the struggle amounted to a juggling act where I was not able to pull off the time, resources, or creativity needed to maintain my cover. This duality, however, brought on a day-to-day life of surrealism. The daytime responsibilities of, say, attending a planning commission meeting with a group of constituents, chairing the Metropolitan Planning Organization, serving on the United Givers Way Board and Boys Club Board of Directors all in the same afternoon reflected a "work ethic" lifestyle. It was imperative that I gave the appearance of the soundness of judgment, cleanliness in attire, and sobriety of thought ... and I did for ten solid years.

The contrast was stretched endlessly. My mental capacities were tested to the extent that even today I cannot explain how it was that I managed to escape disasters that lay before me at the time. For a considerable period, neither my wife, Phyllis, nor my children or closest friends, were aware of the constant struggle in which I was entangled. Given that I was a City Councilman, many people held me in high esteem; indeed, I held the respect of friends, and even thugs and enemies of the status quo. Many of these same people, who knew my secret, were inclined to keep it and not rat me out because they saw me, despite my flaws, as their champion against the status quo.

But winning the battle against a foe that was internal made the fight against business powers or political rivals seem like sport. Fighting against injustice and pursuing the needs of the poor or elderly had always come natural to me, and sometimes the reward was as much in the battle as in the benefit to others. But the fight against the "horse" was more about not losing than winning. Gil Scott-Heron expressed it well in his song "Parallel Lean" which described the torturous psychology addicts face every night.

People have so many stereotypes about what an addict looks like: disheveled, wandering, unpredictable or hyperactive, aggressive, and unscrupulous. I survived, in part, because I was able to defy the image of what people expected. So many doctors, lawyers, corporate leaders, college professors, appointed and elected officials walk on the edge of alcoholism, illicit drug, or pill addiction. However, the public generally would not accept this truth, even if it were placed squarely in their faces. Only when someone is caught do we believe it. If it is

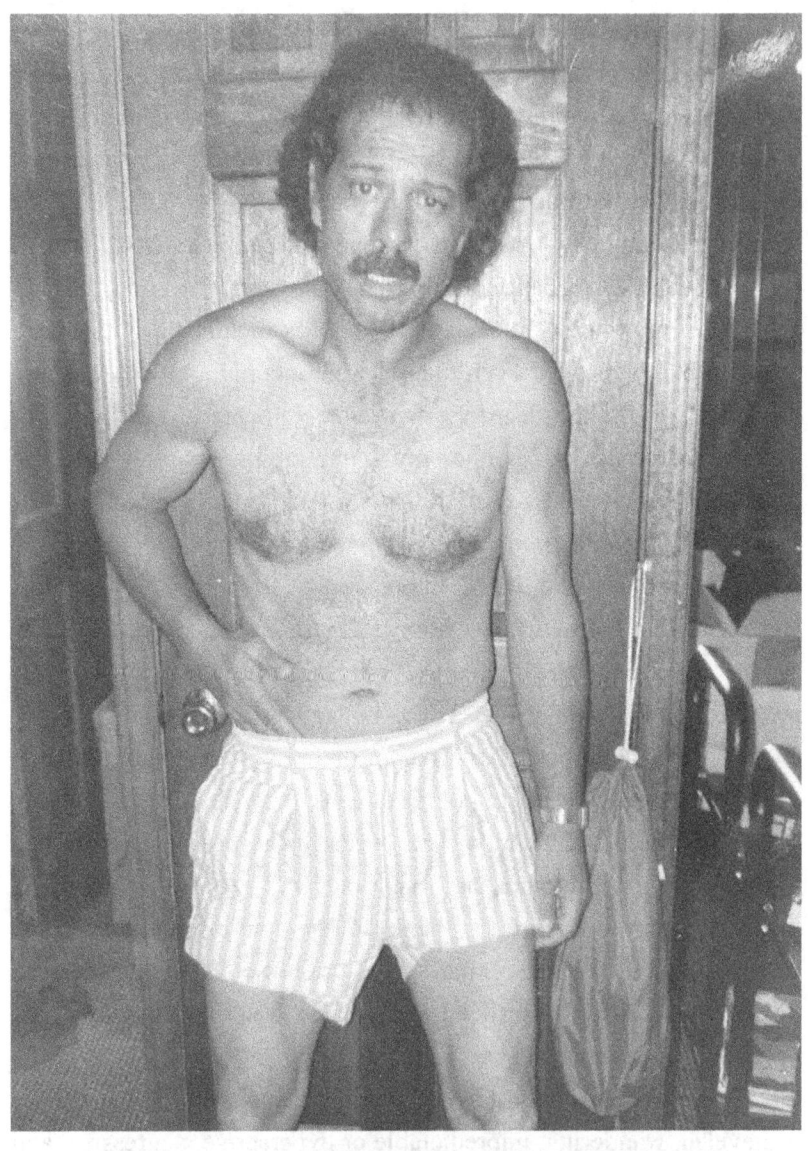

The fight very few saw, and even fewer understood: Withdrawal, a misery beyond words. But as bad as I looked I still looked good — one of the reasons I was able to hide it for so long.

someone you know, well, you make up excuses. Moreover, if the addict is someone you don't like, you unmercifully lambast them and swear that you never knew them.

Many think addicts are simply after a "high" and can't resist the feeling. However, using heroin, after just a short period, is about avoiding the loss: the lack of heroin—and the horrible pain that comes. Just as someone may take a daily medicine to fight off the pain of arthritis, the functioning addict is often unobserved, even by many family and friends. It is the withdrawal that is utterly visible and pathetic. Whenever I was "dope sick," I made myself scarce to the public. I never allowed people to see me in that shape, but once I was able to secure the drugs, I became functional. I would very meticulously shower up, pick out a clean white shirt and one of my tailored Cardin, YSL, or Cassini suits, clean my fingernails and teeth, and then present myself to the public as they expected to see me. Let me try to describe, with my most sincere desire not to tempt anyone, the experience:

Within just the passing of a moment, the uprush of soft warmth consumes your loins and moves from the stomach to every inch of the body. And the euphoric bait that is heroin's trap has you. As Freddie Nelson used to say, "'Your whole world changes," and he was right. It was a feeling I have never felt before. Never had I felt a sensation so euphoric that every physical desire was fulfilled and continued to soothe every need. With shame and remorse, I admit to such pleasure, to succumbing to the bait that is irresistible once the bait has its hook in you. The flesh has no weapon against heroin, even as its annihilation is as certain as its complete ecstasy. Complete surrender is an unavoidable end. Nothing in life is so strong an imprisonment as the body's captivity by this drug, which becomes every means to an end and an end by any means. The desperate struggle to acquire the feeling knows no limit, but the consequences of failing the struggle will never know such pain and anguish.

In the early moments of the onset of withdrawal, the fear is stifling and sends the mind and body into a single-purposed existence. The six, seven, even eight hours or more of bliss evolve slowly and eventually morph into a zone of indifference, followed by fear.

The first sign is the yawning and the leaking drops of irritating tears slipping down the outer slit of the eyelids. The ride is over. Then, the untouchable nerve endings beneath the skin begin to gather inside the palms of your hands, at the bottom of your feet, the middle of your thighs, and lastly, in the middle of your lower back. And when that tingling turns into a distinct, bothersome sensation, you know what's coming next! Pain! A very irritating, annoying nasal drip begins at the back of your throat, and even more pain is imminent: more pain! I used to call them "ganglion armies" because they felt like thousands of nerves gathering in the hands, thighs, and feet that by no means could be rubbed, scratched, or relieved. These ganglion armies become restless; the pain becomes unbearable and excruciating. Nothing can assuage this misery because it is within the parts of the body where nothing can be touched.

The tiny beads of perspiration create a sticky, overall sensation that serves only to exacerbate the pain. In full-blown withdrawal, the body is rapt with a pain comparable to wrenching blows. Vomiting and uncontrollable bowel movements follow, and you are there: hell, where any prayer for sanctuary is futile. These conditions last three to four days and sometimes longer. The physical pain and exhaustion cause the onset of very powerful urges: anger, sadness, futility, hopelessness, and strong, frequent thoughts of suicide. These suicidal urges are strange because, even though they have occurred in past episodes of withdrawal, and, despite the fact that you know they will and should eventually pass, they are really genuine and inconsolable. I made a thousand resolutions never to use heroin again in my life! Never, never, never again! "God, if I make it through this ordeal, never again will I pick up heroin. There is no pleasure on earth worth this pain and brutality of withdrawal."

"The bottom" can best be described like the experience of lying on a cold basement floor, balled up in a constricted knot, unable to eat, unable to sleep, and coveting no desire to live any longer. Unfortunately, some people will experience this ordeal many times before they quit.

Sharing my personal feelings about these aspects of drug use is not easy. The brief and temporary euphoria cost more than I could predict or want to imagine. My two loving children, Karl and Nichole, and my six grandchildren are marvelous blessings to me and they will, undoubtedly, become a credit to this community. With talent, courage, and enormous consideration in their hearts, I am very proud and thankful.

Much of the last two decades of my life has been committed to the prevention of drug use and saving lives from the abuse of drugs and alcohol. I regret if I were ever possibly the reason someone decided to use drugs. The prevention of drug use, and saving lives from it, is the bottom line.

The bottom line of this message is also that the negative consequences of any drug use far outweigh any illusions of benefit. The brief artifices are just not worth the long-time cost and consequences. I have been blessed, and I consider myself to be a lucky man to have lived long and to have people in my life who continually love and support me. Yet had I never used drugs, there is perhaps no limit to what I might have accomplished. I am not complaining about my station in life; it is what I've made it, but it is not unrealistic to say governor, U.S. Senator or congressman could have been within my grasp. But that is part of a lesson that I hope teaches and reminds us all our frailties and motivates our strengths and talents to overcome.

CHAPTER 8

Don't Blink, Just Act

There were times when I would have a reflexive response to an issue or problem, a visceral reaction to something that was so evident I couldn't maintain the typical politician's mild manner: the bullshit we see all the time around obvious problems. When a new, young U.S. Senator, Paul Trible, Jr., came to office in 1983, he wanted to establish a new political precedent for representation at the Federal level. During the early '80s, race relations were suffering, and some Southern politicians began an effort to improve things with their Black constituents. Trible, who had only been a congressman for a couple years, was suddenly a U.S. Senator, a quick power in America for such a young man. One of Senator Trible's big ideas was to invite the members of the first Black-majority Richmond City Council to a tour and a sit-down at his office on Main Street in downtown Richmond. It was something offered to provide a photo-op, as much anything, for the Senator and smiling Council members with as many of the news media as possible being present. The young Senator wanted to impress, or impress upon, us with what real power is and, I found, real arrogance.

It was a cool, chilly morning in Richmond, and we had a bus transport us from City Hall to his building not far away. We were ready to share ideas and concerns with him. The weather was as bright and crisp as one of the White councilmembers; Carolyn Wake smiled nervously at me for a moment from across the bus. Mrs. Wake was probably wondering how I would behave. She was very proud of the new Senator, and his invitation, and may have been thinking, *How will Mr. Richardson act? Will he be the gentleman he is capable of being, or will he follow his proclivity to confront White authority?*

We arrived, and initially, the tour went well. the long, narrow corridor to his office was impressive with large windows and supporting offices for staff. With television cameras awkwardly placed, print and radio media positioned themselves to see the new Senator address his admiring subjects.

We gathered around a large coffee table Trible had arranged for the media's attention of this ostensible outreach to the Black-majority Council of Richmond. Mrs. Wake, now relaxed and pleased, appeared so proud of this young, conservative Christian politician. Trible, all puffed up and full of pride, began to explain his platform, and his solid support of President Reagan's economic policies. Henry Marsh, Walter T. Kenney, Claudette McDaniel, and Willie Dell sat, uninspired, and listened. I sensed White councilmembers Henry Valentine and Wayland Rennie were not particularly pleased but rather envied him being so young at his status so quickly. The Senator went on with a conspicuous arrogance, treating us as schoolchildren in his large, plush "principal's office." But Carolyn Wake was tickled pink.

Trible started his well-rehearsed speech about President Reagan and how his economic plan would succeed. Oh boy, he went on and on, getting more pompous by the second. It was all I could do to restrain myself—and Carolyn Wake—smiling so proudly, looked over at me. She could tell something was going amiss. Trible continued boasting with the confidence of General Patton, "A rising tide lifts all boats… *blah, blah…*You see, it's the trickle-down theory that works. We've all got to tighten our belts a little."

My mouth dropped and I shook my head in the negative. Carolyn looked at me with an expression of horror when I sat up in my chair. "Trickle-down theory, trickle-DOWN theory!" I said loudly as I rose slightly. "Look, Trible, face it! We've got people in Richmond starving who can't eat, people freezing who can't heat! You want people to tighten their belts who don't *have* belts anymore; there is nothing trickling down! It's crazy economics and it ain't gonna work!"

Carolyn broke in. "Mr. Richardson, that is not true! You're being so melodramatic. There's no one starving or freezing in Richmond."

"Maybe not where *you* live," I responded. Mrs. Wake saw the side she had hoped against, the no-bullshit fighter I could be. I was still young, in my early thirties, and maybe still naïve or a little ignorant to the decorum of political hierarchy. But sometimes ignorance can be brilliance.

Mrs. Wake settled back in her chair and attempted to apologize to the Senator. He, of course, acted like he was the adult and he understood unruly children, smirking at some invisible person in the room. I had pretty much disrupted the cordiality of the event and we all returned to the bus as some members muttered about my overreaction and how embarrassing my behavior was.

That afternoon, I called Bessie Jones, my Richmond Community Action Program (R-CAP) Coordinator, and asked her to get me the names and addresses of those to whom we delivered coal, wood, and food to each day. I told the members of the media who had been at Trible's office to meet me the next morning on the R-CAP bus, that I would show them the people who "weren't cold, weren't hungry," who could tighten their belts while waiting on Trible's "trickle."

The tour the next day was sad, an unbelievable depiction of destitution in Richmond: men huddled under blankets inches from stoves next to broken windows covered with wind-beaten plastic; old women in beds next to coal stoves—without light or electricity! Some had little to no food and had anxiously waited for our delivery. It was an America not recognized by most, and as such, non-existent to many. Even today, many Black politicians and candidates seem averse to take themselves and others into that world.

The scenes totally shocked members of the press; they had not seen these things even in their coverage of the "poor" in Richmond, which was rare in and of itself. Because the chances they had reached deep into the conditions of the poorest of the poor was, well, poor. Only groups like R-CAP knew of these people, knew that these people existed and needed help. Diane Freda, a very pretty reporter for the Channel 6 TV news, went with us and interviewed me after the tour.

"What do you think Mrs. Wake would say about these conditions we've seen?" she asked.

"Well, metaphorically, it's like dealing with a mule: you first have to hit them across the head with a two by four, then you try to reason with them afterwards."

"Are you trying to call Mrs. Wake a mule?!" she asked with an incredulous grin.

"Nooooo, no, no! She's just ... a horse of a different color," I said. She and her crew laughed, and that evening they gave Richmond, Mrs. Wake, and the Honorable Senator an idea of just how tight the belt is for some in America.

From the day I declared my run for office, my uncompromising commitment was to the struggles of the poor and downtrodden masses, my inner Zorro ever pressing on to uplift the least among us. The least among Richmond's citizens were those to whom we delivered food and coal each day—families that remained utterly invisible to Senator Trible and Reagan's rising tide to raise all boats. Too bad if some were devastated with leaks.

MLK Holiday

In 1981, the consideration of a holiday honoring Dr. Martin Luther King, Jr. (MLK) was on the minds of many Black folk, certainly in Richmond, and around much of the country. But five years before it became a national holiday in 1983, I approached Mayor Henry Marsh with my desire to introduce the Martin Luther King Holiday Bill in Richmond. It was 1978 when I entered his office in a highly spirited and jovial, yet serious mood, to do business. I said to Mr. Marsh that I intended to initiate a bill to create a holiday for Dr. King's birthday, stipulating it as a fully paid day off for city employees. His response caught me completely off guard and stunned me with disappointment. "We do not need that right now," he said. "You are going to create unnecessary rancor and bitterness between the races, and we cannot afford that racial polarization right now. We have bigger fish to fry."

Henry Marsh was a member of City Council when I was a senior in high school. He was perceived as a hero and trusted community leader, so, one could imagine my disappointment, confusion, and letdown to hear him tell me we did not need an MLK Holiday in Richmond. I thought he would be proud of my idea, but he said *no, we don't need it, it will only create conflict between the races.* Angry and disillusioned, I found myself arguing with him about why we should not have to wait for White people to accept our dreams before we realized them as lawful legislations at the local level.

"Henry, if we only introduced laws they don't oppose, there would never be any change! The people who voted for us think different things, have different ideas, different values, and different heroes," I said.

I had already spoken to Claudette McDaniel earlier that week and shared my rationale, so when Henry responded about White backlash, I felt awkward and out of place explaining to an experienced Civil Rights attorney the justification for this legislation. With his rationale steeped primarily in the argument of having "bigger fish to fry," and not creating an atmosphere inimical to the progress of greater achievements, I told him that a very different group of people voted us into office, and following 250 years of absolutely no involvement in the decision making, we were now in a position to make a difference. I said, "Henry, if we are going to vote the same way they would have voted or wait until they recognize the virtues of our right to choose our heroes, why did we have the election? To wait for their approval of something that they are inherently opposed to defeats the meaning, purpose and validity of the election of March 1977." In the middle of my breath, I caught myself and stopped talking. I realized how absurd I sounded attempting to explain something that he was more aware of than I. The argument was brief, but poignant, and it ended by me saying, "I wish I had never heard you say that to me, Henry." There was no one else in the room when we spoke and I left without telling him I had already submitted the bill to the law department, and that it would be introduced at the next Council meeting.

I was young, a bit naïve, and inexperienced, but despite everything, I still maintained trust and respect for Henry's political judgement. There was a possibility that his viewpoint might have had some validity, but all things considered, I found it ironic that two Black men were debating the question of something that should have been obvious to the both of us, and all we needed was the political will to do it! However, after all the back and forth and other support, when the vote came up at the next Council meeting, Henry supported the holiday with the rest of us. But it still left me a bit dubious about his motives.

I later discovered that Henry's real motive for attempting to delay or postpone the introduction of the Martin Luther King, Jr., Holiday paper bill was around an issue of credit and pride of authorship. He did not want the credit for patronage of this bill to be attributed to me. And rather than asking me to allow him to be co-patron, he attempted to deceive me. I would have welcomed his patronage and supported the idea of co-sponsoring; furthermore, it would have endeared and strengthened the dubious status of our relationship at the time.

The one thing that disillusioned me the most about the elements of influence and power among the political environs, so polarized by race, was the inability of many Black leaders to set aside personal ambitions for the sake of unity. Who receives the credit for a given achievement often becomes seen as more vital than the achievement itself. I do not exclude myself from such criticisms. We all want credit for the good works we produce. But some do not draw a line between getting credit and doing good.

Because of my age and inexperience, I did not perceive myself within the context of some sort of competition with the other elected officials like Doug Wilder, Henry Marsh, Willie Dell, or others. Nor did I with noted community leaders who had previous involvement such as Oliver Hill, Sam Tucker, or even Saad El-Amin who had been an outspoken proponent of the sixties' Civil Rights Movement. To have been elected to City Council, and in a position to determine change at the age of twenty-nine, was sufficient ego nourishment that I only saw myself as a unique cog in the larger wheels of the political machinery. I had endured the Vietnam War, attended Black Panther Party meetings, heard the eloquent and emotionally-powered speeches on racial injustices, and truly believed that change was necessary and would only be accomplished through unity. I was oblivious to the personal power struggles between other Black leaders and their individual desires to be "top dog" on the porch, so to speak.

It was during those days that I wrestled with my intention to reveal to Dale Wiley and Justin Moore the idea of taking down the statue of Jefferson Davis, a proposal that, again, would hardly have had Henry's support given his deceptive and timid nature about the MLK holiday. That idea truly just might have to be put on hold much longer than I had expected—much longer, indeed.

Henry was also against my 30% minority utilization plan: providing 30% of City construction projects to minority contractors. He said we did not need the policy, that we could achieve it by directing the city manager—which I found absurd. Years later, he was not supportive of the idea of placing the Arthur Ashe Monument on Monument Avenue, and mislead Walter T. Kenney about it, even though Walter believed it was right. I could not believe neither of them came to my aid or lifted a finger to help as I argued with many racist, hostile Whites who were dead set against a Black man on their precious "Bigot Boulevard."

The other four of us made the faulty decision to place our faith in Henry, trusting his wisdom and legal judgement explicitly, and never discussing those aspects fully because Henry was the experienced attorney among us. An example of this is when Henry had the idea that we grant ourselves a $200 dollar a month increase called "extraordinary expense." I asked him why we didn't just vote ourselves a raise. It was legal, and I was certain we worked hard enough for it. Henry said the raise wouldn't take effect until the next City Council election, plus the public might not accept it and vote against us. I said, "Not my public. They know how hard I work for them and they would still vote for me!" The other Black members of the Council quickly dismissed my suggestion and, following a few brush-offs by Henry and the others, I went along with the mayor's legal judgement.

We all voted for this idea, but the White members were against the measure. The vote was five to four, and we began receiving the $200 dollar a month check along with our regular pay. After receiving this extra pay for a period of time, a group of citizens sued the Black majority alleging that it was illegal. The Richmond Independent Taxpayers Association (RITA) carried us to court. We never gave it a lot of thought, assuming Henry knew what he was doing; everybody just forgot about it until it came to the court date, nearly two years later. The judge decided we had to pay all the money back—with compounded interest! I nearly shit a brick! Where was I going to get over eight thousand dollars?

Thanks to a few good friends of mine, when the final bill came due, I was able to pay close to $10,000 back to the City. RITA, like salt in a wound, celebrated at the Jefferson Davis statue on Monument Avenue. I wondered how in the hell this happened?! But no one had ever discussed the possibility with Henry, and of course, he never said anything to us. I started to wonder about Henry's legal acumen and made sure we had second opinions after that.

Another one of Henry Marsh's legal missteps was the Hilton Hotel lawsuit. It was brought against us by two White hotel owners who sued the City over our Project One decision to exclude other hotels from being built in the development footprint of Project One. Henry Marsh was our go-between who, for the most part, only informed us but seldom allowed us to indulge our concerns. We had hired Rouse Consultants to manage the development, but they could do nothing without Henry's approval because he carried the five city council votes.

At any rate, much like the expense account issue, we relied

Cease Fire! Cease Fire!

on Henry's judgement, and Rouse was acting by the dictates of the mayor on major legal decisions. They had brokered an agreement with Marriott not to allow any other major hotels to develop in the area where another developer wanted to build a Hilton Hotel. We lost that case in court also, but this was not completely Henry's fault; he had other players involved and they all should have seen the anti-trust violation. We ended up repaying almost $2 million in damages.

A rare, pensive no comment in the late 1980s. © Richmond Times Dispatch

Henry, Doug and Maynard

Often in life, we like to focus on the amazing, historic, or grandiose accomplishments to offer for posterity, and if I touch on those items, so be it. But the ordinary, insignificant, smaller aspects of life can sometimes be more revealing than some of those dynamic achievements. When Roy West defeated Willie Dell in the

Third District council seat, it opened up for him the chance to take the Mayor's Office as well. Henry had cherished the mayorship like a dog with his only bone. Since the City Council members elected the mayor at that time, great speculation—and doubt—arose as to whether Roy West would vote for Henry to remain mayor. With four Black votes supporting Henry and four White votes against him, Roy was "in the catbird seat." The Richmond press had been relentless with criticism of Henry, lambasting him as the virtual anti-Christ because of his heavy-handed dealing with the White minority members of council.

Henry was pretty mild and conservative in the eyes of Richmond's Black citizens. To White folk, he was seen as arrogant and disrespectful, especially in the context of the bogus genteel Virginia symbolism they fancied. They preferred, and needed, someone like Roy West: a lackey. Henry Marsh was a bit shaken by Willie Dell's loss but, like the other three members, could not know for certain what West would do with his vote. As the July 1st vote approached, Henry had been quietly lobbying behind the scenes to secure Roy's vote along with the other Black council members. However Roy West would not meet with Henry.

At the time, Doug Wilder was still a State Senator and the highest-ranking Richmond elected official—with substantial influence. However, during his terms as mayor, Henry had gained considerable state and national acclaim as well, even appearing on the front page of an issue of *Ebony* magazine. President Jimmy Carter had relied on Henry for Black support in the South. With this heightened public status, he had gained a relatively higher political regard than Doug. Meanwhile, Henry would show no particular deference to Doug, even as a Black State Senator, which, given the rivalry in the history of their relationship, got under Doug's skin. The two had always maintained a dignified rivalry, but I could discern the growing undercurrents of a new tension. I will say Doug carried any resentments with a distinct care, in public especially; he was always the gentleman. So, Henry's defeat at the hands of Roy West for the Mayor's seat placed the Senator in the auspicious posture of a little payback for Henry's indifference toward him.

Doug had agreed to meet with Henry the morning of the Council vote at the Senator's office—a last look at how to thwart Roy's chances. It turned out Roy's chances were, as history has told, full; he won the office of Mayor of Richmond by casting the deciding vote for himself along with the four White members on council. After Marsh met with Wilder that morning, he came to me later that afternoon totally broken and depleted of any spirit at all. The only thing missing was actual tears. Like a child telling on someone who had stolen his prized possession, he said to me, "Chuck, you know what he [Doug] did? He had told me to be there at 8:00 am, so I got there and the secretary had me sit on this tall-ass chair in front of his desk. My damn feet didn't even touch the floor. I sat there and realized there was nothing on his desk but a block of wood—inscribed with the words. 'I Don't Get Mad, I Get Even.' I sat there almost an hour and he didn't show up!" It was a sad story that is classic Wilder. Had I not seen the pain on Henry's face, I would have been on the floor rolling in laughter.

While Henry and Doug were very prominent and successful elected officials that I had the good fortune to have been associated with, it was my brother-in-law, Maynard Jackson, who by far gave the most lift to my legislative accomplishments. I came to rely on Maynard for consistent, ongoing, meaningful advice and information on laws, policies, and legislation regarding urban affairs. When I contemplated the introduction of the MLK Holiday in Richmond, Minority Utilization Plan Proposal (The Plan), supercans, and tax abatement for the elderly and disabled, it was Maynard to whom I looked.

Being close to Doug Wilder, I was fortunate to have ample access to his schedule. Doug was creative and would not hesitate to make a full-frontal assault. At other times, he was most subtle; his political acumen was second only to mine... just a joke. On second thought, no joke (smile).

When the City Council decided to honor Henry for his terms as mayor as an official function not too long after his mayoral defeat, Maynard was the keynote speaker. It was held at the auditorium formerly called The Mosque at the City's expense and was highly publicized. It was a grand affair, and it gave my pal, Doug, an opportunity to demonstrate some of that understated political acumen. It was a formal event with suit and tie required at a minimum. Doug nonchalantly sauntered in, unaccompanied, in a maroon sport jacket with a CIAA football emblem on the chest pocket. It was, again, all I could do to contain myself from laughing.

Doug had a presence that usually excused his disregard for attire at times, but the implication of the CIAA emblem was full-frontal. As co-host, I graciously ignored the slight and took no offense. I considered it an altogether fitting and proper gesture of a political "no vote" of confidence and enjoyed the evening. Doug excels at that type of nonverbal communicating, for those open and keen enough to appreciate the messages.

At any rate, things of this nature speak to the essence of who we are, our real voices, as much as an hour-long speech. I'm the type that would verbalize my feelings on a one-on-one basis, as I did at a legislative reception I once attended with Doug, a few City Council members, and state House members. I was standing with Walter T. Kenney, Benjamin Lambert, and a couple other brothers when Doug walked up. Meaning no true harm, I greeted him like brothers do sometimes on the street corner jivin' and said, "Hey, motherfucker!"

This can be a term of endearment depending on how it's delivered and by whom, to whom. I didn't think my relationship with Doug was such that he'd take any real offense. But I had been going through a particularly tough period and the press had been pretty harsh. At the same time, Doug was receiving consistent plaudits from them.

In any other circumstance, I'm sure he would have brushed it off, but he could probably also tell I was a bit pissed that he had failed to stand by me during such adversity. Though I would never have said it outside the small group of brothers we were, my comment had the intended effect. The smile on his face disappeared at my "term of endearment". I continued to smile and the evening passed without event, as did the next two days. That is, until I received a call. "Brother-in-law, how ya doing?" It was Maynard from Atlanta.

I said, "Well, what could I have done to deserve the good fortune

Cease Fire! Cease Fire!

of receiving a call from you, Maynard, your honor?"

"Chuck, did you call Doug Wilder a motherfucker in public?!" Now, to understand the impact of that question, one must understand Maynard Holbrook Jackson Jr., is a man of exquisite sensibilities. Always poised, polite and mindful of self-respect and dignity, he would search and find any words to convey resentment before reducing himself to such vulgarity.

What Maynard didn't understand was that Doug and I often used such language in each other's presence—behind the scenes—with vernacular that made such a word common and acceptable. Maybe the way I used it was a little strong for the occasion, but not necessarily for the people who were in our immediate presence. Certainly it was nothing he should have run and told on me about, as if Maynard would give me a spanking for cursing at my teacher in school.

Doug had done something that deeply hurt me. It was something, as a friend, I would never have done to him! So, when Maynard asked me that, I simply said, Yeah," and waited, saying nothing further. In my long pause with no explanation, Maynard realized he was getting into something that was no business of his. I had answered the question point blank: "Yeah," and waited for his response as if to say, *yeah, whatcha gone do about it?*

Then he asked, "Why?"

I wanted to call Maynard by his full name—like he was the student. I think he was taken aback until I laughed and said, "Aw, man! Doug's on the rag about something and took it all wrong. Maynard, don't worry about it! Me and Doug just fine. We're cool, Maynard."

He said, "Oh..." It was the only time in my life I had the upper hand on Maynard Jackson, where I had all the answers, and he was left at a loss for words.

"How's Valerie and the baby?" I asked. Valerie-Amanda was the apple of his eye and I knew I could change the subject asking about her. We chatted a little while just fine and I got off the phone thinking: *That little bitch motherfucker Doug went back and told some bullshit like that!* I was really pissed at Doug, but ... still, you gotta love the guy.

Chuck Richardson with Monte Richardson

...and Uncle Roy

From 1977 to 1982, there was a special significance in the pride of Richmond's African-American community. It was not a perfect period of time. Mistakes were made, but by and large there was a collective sense of achievement and dignity that was shared by virtually all of us during many public events. That pride and sense of progress was something the Black community had never felt, and to that extent, have not felt since. Although Henry Marsh was Mayor, it was a feeling that transcended his individual achievements as well as the collective impact of the other four Blacks on Council.

When Roy West voted for himself as mayor, the celebration in the White community hurt us as much as the political loss itself. Roy West is one man for whom I feel a genuine sadness, anger, resentment, and political animosity. He set Black political progress in Richmond back fifty years from the standpoint of self-esteem, confidence, and unity. His singular ego deflated the spirit of Black folk as much in 1982, in its own way, as would a lynching of Negroes on Broad Street at high noon. There is no doubt in my mind that he must have spent sleepless nights and hours of his days gazing into his past with great remorse and a devout desire for a chance to redo some of his history.

His name was synonymous with "Uncle Tom," a term in the Black community that describes an egotistical, highfalutin Negro believing he was "more-smarter" than the rest, anxious to please his White master at the expense of his own people. He was almost as bad as the character Samuel L. Jackson played in the movie *Django,* the "house nigga" who betrayed Django and informed his master of his plot to rescue his wife. There was a saying about "house niggas," that when the master had a cold, he would ask, "Is <u>we</u> got a cold, sa?" West was pretty much that way; if the White members of council had a cold, he sneezed. Roy was under an illusion that he was "more-smarter" than all the other colored people in Richmond, usually speaking with pedantic arrogance, demonstrating to Whites that he was as intelligent as they would tell him he was. Their standard for his intelligence required a component of ignorance about his own people, however, and a lack of any empathy towards them. Roy thought he was using *them*, but the Whites played him like a flute in a sixth-grade music class.

I remember that July morning when Roy West, with the four White members of City Council, voted himself Mayor of Richmond. A Black female reporter requested an interview with me the next day after a dedication ceremony at the old Henrico County office building downtown. I was there in a three-piece suit with the temperatures probably in the low nineties, and we met out under the sun. I was almost always in a jovial mood for television reporters. That morning however, in that heat and still smarting from the political pain of the day before, I was in not in the best mood.

The first thing the reporter asked was my reaction to Roy voting for himself with the four White members. Already sweating, I did something rarely done in the Black political world. I said, "Roy West is an Uncle Tom. Voting with the White members he has established a coalition that will be the Council's faction for the ensuing term." The reporter was a little startled. Just a little, because media folk were used to me speaking boldly. And what I said happened—exactly what happened, a relentless five to four voting pattern with Roy West and the four White members versus the four Black members.

I called Roy, "Uncle Tom." He never outlived it, a classification he earned in full, and stands even today as a first ballot, Hall of Fame "Uncle Tom!"

C-SPAN

In 1985, the Richmond City Council was selected to appear on a new television program called *C-SPAN*. At the time, I had no idea what on earth "*C-SPAN*" was, except it was something new and apparently about politics. First, it was on cable, which was not as broad-reaching as now, but it could reach across the country and let almost anyone see "the sausage" being made in local and Federal government. Our meeting was to be televised from one of the State Senate rooms at the Virginia Capitol. In Richmond politics, Roy West had just defeated Willie Dell for the Third District seat and then dethroned Henry Marsh as Mayor. Roy West, as the Mayor, and as the deciding vote on a five to four council make-up, was doing a pretty good job of humiliating Richmond's Black leadership by handing over the world, so to speak, back to the White oligarchy in the City. Roy had deprived Black Richmond of the pride and dignity with which they had once walked proudly since the creation of the nine-district system and the fair representation of the city's population, giving Richmond its first Black majority in city government in 1977.

Unfortunately there was an actual sad hatred for Roy by all four of the other Black members of the City Council. Willie Dell, Claudette McDaniel, and Walter T. Kenney would not speak to him. I was different; I'd call him an "Uncle Tom" to his face. He once commented to the press that he resented breathing the same air in the room I was in. Many in Richmond did wonder if he was breathing the same air as the rest of us. To make matters more contentious, William J. Leidinger, the former City Manager that the original five Black members had fired, won election in the Second District and was now an adversary to the Blacks on Council, spare one of course. There was sufficient emotional resentment to start a small provincial war around Roy West's stance on Council. We did, however, remain civil while the television cameras were running.

The meeting began cordially enough with a setting comparable to a Hollywood production, movie makeup and all. The room included writers from the papers, broadcast reporters, and a small group of local civic leaders and citizens. Each of us was allowed to identify ourselves. The commentator began asking innocuous questions that, while maybe having generic value, offered no picture of the fundamental issue

Cease Fire! Cease Fire!

in the minds of all its members. Henry Marsh was embarrassingly uncomfortable but maintained his poise. He tried to carry himself as the legitimate, yet almost useless, leader of the once powerful group with whom he sat. Henry was never a street fighter or someone who would openly go for the jugular, but he was hurting after his glorious rise to the mayor's desk of the former "Capital of the Confederacy" and the ignominious fall at the hands of another Black councilman.

I had little patience for protracted decorum or protocol, nor was I aware of the viewing range of this new *C-SPAN*. I had no idea it was national. Not that it would have mattered; my focus remained on the obvious truth of what Roy West was doing to the progress we had made since our historic victory eight years earlier. In any event, the discussions had gravitated to the balance of powers and the manner in which we were progressing as an interracial governing body.

In retrospect, I probably could have been more diplomatic, given the type of stage we occupied that day. At the same time, I said what I felt and what best described the dynamics of the Council at the time.

Me next to councilmembers Carolyn Wake, Andrew Gillespie and Roy West, C-SPAN 1985. © C-SPAN

While Carolyn Wake and Bill Leidinger were attempting to protect Roy West for his "sell-out" politics, I gave a very direct and forceful description of the Council's Black/White relationship. I recall stating that there were no negotiations, no give and take because Roy West insisted only in giving in to White interest—and taking from ours. "He gives them everything they want by voting with them and against us. They might as well have a White vote majority since he was elected," I said passionately.

The Black members had reached a boiling point, and I just made it plain on *C-SPAN* in 1985. Mrs. Wake spoke of the progress that had been made since the '60s, how she now lived in a mixed neighborhood, how wonderful things were happening between the races, and that she resented the suggestion that she voted based on the race component. Speaking immediately after her, I pointed out that the measure of political leadership is not so much in our attractive rhetoric and singing "Kumbaya" while holding hands. I said, "The test is in the substance of what we do, not the pretty words and saying we're coming together. The test is, did you approve twenty-five percent of the Sixth Street Marketplace for minorities? No! Did you initially vote for the MLK Holiday? No, no you did not, Mrs. Wake. Did you vote for projects that would have enhanced the employment opportunities for minorities in City of Richmond? No! And there is a list of items that when you come down to the substance of it, makes a difference." Mrs. Wake sat disappointed but dignified, while Gillespie, West, and Leidinger stared down at the table, at the ceiling, or fiddled with their fingers in their faces like annoyed teenagers.

I can recall Mrs. Wake, sitting next to me, quickly becoming incensed at my comments. She sat there leaning back, eyes wide, as though I was about to jump on the table. "Oh, Mr. Richardson, why do you always do that?!" I didn't understand what she meant at first until I looked over and saw Henry, elbows on the table, hands bent in front of his face concealing a small smile and I realized I had dropped the proverbial "turd in the punch bowl." Roy West sat as if he heard nothing, as if my words didn't dignify a reaction—playing his role.

Cease Fire! Cease Fire!

Leidinger fidgeted and sighed with an overtly indignant sneer on his face, admonishing the *C-SPAN* moderator for not pulling the reins on the "mud-slinging Negroes" (my word) embarrassing the council. Sitting next to him, Mr. Gillespie, with his trademark antebellum drawl, also begged the moderator to realize that a few members of Council were playing out a power struggle, and it did not reflect the character of Richmond. Mrs. Wake, who was a nice lady, was suggesting I had once more said something wrong in front of the whole world that embarrassed the Council and the City. But the Black councilmembers knew I was right, Black Richmond knew I was right, people from North Carolina to Texas knew I was right. *C-SPAN* had put out across the country what I always do, according to Mrs. Wake. One man from Nebraska called to say he saw me "kickin' ass" on TV.

It was my style, and Mrs. Wake knew it too well from the earlier "embarrassment" in the office of an arrogant freshman U.S. Republican Senator, Paul Trible. I derailed that in front of cameras, too. I learned about *C-SPAN* that day, and maybe, a tiny piece of America learned about politics in Richmond and Chuck Richardson.

Jesse Jackson with me in Richmond, 1984.

Chuck Richardson with Monte Richardson

Catching a Purse Snatcher

Some events in life don't seem to be real, but rather something written for an action movie. What happened to me on the night of November 19, 1984, I would never tell anyone about because they might not believe it. However, since there were four other witnesses and it made news the following day, and since I received a police commendation, I guess it might be accepted as true.

On that night, I was driving up Harrison Street in the Fan District of Richmond with two of my friends, Bernice Travers, and Michael Ziglar. When we drove across Floyd Avenue, walking up the sidewalk on the passenger side was someone I recognized, Mrs. Nina Abady, an old schoolteacher of mine from Virginia Union. Mrs. Abady was with a gentlemen friend I didn't know. They had just attended a Virginia Commonwealth University (VCU) function and were enjoying the stroll to their car on the pleasant fall evening. I slowly maneuvered over to say a quick hello from the car. Just as we came upon them, two Black youths ran beside Mrs. Abady, snatched her hand purse, and rushed past my car. I immediately hit my brakes and jumped out of my vehicle. Ziglar, without hesitation, hopped out of the passenger seat. We bolted in hot pursuit on foot, dodging cars as the young man who grabbed the handbag had run behind my car, across the street, and down West Avenue. I wasn't far behind him with Ziglar right behind me. Meanwhile, my car was left running in the middle of a busy street with a bewildered and shaken Ms. Travers in the middle of the front seat.

Not the track star I was in high school, while I was gaining on the kid, I was beginning to lose faith that I could keep up. A cross street came up and the kid took off down this side street, but he, too, was out of breath. Apparently he was not a track athlete at all, just a thief! Exhausted, the kid ran behind an old, parked Saab and stopped. I also stopped and could do very little beyond stand there, leaning forward with both hands on the Saab, panting like a racehorse. The tall dark-skinned kid looked at me as he stood breathing hard while he rustled through the purse quickly, looking up at me every other second. There was a garage light just over the kid's head behind him and he could see my face, but I couldn't see him very clearly. He probably could tell that I was more exhausted than he was.

He was rummaging through the purse, glancing up at me, and back down while I was pulling at my necktie trying to get more air. He said, "You that ... that, Chuck Richardson guy ... ain't you?"

I could barely breathe, much less talk. He made a quick fake move back to the rear end of the car, but after the long sprint, my legs were frozen. I couldn't move. Still gasping for air, I could feel my body rising up and down with each breath. His youth was his advantage, and he knew it, watching me struggle to get my breath. Then he said, "Why you gon' help that fat White bitch?"

I wanted to jump across the car and strangle the kid, but I was so exhausted my legs would not move. Finally, my exhaustion gave way to my anger and I said, "That lady, Mrs. Abady, works for her money and you so lazy, nigga…you'd rather steal her purse than get a job." I took another breath while he continued hunting through her purse. I kept it up. "That lady's honest," I said as I took another deep breath and continued "You a fucking thief," took another breath and said, "and you want me to let you go 'cause you Black?! Nigga, you ain't shit!"

He made another fake move, dropped the purse, and darted in the opposite direction from behind the car and up toward Park Avenue into the dark. I could only look as he ran off. What seemed like ten minutes of hard breathing actually took little more than ten seconds. Three or four minutes later, Ziglar came trudging up the street. "I couldn't keep up, man." He couldn't believe I had the purse.

When Mike and I returned to the scene of the crime, Mrs. Abady was all worried that something had happened to us, as was our companion Bernice. When I told Mrs. Abady I had the purse, she said with her customary affection, "Aw, darling that's all right! Wasn't anything in it." She smiled and thanked me as I looked to the sky and smiled, too, only slightly out of breath.

A young Black reporter in Richmond in the '80s described a scene she witnessed once at a Council meeting where I jumped into action. I didn't stop a thief or berate an attorney, but she thought it was emblematic of my style. Her name was Hazel Edney, and she tells it like this:

"That's it! That's it!" Chuck told the tall White fella whose arm Chuck had grabbed and held while looking square in his eyes, making the admonishment. It was movie-like, almost unbelievable. People gasped and every eye in the room was wide and unblinking. It wasn't a bar or party—it was the Richmond City Council chambers. As a news reporter during the '80s, I had many opportunities to witness verbal disputes in this racially polarized Southern town.

I was at a scheduled city council hearing where the public was invited to speak for or against an issue when a heated debate erupted between a group of elderly Black women and some middle-class homeowners from the "Fan" district, which ran from the VCU campus west toward Boulevard. It was not necessarily a racial issue, but then, few things escaped race ultimately. The speakers who had lined up at the front of the chambers became intense, arguing openly. Insults started to fly, and things became very personal.

The dressed and professional demeanor of the council members who sat raised and beyond a rail, maybe twelve to fifteen feet in front of the speakers, was becoming edgy. Councilman Richardson, "Chuck," who was dressed as usual, replete with a double-breasted suit and polished boots, looked on intently. One very tall, well-built White speaker, young but balding, and a bit sophisticated, became arrogant and intimidating with his two friends towards a small but spunky group of elderly Black persons. The tall White man had said something at the start of his remarks about how "when speaking, one should never follow children or dogs." Whatever he may have meant, it was taken as an offense and one old Black man bristled at him and an altercation broke out right down at the speaker's podium. The older, smaller Black man in the midst of the crowed group raised his

Cease Fire! Cease Fire!

fist and the tall White man raised his, poised as if to strike.

Suddenly, out of nowhere, sweeping around councilwoman McDaniel's seat, leaping over the four-foot rail, sailing in the air with his double breast jacket flying wide like a cape, his long hair floating just above his shoulders and a milli-second flicker from his polished boot-style shoes came the councilman. Chuck leaped over the rail and landed squarely between the two men grabbing the arm of the very tall, younger man before he could swing. The two jerked their arms briefly and Chuck raise his voice: "That's it! That's it!" Everything stopped at once and the chambers became deadly silent. The two men slowly backed apart and Chuck slowly released the man's arm. Then, the crowd settled back in their seats.

Chuck continued to look at the man while he took his hands and simultaneously stroked his suit jacket twice, then adjusted his tie and returned to his seat—by way of the steps. It was the most action-packed public hearing I'd ever attended—where a fight was prevented. Chuck was the flamboyant "bad boy" of Richmond politics, embraced and glamorized by a lion's share of the Black community but demonized by most of the White status quo. He was, in some ways, not unlike his childhood hero, "Zorro," the Disney TV Western star of the '50s, a normal person in the day but a brilliant, skilled fighter for the poor and the oppressed by night. Zorro had a beautiful, fast, black stallion named "Tornado," and Chuck drove a beautiful black Lincoln Continental Mark III.

The similarities in the fictional TV character and Chuck Richardson would lead one to believe that subconscious influences were at work in his life."

Chuck Richardson with Monte Richardson

Feeling strong again to continue serving the people every way I can - like here with Habitat for Humanity. © *Richmond Times Dispatch*

CHAPTER 9

An Infinite Debt

During the early to mid-'80s, I was making a name as a fighter for the poor, elderly, disabled, and Black citizens of Richmond. Very few were aware of my most difficult fight, the one within. Even those who might have known probably felt there was a greater fight being won keeping it "on the down low." The biggest problem for me at the time, besides the addiction, was the suspicion of the police. I had to place myself, necessarily, in the scope of their scans and sources in the vice squads, which, by snitch or by spy, kept a degree of surveillance on me. I had to be ever cognizant of them.

It was a type of "cat and mouse game" that was a hidden part of my role as the dynamic "Zorro" of Richmond politics. Most of the time, I scored dope with one of my friends, something that was never casually done but it was somewhat routine. Plus, there were a significant number of Blacks in the police department and vice squads, and there were likely times they looked away or felt conflicted about nabbing someone admired and beloved by so many in their own communities. Also, others saw it as a type of game, a challenge for their big detective egos, harassing me because they disliked my personality. Ironically, it was actually a kind of addiction for them; but *they* didn't have to conceal it.

One hot summer weekday morning, I went to score with one

of my good friends, Blackie. We met and drove to a place in Church Hill, picked up our shit, and headed back across town to a restaurant called Infinity. Driving west from Church Hill, we passed by City Hall rode on up Broad Street to the West Broad area. As soon as we passed City Hall, Blackie, who was driving, noticed the appearance of plainclothes cops in one of their typical rental car vehicles following us. It was not hard for us to discern undercover guys after a couple years of "cat and mouse." Blackie started to get nervous, urging me to "throw the shit out, man!" I told him, "Keep going; let's see." I was dope sick, and was not going give it up at the first scare. I told him, "Fuck it! Keep going! Let's see what them muthafuckas do."

Blackie was convinced they had seen us do the pickup in Church Hill and pleaded with me to get rid of it. I thought about what time it was: 11:00 am. There was a police precinct just near City Hall and there was always a shift change at 10:30 am each day. I had to think they had just started the shift and happened to see us as we passed in their view—and decided to fuck with us. Blackie was getting pissed at me, demanding I throw the stuff out somehow. Being dope sick, I wanted to trust my hunch and told Blackie to just keep going.

As we headed out Broad and passed Fifth Street, they were still with us and Blackie was having a fit. It was getting hot, really hot, and he and I started to sweat like dogs in our open windowed old Buick with no air conditioning. After a couple of blocks, I said, "Fuck it. Pull over." Blackie argued for just a moment and I said again, "Pull over, right here! Let's deal with these motherfuckers." We pulled over to an area of loading docks for trucks just past Harrison Avenue.

As we came to a stop, they rolled right up next to us, pulling close to my door so I could not open it. I looked at the driver as he rolled down his window and saw it was someone I knew, a jerk named Ronald Taylor with whom I had gone to middle school. I never really liked Ronald back then and he had not changed. Now a detective with vice, he seemed to enjoy hassling and beating on young guys while making bust for ten-dollar bags of reefer.

I'm in a white shirt and tie, sweating like a white-mouthed mule with my window down, and I looked right at Ronald. He says, "Can you stand a search?"

I kept a straight face and said back, "Can you stand to search me?"

As a councilman, and his boss in a sense, he knew if he searched me, and there was nothing, I would have his job. It was a sort of standoff, a poker-faced challenge I made. Ronald liked his job: being plainclothes brings a power that plays with people, riding around in a new car with air conditioning and privileges that come with being a detective. However, I liked my job, and knew if he searched me, it was over.

The whole time I am sitting there holding the dope in my hand in aluminum foil, sweating almost through the foil. Blackie is almost frozen in the heat, hands locked on the steering wheel, looking straight ahead like he had been ordered to do so. The water was starting to mat my hair on the side and I could feel a cool sweat bead roll right down the center of my back from the shoulder blades to the crack of my ass. "You sweatin' pretty hard there, trooper," Ronald said. He tried to be calm because he no doubt was, figuratively, sweating the situation, too.

I said, "Look, I don't have the luxury of a city paid, air-conditioned new car to ride in on hot days like this. It must be nice ... you ridin' round beating up on kids, messing with people with a pinch of reefer."

I could see Ronald, and his partner, another brother named Tabbs, had that same look you might see at the poker table; who's bluffing who? It was like a moment where you knew you had committed yourself like a falling skydiver: suddenly, uncertain if his "chute would open." As Ronald put it, this trooper was sweating hard —but I was determined to be cool.

At that moment, as if we both were dealt the ace we needed, the radio crackled in his car, "Unit 48, what's your 20? Need assistance ASAP at Broad and Lombardy."

Tabbs said, "Come on, man! We gotta go, he ain't got shit." Ronald rolled his eyes at me and backed up; then they sped off.

Blackie released his grip and almost grabbed me and yelled, "Man, why you gotta always fuck with people ... goddamn! I was 'bout to pass out! Shit, nigga!"

We went on to the restaurant, both of us feeling like, and looking like, we had walked five miles through a desert. But we had arrived at our Oasis, a paradise in tin foil. After Blackie gave me the hit in the arm, he looked at me as I relaxed and said, "Your whole world changed didn't it, Chuck?"

As I felt better, I went home, cleaned up, shaved, put on a fine ISL suit and my Bally boots. By 2:00 pm I was in City Hall at, ironically, a transportation committee hearing, where we considered the exorbitant cost of rental cars—like those used by vice squads. Like nothing had happened to me that day, I motioned for a drastic cut of those type rentals: air-conditioned, new, comfortable, unmarked undercover cruisers for cops like Ronald. The motion passed! It made sense for the committee, and for a hard-sweating trooper—who had gone from mouse to cat.

But, I have to say, luck was on my side. It is not always the case, for either cat or mouse, and very sadly I have to mention the fact that officer Ronald Taylor was killed on-duty several years later. He was making a typical traffic stop when the driver shot him as he approached. I didn't like Ronald, I thought he was a jerk, but he and his family certainly never deserved that. I hope they have found a measure of peace somehow.

If You Think It Hurts Now, Wait Until Tonight

I was still a fairly young man during the mid-'80s and, despite an addiction virtually unknown to everyone, was seen as a vibrant, relatively healthy Vietnam vet. With a Purple Heart, Cross of Gallantry and Combat medal, a Vietnam vet like myself and others like me were beginning to receive long overdue recognition for our sacrifices. But

Cease Fire! Cease Fire!

that service had left me, as it did many, with post-traumatic stress disorder, something not officially diagnosed for another twenty years. I can't say what role that may have played with my heroin use, but it couldn't have helped. I had, and still have today, many sleepless nights, with dreams and flashbacks to horrible things—like the face of a little girl that lived in the middle of a war.

No one else has ever known the nights I have cried with that little girl's face emblazoned in my memory forever! Nights I can't imagine that anyone has ever paid the price as great as I have for this one murder. When people say war is hell, I know what they mean. Not so much the brutality of its conditions, but the incomprehensible injustices of war. The lack of explanation, or reason, or unfairness is the hell of it. The inability to rationalize anything about it!

Maybe the little girl should not have jumped to run. Maybe she should not have had on black pajamas. Maybe the Lieutenant should not have given the order to shoot. Maybe war is an excuse and maybe it wasn't. "It was not my gun that hit her," I had said. "It couldn't have been my gun."

One of the other Marines said, "No other gun could do that but a '60, Richardson."

"Good shot! It was a gook!" another said.

He didn't know the half of it. Neither he, the Lieutenant, nor any of the others could know how I felt at that moment. No one else has ever known until this writing. Not my best friends, man, or woman, not my wife, Phyllis—no one.

In the jungles of 'Nam, we would often cover the same area more than once, coming across villages and villagers we had seen weeks or maybe months before. We would sometimes befriend kids and the elderly for just an hour or so and move on. Sometimes, it was only after interpreters would explain the meaning of the words that would we understand their behavior.

We were at this place on a search-and-destroy mission late one evening, when everything looked like everything we had seen, but as Marines, our guard was on full. Suddenly, a short figure darted across the bush from the trees and the Lieutenant ordered, "Shoot! Shoot 'em!!" We instinctively turned and fired our weapons.

Following the loud burst of gunfire, when the smoke had lifted, we ran over to see what we had gotten. I recall running over with my long roll of M60 ammo still hanging from the gun chamber swinging as I ran. When we stopped, a little girl laid there still alive and conscious, but her body was all but in half at the torso. Blood was covering where she lay and all around her. She was uttering a word and her eyes looked warmly right into mine. She just looked into my face and said a word, just one word. I was in a state of bewilderment because she looked at me as if she were uttering this word to me. Then, the others looked at me and she got the word out again. In a moment, the little girl was gone, and I turned to the interpreter to ask, "What did she say?" He couldn't speak to me at first, and then I asked him again, "What did she say, man?!"

"'Daddy', she said, 'Daddy.'"

At first, I thought she was calling for her daddy. Then my fingers became numb, my gun strap slumped from my shoulder, and a pain gripped my throat like a large steel rod bursting from my neck. My heart felt like it had been pierced by a hot sword and my stomach burned down to my pitiful ass. It dawned on me; she wasn't calling for her daddy. It was the little girl from a week or so back, in this same damn village who had tried to teach me a word the last time we were there, and the word was Daddy.

Nobody else knew what had happened between us, and I realized in a single moment that I would never, ever feel the same again. I couldn't cry in front of all those Marines and I couldn't move. Now, even fifty years later, the steel rod returns to my throat, and her eyes sometimes awakens me, and tears flow until I'm unconscious. My consciousness has paid and will continue to pay the price of her death until I am where she is, wherever that is. Because, for her that day, Zorro was not there to help.

The feelings that crush the spirit can come at any time. When in revelry of my mind, daylight assuages the feelings of sadness, guilt, remorse, and loneliness. But the sleepless nights, the nocturnal nature of my mind, brings to bear the sights and sounds of the cruel and painful sins committed against my fellow human beings. The darkness just seems to intensify the depths of hurt and devastates the soul's desire to live.

Bobby Womack wrote a song that best describes the darkness and pain when it becomes insufferable. "If you think you're lonely now, wait until tonight ..." The words are so true. I used to fill my days with people—friends, crowds, and excitement—just to keep the night away. I feared the memories that would invade my thoughts. Even today after so many years, like a baby fearing the loneliness of night without its mother, I attempt to extend the daylight hours. I need people around me, talking, telling jokes, laughing, dancing—anything to ward off the unavoidable night, or the other recurring memory: the scene of two little boys, one maybe five years old, the other no more than three, caught in the middle of a dirt road and the crossfire between the V.C. and Marines. The unbearable memory of the older boy's futile attempt to protect his baby brother and himself—and my futile yells to stop the firefight.

"Cease fire!! Cease fire!" I called out, but there was only the relentless burst of automatic fire from one side to the other. I was trying my best to get the attention of Marines who might look away from the fight. "Cease fire! Cease fire! There are kids in the road! Cease fire!"

My screams of "Cease fire" were in vain. Neither those words, nor any prayer, could stop the intent of our commanding officer who yelled at me, "Fuck it! Too bad! I want a high body count! Their asses ain't getting away!"

I yelled again at other Marines, trying to time my shouts with the brief seconds that weren't shock waves of automatic fire. But nothing ceased except the lives of those two boys. The sight of what looked like two rag dolls being kicked across the road while dust and foreign bullets of war tore across their bodies was a sight that was unforgettable—and unforgivable. And afterward, how I laid on my back with my arms spread wide, looking into a clear blue sky. I spoke to it: "Are you really out there? 'Cause if you are, you a dirty motherfucker."

War can make you curse God because war curses you for ten thousand nights. Some nights, I stop fighting it and find a place to cry out, to scream to God to take these painful memories away, with a devout prayer that I did not have a heart that hurt this deeply. But the visions don't leave; they linger without answers. Nobody knew, save my faithful wife, Phyllis, that happy-go-lucky Chuck was (and still is) fearful of the night. We attempt to convince ourselves that it was someone else, someone else's weapon, but when realization sets in and the night falls, the light of the truth reveals that it was your gun; it *was* you!! No screams or tears will expiate the guilt; it continues, and no matter how much it hurts ... wait until tonight, with or without sanctuary, wait until tonight.

CHAPTER 10

The Fog of More

—

One way I was able to extend the daylight, so to speak, was to be where the energy was: crowds, conversation, and music. It was during the '80's musical explosion when Stevie Wonder; Earth, Wind and Fire; Toni Braxton; and others were the soundtrack to integration and the cross-cultural revolution that began to take place and provide escape. It was happening rapidly around the country in many cities, but only a few places in Richmond took advantage of its benefits, and the Stonewall Café was one of those places.

It was a progressive crowd that didn't have time for hate, prejudice, or bigotry, although those remnants dove-tailed every corner of America. But what dominated that crowd was fun, pleasure, entertainment, new ideas, and excitement. Power, influence, money, and the best-looking people anywhere in Richmond, Black or White, came here after dark.

For a brief period in Richmond's history, it seemed that a whole new paradigm of business, politics, and power would take off from this little corner at Lombardi and Main Street, but for some enigmatic reason, it would not. For a while, the evenings were filled with excitement, enthusiasm, energy, and fun: the recipe I needed to delay my dark night. One particular evening was filled with excitement and unexpected events. Women seem to be pulled by the lure of power that surrounded the circles within which I moved. The way people enjoyed just being near you was something special, but I also realized that I needed to keep my head about me or I'd easily fall prey to some sexual trap to which every young Black politician was subject.

The Stonewall Café was owned by John Ross, the son of a wealthy Richmond merchant. I had helped John secure all the necessary permits and approvals to open the Café while I was in my third term of office. I had run unopposed and, at thirty-three years old, was at the height of political strength: the titular leader of the Council. It seemed I could do no wrong that year. During one chilly December evening I wore my ¾-length camel-hair particularly well as I entered the café. As usual, John greeted me as he did most of his guests at the door. He would always walk a small distance with special guests to enjoy the presentation and status it gave the nature of his establishment.

It also gave prominence to the times in which we lived, and the unusual appearance of racial progress, real or imagined. That evening as I entered, I immediately felt a discerning eye which followed my every move. I would get looks at public places and I'd just go with the flow and not let their gazes dominate my attention.

Even with this in mind, there are times when nothing will stop the male libido. With this one special woman, who would not stop looking at me, I had to respond to her. She kept gazing across the crowd at me like she wanted to be sure I got her message. As I moved closer to speak to this young, not yet thirty-something, well-spoken, highly intelligent lady. I noticed that she was seated not on a bar stool or a table chair. Arranged next to a closed wheelchair, she sat at a table—disabled and unable to walk! Although I was somewhat startled, her profound beauty continued to mesmerize. This conundrum was one I'd never previously beheld: a woman of great beauty and charm who from all indications was as dubious of me as I was of her. My compunction was overwhelmingly confusing and diminishing. To break the spell, I asked her if I could take off my heavy wrap.

"I was hoping you would get to that at some point of the evening," she said with a devastating wink. Amid my considerations, she looked

Cease Fire! Cease Fire!

at me and said, "Come on, you're a big boy; you can handle this. Decide what you want and take me from the eyes of these haunting wolves."

Her name was Lydia, and I had never seen someone who possessed the looks of a soft-spoken damsel in distress speak with the timbre of a Wall Street stockbroker. She was relentless in her desires and I was not unmindful of the mostly White eyes that inconspicuously followed my every move. Her beauty was so rare, I was transfixed momentarily but had to maintain the significance of where I was, and who I was, despite everything that had occurred over the previous five minutes.

With an attraction I could not resist, the acknowledgement of the situation and the logistics was becoming more than my conscience could bear. She seemed to read my thoughts, then said to me in a soft whisper, "You can handle this; you're a good man—and I've been watching you all evening."

I knew then that we would leave together. The dilemma was not a small task before me: to do nothing in the face of a grand opportunity or do it all without compunction. The question before me was, would I serve a greater principle or a weak passion?

She asked if I could assist her to her vehicle, and she would meet me some place. I was astonished with her capable means of mobility and self-sufficiency. She was garbed with a dark fur coat that covered most of her lower body and detracted the would-be sexuality of her feminine aspects. As we made our way through traffic, she led me towards a gated community and directed the gatekeeper to allow me through as I followed behind her. When we pulled into the parking area, I quickly exited my vehicle and got into her car. I sat in the passenger's seat of her Mercedes Benz and whipped my coat over my legs. I reached my left hand behind her head, pulled her face directly to mine, and gave her a long, slow, soft kiss. It was more sexual, more arousing, and manlier than the best fuck I could have ever given her.

After the kiss, I leaned slightly away. As beautiful a creature as she was, as much as my imagination had driven me wild thinking about caressing her body, kissing her lips, and feeling the fall of hair between my thighs, I was being haunted. The image of her lifeless legs and non-responsive thighs, the strangeness of motionless hips and weak back, was unnerving. I began to fear it simply because I had never known it. I gave up, lost my will to continue the path I had envisioned, afraid to demonstrate the confidence and commitment she had shown all evening. This had to be something men and women have at some time considered about sex, and I am ashamed to confess, with all else, my ignorant regard. Big, bad Chuck Richardson; Marine war vet; seen it all yet, unable to accept for one hour what she must live with through each hour of her life. I had never, ever felt this before and realized that I could not go through it.

My desire for her was overwhelmed by my inability to serve due to my hesitancy. Most importantly, how, if possible, would I not hurt her feelings at the same time, and depart while leaving the both of us with our dignity intact? With all the strength of resistance I had left in my body, I told her that I was a married man and had thoroughly enjoyed her company but...

She seemingly understood. It may have been something that was just another aspect of her condition that she was used to ... or at least understood. I never saw her again after that night. It was a one-night (under)stand, on her part particularly.

My indiscretions with other women were typical affairs based solely on carnal desire. It would be the height of hypocrisy to profess that I loved any of those individuals. During that stage of my life, I hardly had any concept of love beyond Phyllis, and I doubt that few, if any of us, do when sex is the primary aspect of the relationship.

Physical beauty and desire are the foundations of lust. And it was this strong but shallow desire that influenced my behavior far more than love. At first sight, Lydia, like so many other of my sexual encounters outside my marriage, stimulated that yearning. And it was lust at first sight, not love.

Though I possess a more mature concept of love and of life now, at that time I acted as a child in a candy store, where the candy was jumping off the shelves, into my pockets, and often straight to my mouth. I truly wanted to be a good, faithful husband when I returned home from Vietnam. It might sound like a corny, old, tired lie, but on the top of a mountain in the Quang Nam Province of Vietnam, I made a deal with the Lord. If he delivered me safely home from the treacherous conditions of this war, I would return home and be a good and faithful husband to Phyllis.

Having seen so much misery, experiencing horrific and death-defying instances of survival, I was willing to settle for just being alive. I can recall saying to God, "Just let me make it through this and I'll be a good man for one woman." That was how I felt on the top of that chilly, wet, dark mountain on New Year's Day in 1970.

It may be unreasonable to say I was a good husband, but I loved my wife, Phyllis, unconditionally. As gorgeous as she was, Phyllis's inner qualities were a greater reason to love her than any of the physical attributes of those other women. There were some real beauties, however, like Veronica, Joanne, Rosemary, Belinda, Maryanne, to whom I had developed a degree of emotional attraction. A few tested my marital bonds. The real criterion that determined the longevity of a sexual relationship transcends the sex itself; that much I realized even at that young age. Had I not recognized this, and had Phyllis not been so attractive inside and out, with a saintly tolerance, I may have moved into an illusion of love and made a dumb mistake that would have changed everything.

Many men, throughout the annals of history, have been led to an ignominious downfall as a result of a sexual illusion. I think I was blessed in that I did not possess the ability to be cruel to the "candy," if you will. No matter how much I abused the heroin I consumed, I could not hurt the heroin, but a human being was attached to the other end of my sexual pleasure. The more I indulged with that other individual, knowing that I would not leave my marriage, the more cruelty I would impose on her life.

As selfish, jealous, and determined as I was to get what I wanted when I wanted it, I always told the women there was a limitation to our relationship because I was married. *If you wish to continue seeing me—after the fuck—you do it, as will I, at the risk of losing something we both cannot have.* I always made it clear from the outset that my home, children, and wife were my priorities. I couldn't have done anything more; as beautiful they were, I knew I could not become but so involved. I set my own limit. However, there were other relationships that went too far and lasted too long. There was no joy in heaping that type of emotional misery on another human being.

Nonetheless, the number of sexual episodes between 1976 and 1995 in my City Council years was criminal and I was oblivious to any emotional involvement in my escapades. It got to the point where, at times I was having sex three times a day with three different women, separately. A lot of men boast and brag of their exploits as if trophies. However, mine were not conquering exploits, but rather a man presented with outrageous opportunity from consenting adults who became reckless. In a complicated world of sexual interplay where stimuli are in constant demand for a response, the male species is so often in a no-win proposition. Does that sound like an excuse?

I observed back in high school at Henrico that the White boys never spoke as bodacious braggarts regarding their fathers' extramarital affairs. In fact, as I recall they were very protective of their image of being monogamous. Often in the Black community, young males would readily acknowledge and almost boast of their fathers' sexual prowess with a sense of strength and pride.

I am certain that the explanation for these attitudes is deeply rooted in the damage to so many of the family values during slavery There is a historical tradition to ignore the many detrimental aspects that slavery had upon the Black family unit. And even when made painfully clear through sociological explanations, social scientists prefer to dwell upon the effects and ignore the causes.

In hindsight, when listening to Black boys in the Providence Park community speak about their fathers, then hearing White boys at Henrico High speak otherwise, I now consider the crux of the issue to be slavery. Slavery had so decimated the fatherly role in the Black family that as an individual, he had few means of portraying his manhood except through his sexual exploits.

It is not at all that Black men are less moral or possess less strength of character. Rather, when placed in a position to express or exhibit his manhood, the means of demonstrating it is restricted. The difference between men in the community in which I was raised and the one in which I was educated was stark. Black men could not boast of stocks, bonds, real estate holdings, titles or positions of power, large homes, or lucrative businesses. Instead, they boast of carnal pursuits. I am not trying to psychoanalyze, excuse my behavior, or imply in any way some merit to the racist stereotype of the sex-crazed Negro. I am simply wondering about myself.

The question for the female species is this: at what point does sexual attractiveness cross the line of flirting to becoming a lure to some men? This is a serious question that cannot be taken lightly. The sexual drive is a powerful force and will subdue most men. So many have fallen and succumb to the urges of sex.

The deal I made with the Lord on the mountains in Vietnam was unrealistic. When God made man, to perpetuate the species, he had to make sex an urge more powerful than our will. We are already doomed to the temptations of a woman's beauty and the weakness of our own willpower. Just a small flirtatious gesture by a woman can be misconstrued by a man into what he would want to believe it to be rather than what it is. Once a small appearance of a suggestion is perceived, it becomes almost impossible that he might change his course of pursuit.

Our reluctance for both men and women to engage in open and honest discourse pursuant to our feelings regarding sexual desires, combined with a woman's desire for sex being considered by some to be taboo, mean much remains hidden and misunderstood. Thus, undisclosed thousands of cases of hurt feelings, destroyed relationships, lost jobs, broken families and friendships, and many other misunderstood indignities regarding sex remain.

Only a greater power than myself saved me during that period of my life; I am blessed in that regard. I rationalized my indiscretions with Phyllis by reassuring myself that she knew my commitment to her was solid. Phyllis was strong. More than once she commented to me, "I saw that look that woman gave you tonight."

I would say, "Aww! It didn't mean anything."

She'd respond, "It may not have, but my concern was the way you looked back at her... that meant something."

Phyllis was so perceptive, so wise. Although she knew what was going on, she was straightforward yet kind when breaking me down. Yes, she broke me down—more than once. There was one time, I'll never forget how it happened: we were upstairs in our bedroom and she was quite quiet. I had been lying to her about something regarding my behavior and she knew it, and she knew I knew it.

"Look Rich, I know you, and I see things; you're handsome, charming, and a good human being," she said. "You are lovable and irresistible, and you can't resist all the things that come before you." She moved around the bedroom as if her words were futile and she didn't care if they were. Walking over to me, she softly glared at me as if sympathetic to my pathetic lies. Then she suddenly reached up, grabbed me by my necktie, pulled me right up to her face and revealed a blade! She held it to my face and firmly said to me, "So, put that thing in me or I'll cut it off!" After a second or two of eye contact that spoke through years, she backed up slowly, lowered the blade and sat on the edge of the bed, defeated not by anger but sadness.

There were several seconds of a weird, almost magnetic pull of the love between us that was pure and longstanding as she dropped her head in a crushed posture. As she sat quietly, she placed the knife across her wrist, pressing into the skin then releasing, and then, as if confessing, said, "Or I'll use it on me." All I could do was kneel and hold her close to me, conveying my full apology with an embrace my empty words could not convey. We looked at each other and I felt a forgiveness I didn't deserve.

Phyllis made sacrifices that, to some, may seem unreasonable, but she was able to understand the impact of war, the impact of my presence on council, the big picture of my role, and hers. Though I was weak in a carnal way, she gave to me a comfort I never found

Cease Fire! Cease Fire!

elsewhere. Boy, did we make love that night! There is nothing like having sex with someone with whom you make love.

Undercoated

Many inconveniences can go along with being well-known and recognized, not the least that I had to move about in the darker worlds of crime, drugs, and suspect areas. Trying to remain unknown was as bad as being well-known because anybody could be the police. Everybody was a suspect as someone could recognize you immediately. My particularly unique problem was obvious to everyone who knew me and who understood that, with my addiction, I had to obtain drugs but that I couldn't go into the drug areas myself! I always needed a middleman to score the drugs. I remember my friends, Charles "Blackie" Alexander and Donald "Popcorn" Minor, describing how on separate occasions, the vice squad cops would become angry when they, or other friends of mine, refused to give them information that would set me up for arrest. Even when the cops caught Popcorn scoring for me, after he had ditched the drugs, he denied everything. The policemen had walked up and down the alley looking for the dope, but they couldn't find it. So, they had to release Popcorn, but before doing so, they threatened to charge him with all types of drug offenses. But he was as smart as they, and never broke.

One day, near Woodville School on 28th Street, the police chased Popcorn as he was returning from scoring for me in the Creighton Court Projects. The vice squad chased him for four or five blocks, but he dumped the dope. I always paid for both of us because I would never accompany him; typically, I was waiting in the car. This time, I waited and waited and thought that he had taken the drugs, gotten high, and was going to return to me with some bullshit excuse, as this kind of behavior had happened in the past. It took him so long that I was convinced that he had "macked" me. I remember sitting in the hot car, tapping my fingers to some music on the radio and glancing around, talking to myself, preparing what I would say to him, and how I would jump in his shit when he got back.

But when Blackie returned, he was out of breath, with the perspiration rolling off of him like the chain gang in a coal mine. As he dropped into the seat beside me, his head fell back, and he closed his eyes. I didn't give him the normal excoriation and cussing out; I knew it wasn't warranted this time. Eventually, we would have to try again because when you are dope sick, you have no choice.

The drug dealing enterprise is all about money and, no matter who you are, you must pay for the product. But there have been, and still are, times when I can't get past moments of indescribable guilt! I would do heroin and, for the most part, became functional. So, it was an on-and-off, good guy-bad guy scenario. As a City Councilman, it was a magician's trick, a magical act of transforming myself from a clean cut, three-piece suit, necktie-wearing, trustworthy citizen recognized city-wide to a dope scoring drug addict.

What made it worse was that it was imperative I always find someone who I trusted to go buy the dope. Usually, a long time, well-known trusted friend, male, or female, would go directly to the dealer and purchase the drugs for me. Moreover, in a sense, I carried a double habit because each time I used, I was obliged to secure enough dope for me as well as the other guy who was securing it. Sometimes, if you couldn't trust a certain friend because they were hurting as bad as you, you had to accompany them and face whatever you had to face. That "magical" transformation was not possible all the time. Sometimes when the habit was crushing me into a puking-sick misery, still in my suit and tie, I couldn't just run out to my local pusher man and expect him to trust me, much less at night.

One night, I had to go with Popcorn and another friend named Bee Bee to score. That night, I was sick, dog sick, in a suit and tie crouched in the back seat under a coat, sweating, aching, vomiting. I didn't want the guys to run off with my money and the shit, too, so I rode with them in the back seat to Fulton, down where those "gangstas" shoot cops. I had the money, Popcorn knew the dope boys, and Bee Bee was the driver. Since I was light-skinned, it was a strike against us already being deep in the hood. We argued over the money all the way. I was ducking up and down with the large overcoat pulled over my head, worried the whole time that my boys might get their heads together and figure a way to cut me out, so my concern was watching my money and my "friends."

Anyway, when we were near the hook up spot riding slowly, I saw the dope man, "Polio," with his boy (gunman) walking. Polio usually had one of his boys with him to cover his ass in case someone tried to stick him up. Slinging dope was a complicated and dangerous business in the hood, especially in Fulton. They walked over to the car.

"Hey, Corn! Wha's up?" Polio said.

"Hey, Polio! Wha's goin' on?"

"Little man name here is Cat Man," he said. Cat Man was slightly crouched with a high-collar, dark trench coat. He was quiet and just looked around while Polio got his package out.

"You said you want three, right?"

"Yea! Hurry up, man, hurry up!"

Meanwhile, I was trying to be still and quiet under that hot coat. Then, all of a sudden, "CLICK!" A .357 Magnum was cocked and was resting right in my face. Another barrel in the same damn week was looking me straight in my face. Of course, I didn't budge.

"Who is this motherfucker in the back?! Nigga, who the fuck is this, Corn?! You tryin' to set me up? Youuu Muthafucka!!"

"Hold it, hold it, man! Hold up, Polio! It's Chuck, Chuck Richardson, the councilman. Hold up, brotha! You know he can't be seen out here, man! That's why he under there. It's Chuck. Don't shoot, man."

"Shit! Let me see, goddamnit, let me see. Who the fuck is you, nigga?!!" Polio said.

I could almost feel the clinched position of his mouth that barely opened, speaking through his teeth. I was really sweating, sick as shit by that time, and frozen by that .357 Magnum inches from my nose in the quivering hands of Cat Man.

Although it was dark, I could see the streetlight reflecting off the barrel's tip. I pulled the coat from over my head.

"Mothafucking Chuck." Polio tells Cat Man to put the gun down. "Put the gun down, goddamnit. That's Chuck Richardson." He walks over to the back door and opens his arms, tilts his head, and looks at me like an old friend. "My man, Chuck ... gimme some love, nigga. Gimme some love. Cat Man, do you know who this is? Dis dat nigga, *the* nigga, Chuck Richardson."

"You lyin'! I heard of him but I ain't never seen him in person. Goddamn, Chuck Richardson," Cat Man said slowly.

"Git down, Chuck, git down," Polio said. "We don't want nobody seeing you. You say you want three, right? Git down, Chuck. Nigga, you all right. Put the Mag away, fool. Chuck, my man, what the hell you doing out here like this, Uncle Chuck?" Polio asked as he held on to the drugs and stuck his hand out to Popcorn for the money. I was sweating like crazy, but I think it was more from being dope sick than being scared.

Popcorn asked, "Hey, man! Can you give me a break? We a little short."

"Short!" Polio barked, "You come out here with this mutherfucker and you short?"

Popcorn laughed and said, "It ain't but three dollars, man."

Polio cut him off, "Look, mutherfucker! When you come down here in Fulton, you better have the right money ... but since you with my man, I'll let you go."

Popcorn said, "Okay, man, but we got money for three eggs, seventy-two dollars; that ain't but less than a dub ($5.00) short."

"Okay, okay man! Get him the fuck outta here and don't y'all jive asses bring Chuck out like this no mo'! Ha! Ain't dis some shit?! Niggas ridin' round wit' the *baddest* nigga in Richmond—and he short." The whole group broke out into relieved laughter.

"A'right. Let's go!" As his driver pulled off, Polio the dope man, who was obviously high himself, said, "You be cool, Uncle Chuck, and keep yo' ass down, brother. Get the fuck back down."

After we left the neighborhood, B-B said to Popcorn while laughing, "I told you not to bring that mutherfucker with us."

Popcorn replied, "I know it, but he said he didn't want to wait at home because the last time you went for him, you brought back two eggs won't big as my dick!!"

I rose from the back floor and added, "That's right, 'cause the last time y'all niggas scored for me, I know y'all took some of my dope. I was not going to put seventy-five dollars out here with no goddamn trust! I would rather face them dope dealers any day than trust you motherfuckers with my money. Now hurry up, B-B! Let's get the hell back to the house! I'm feeling like shit." But I must say I did feel better than I had felt twenty minutes earlier.

Busted

Not long, maybe a week or so after my precarious trip into Fulton to score with BB and Popcorn, I was with my other buddy, Blackie, in Church Hill after we scored. We had parked on Ford Avenue, not far from where I lived as a child. Blackie and I hit the "horse" as soon as we could, finding that place I had found first in Vietnam—away from "the world." A few minutes after putting the syringes and supplies away, in the flash of a second, out of nowhere, the police were dropping from the sky, literally almost. It was, I'm sure, a bit enhanced by the high, but it was almost like a scene from an *X-Men* movie: boom! Suddenly, cops on both sides and behind us. It was October 14, 1987, a date like some others in Vietnam that just stick. They must have been aware of what was going on, and when they saw some of the supplies in the seat we had missed, they told us to get out. We were cuffed. They seized the supplies in hopes of getting something to pin us with. Two of the officers were Black; in fact, one I knew from my teen years. They, of course, knew who I was and went about their duty with a slight grin that rubbed me with resentment.

Blackie and I were taken in and I soon had my lawyer, Mike Morchower, help me with bail. A few days later, Morchower and two other lawyers were trying to convince me to plead to a felony in exchange for no jail time. They all said, "Chuck, you gotta take this, man. You don't want jail; you'll lose your council seat for sure." The judge wanted me to admit I had a drug problem and that I would seek help. Only then would he drop the jail sentence but leave me with the felony charge. I thought, *damn, if I plead to a felony I'm gone from council as well*—the council elections would be coming up in May!

I knew if I could get a jury trial, I had a better chance with the opportunity to strike jurors who may already have been hostile towards me. My record of pro-Black causes and stances against the status quo White domination had endeared me to the Black community—and enraged the White community. When my addiction became public, judgments about my guilt or innocence were divided, almost absolutely, along racial boundaries. It would be a gamble I felt confident about, although my lawyers remained incredulous as we prepared for trial in February.

A little more than a week after my arrest in October for possession, almost two months before the trial, and before the facts and evidence were presented, Henry Marsh visited me at my home—the first time ever in his life. In tow was his companion, Walter T. Kenney. I was pleasantly surprised to see that my close colleagues with whom I had worked on the Council for the last ten years would visit me in my hour of trouble and despair. We greeted each not so differently than we had over those ten years; I welcomed them in and offered a coffee or something to drink.

After we dispensed with the formal niceties, Henry quickly got to the point. He often had a way of looking nervous and awkward when

Cease Fire! Cease Fire!

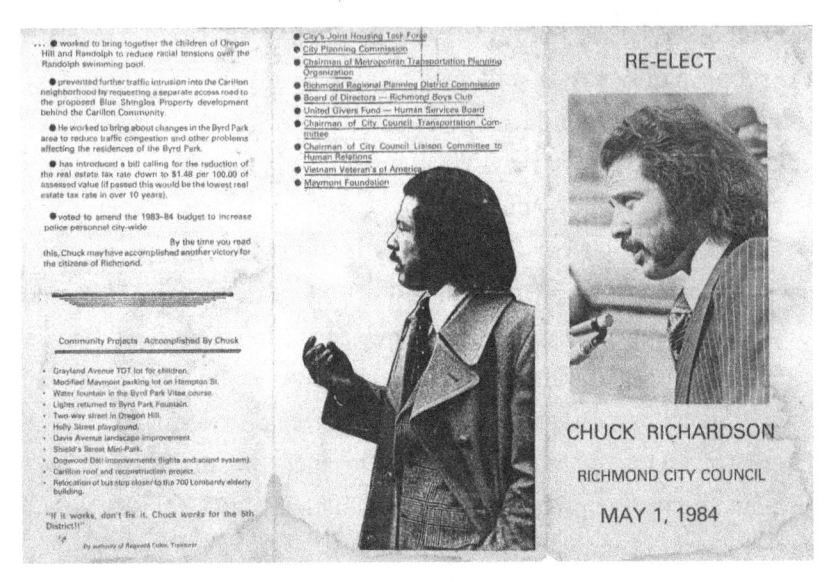

An early re-election brochure.

Early campaign literature done by hand. Old school copy and paste.

he tried to lead, unsure of any follower. He had that look this time when he said, "Your case looks pretty much open and shut, Chuck."

I said, "Henry, Morchower has all the facts and he's agreed to help me pro bono, along with Jim Sheffield. Did you want to join us? Could you help?"

He said, "Well ... Walter and I were concerned about the City... in the event you are not on Council, who would take your place, you know, if you considered resigning. Who would you suggest be your replacement?"

At first, I was hurt to realize after all the shit we had been through, endured together, that they actually weren't concerned about me and my family at all. It was his political posture and concern about the Council that brought them to my home. I was silent for a few moments as I looked at them. I had to control my anger and calm myself to not ask them to leave immediately. As I was rolling through a mixture of embarrassment, insult, betrayal, outrage, and disbelief all at the same time, I kept saying to myself, *What the fuck is this?! All the shit we'd been through, and they pulling shit like this?* I told myself to calm down and talk to, or at least listen to them, before I kicked them out. Henry was smart enough to know my influence and political hold on the very important Fifth District. He knew whether I was in or out of jail, I could influence the election or who would be appointed. He was hoping to determine who would take my place before it was even vacant! At a glance, my case did look pretty bad. Still, I had been Henry's right-hand man on the Council, helping him move a Black agenda—though at times, blocking some of his sell-out garbage.

And now, it was only my friend, Morchower, a White man, who was willing to jump in and help me. It was all I could do to keep my foot on the floor while I watched him squirm on my couch next to Walter. And poor Walter; he didn't know what to say or do. Walter was a good man; his heart was always in the right place. He sometimes just would not show the strength of conviction, especially around Marsh, and Henry often took advantage of it. Maybe that day, he didn't understand he was just along for the ride in case I got pissed and "bitch-slapped" Henry a couple times for coming to my home with this bullshit. But I was cool. I said to him, "If I did resign, could you help me squeak out a living in my struggle?"

"Ain't nothing I can do 'bout that, Chuck… like, that's on you now," Henry said flat out.

Boy was I getting hot! He could have at least said, "I'll see but I can't promise," or something to let me know he had some concern for my future; but damn! It was like he was saying, "you have no value; your political use is zero." I said to him, "You've given up on my case and I haven't even started to fight yet. It's November and the election is in six months! I can still be there with you in May if you give me a fighting chance, Henry."

He looked away, again nervous and awkward, and said, "Well, it looks pretty bad right now."

After a brief moment, Walter leaned forward and said, "Well … think about it, Chuck, okay?"

I stood up, shaking my head not just at Walter but the whole damn scene. As I walked to the door Walter began saying something else, but I cut him off and told them I had important things to do. I opened the door before they were even standing. As I held the door, and they started to walk out, Henry started to say something, but I interrupted him loudly. "Man, get the fuck outta my house!"

For many Blacks in Richmond, my guilt or innocence in this case was not the real issue. It didn't matter. It wasn't that they didn't care if I was clean of heroin, but they knew the game police and the Feds played, and it would not surmount my service to them on the Council. Believing I stood a better than fifty percent chance to convince a set of my peers that I was only with a friend, and there was no proof I possessed anything—evidence was sketchy at best— I was determined to put my faith in my peers. I told my attorney, "No, no deal. I want a trial."

The Commonwealth Attorney, Aubrey Davis, well understood the political and racial dynamics of my situation. He knew, probably surer than I did, that a predominantly Black jury would never convict me. In the middle of the jury selection process, one young, obviously conservative White lady, admitted her open resentment for me. She even stated that my pro-Black politics were so repulsive that she could not find me innocent even if I were. She was not unique, only

The first court fight in 1988, with Jim Sheffield and my wife Phyllis. © *Richmond Times Dispatch*

Weighing the charges and chances with Jim Sheffield and Phyllis. © *Richmond Times Dispatch*

outspoken beyond the others who said with their eyes that they agreed. Judge Duling, forced by the law, dismissed that woman. As she walked down from the jury box, just beneath her breath but loud enough to be heard, she uttered some anti-Richardson sentiment, to which I softly responded, "I love you, too."

Judge Duling said, "Mr. Richardson, that was not necessary. You are out of order!" *I* was out of order.

From that point on, the racial implications were entirely too deep to have a fair trial. The prosecuting attorney, Mr. McNally, called for a recess and met with his team. McNally returned after only a short while and offered a plea bargain. It was unbelievable to my legal advisors. No one had ever placed their faith in a jury that way, believed in the empathy of his peers. I felt like Superman; it was so wild to believe it could happen in 1988, a giant leap of faith in a single bound. This was well before the broad notion, nationally, with the O.J Simpson case and Marion Barry and others, that Blacks, too, could hold the power of peer judgement. A jury of peers: a power that had been denied many countless Black men and women over decades, if indeed, a chance for a jury at all. It was like imagining poor villagers finding Zorro guilty of stealing grain to feed their children. I am in no way equating my offense with that of Simpson or Barry, but my case was years earlier in Richmond, and had much of the same polarizing racial reactions.

This component of peers for the Black defendant is part of the legacy of the struggle for true equality throughout our history since Reformation after the Civil War. John Wesley Dobbs, one of the most effective and celebrated legends of Black Atlanta in the early 20th Century, and also the grandfather of Maynard Jackson, the first Black mayor of a major Southern city, spoke of the key elements to Black progress. He called them the three Bs: The Book, The Ballot, and The Buck. The "Book," meaning education and perhaps the Bible; the "Ballot" as representation and a voice in the government; and the "Buck," which indicated economic power and self-reliance. My case was reflecting the "Ballot": not only the fact I had been elected by virtue of the vote, but the seating of my peers in judgement. This can be a difficult reality for most Whites, even those who understand the legacy of cases like that of Emmett Till, or the "Mississippi Burning Murders." But like the pendulum, the aim of reaching true equality must necessarily, at times, overcorrect before reaching center.

As part of the plea agreement, there would be no felony charge, but I would admit to an abuse issue and agree seek help for my drug problem. That was one of the freest moments of my entire life. I could now stop playing the double role that had become too heavy a burden. Liberation from the life of having to conceal such a devastating secret was like a release from imprisonment, which was not only tearing at me emotionally. Logistically, it had become unmanageable. For the first time since returning home from Vietnam, I was truly free. It was a glorious moment for me, no longer having to live a double life, a living hell. And I truly believed I could break the hell that had contained my body for almost a decade.

The agreement was on a Friday, and Monday, I checked in to St. Johns for treatment, thirty days of very difficult times. I was released at the end of March and had one month before the election. I hit the street campaigning hard with contrite but earnest assurances to my district. April showers brought some damn sweet May flowers; I was re-elected, easily! All through November, January, and February, the constant menu of Chuck Richardson's trials with heroin and the law had played out on the television news, but it was not a game changer for my constituents. I was ashamed to an extent but felt a greater pride in the Fifth District. Many of my constituents understood that I had personal problems since my service in Vietnam. While it bothered many and myself, the question was my Council representation. It seems my constituents were saying, *yes, he might, unfortunately, shoot up, but no one stands up like Chuck, no one speaks more passionately or strongly about the issues meaningful to Blacks, to the poor or disadvantaged than Chuck Richardson! WE WANT HIM!* It was a position taken by most Blacks across Richmond overall. It was more amazing than cops falling from the sky.

The Commonwealth Attorney, Aubrey Davis, went absolutely

Some things were obvious, but they did a great story on my first case. © Style Weekly

crazy. The combination of drugs, the power of Black voters, and a young, in-your-face, bad-ass, Black vet left him without much comment—only a look that spoke volumes. Ironically, and seemingly from a Hollywood comedy script, the powers that snagged me and supported my habit for several months after. After my arrest in October 1987, I was approached by the FBI. They offered to pay me for information on violations of the Hobbs Act, a law addressing white-collar crimes around commerce and property theft. Their thinking, I suppose, was that I may have knowledge of politicians or businesspeople involved in those crimes. I did not. But as an active addict at the time, I saw a huge opportunity to support my habit. So, I thought, *alright motherfuckers, let's play.*

I fed them bullshit and sent them on wild goose chases, accepting close to $20,000 in several payments over the next four months. The whole time I was waiting for trial, Blackie and I were able to supply our habits—on their cash. After I got clean in March, I used about half of it on things at home for Phyllis like a washer and dryer, clothes, and furniture. But Blackie and I would laugh like clowns while we used my cash-cow during the holidays in '87. I know they'd never admit to something like that, especially being used by me, but truth is stranger than fiction... and that's the truth. That free ride ended in February. Poor Blackie had to accept that I was out of the game, and I began a very hopeful stretch of a clean life.

Following my successful treatment, I felt like a newborn baby: clean, fresh, with nothing to hide any longer. It was like a million-pound weight had been removed from my back, and I was happy, thankful, and gratified not having to live that miserable double life any longer. Add to that being re-elected within a month, I felt a redemption and forgiveness I could not abuse. Everyone appeared to be happy for me, except the police and the Richmond newspapers. Following my court case, it was no secret that I had struggled with an addiction, but my admission and decision to seek treatment at St. John's Hospital should have rendered the matter a medical condition and not a situation for police authorities to exploit politically.

The police were actually angry and disappointed that I was clean and sober. They continued to follow me and check for any indication that I might be in relapse. The vice squad actually had people at Alcoholics Anonymous (AA) and Narcotics Anonymous (NA) meetings. It was sad and tragically ironic that individuals responsible for the elimination of illicit drug use were disappointed at my success, hoping and even baiting me back to an active use of drugs. You can never judge people by their appearance, but everyone at those meetings were convinced they were cops. My buddy, Popcorn, did not look like a college professor or a rocket scientist, and the police did not think he was very intelligent. Even with an addiction, however, he was twice as intelligent as those cops. When the police carried Blackie downtown to the Richmond lockup and threatened him in the interrogation room, he held fast. Blackie would tell me how the cops reacted in disgust that none of the people they had apprehended would roll over on Chuck Richardson. Detectives looked at each other with a "who in the hell is he?" frustration.

Once, I encountered a trio of plainclothes cops at a downtown festival. As I passed them, they paused to speak and one of them said to me, "Richardson, you ought to be under the jail!"

Although I was hurt and taken aback at the comment, I managed to maintain my composure. It was in the middle of a crowd of a thousand, and I took a breath and said, "I can understand your feelings and you have the right to express them as I am a public authority. Do have a pleasant afternoon." I looked away to wave at a supporter, slowly walked off, and did not look back. Wherever God was that day, He made a quick dash to get there next to me. Construction was under way at that site and a large brick was right at my feet when that plainclothes officer made that snide comment. It was God who kept me from bending down and made me speak instead. But for every one person who expressed that attitude towards me, there were ten who supported me following my case and reelection.

As part of my plea bargain, I was on probation and had to report to an officer each week. That probation officer would strut, with me in tow, around his office each time to show off his celebrity subject as if he had tamed a savage beast. It really upset me after a few times. I wrote him a letter expressing my resentment, informing him I would not be treated with such an affront like that and would not be at the next meeting. I missed that appointment and once that violation occurred, they had the prerogative to file a charge they chose not to prosecute back in February—and they did so with gleeful zealousness. The charge was possession of cocaine.

When Blackie and I were busted, they found traces of cocaine in the syringe Blackie used to "speedball": mixing the heroin with coke. I never did that: never did cocaine, period. The prosecutors knew that all along, and they knew I didn't do coke. They never suspected anything but heroin from the time they began surveillance of me—back who knows when. However, this was a second chance they wouldn't pass up to get me off the Council and incarcerate me. This time there would, indeed, be a charge, a trial, a jury, and a verdict. It was a second chance, a redemption for the Commonwealth Attorney, after my startling election victory, after he had me admit my addiction in February and believed, as many, it was politically over for me. How I could not be convicted this time was hard for them—the media and most Whites—to grasp.

My defense was the truth: I was not aware of the cocaine; it was something Blackie did inconspicuously. I had no idea until after the arrest that a trace was found in the syringe. That trace, an amount smaller than the eye can even perceive, was now supposedly in my possession that day.

The media returned to high gear coverage and most of the White outrage returned as well. In other words, the newspapers sold well with me at the center of a scandalous, depraved dope addiction. The *Richmond News Leader* even put out a cartoon caricature of me seeking advice. Looking sad and clueless, the cartoon portrayed me in a fictional bid for help—with a space for a written response and the City Hall address to mail it to. It read something to the effect: "His name is Chuck. He needs your help," and it went on with sarcasm about my battles with the courts. It was not about my serious battle with the addiction from which I was recovering, but a humorous mocking of me, inferring the system was letting me get away with something.

The replies flooded City Hall, as close to 15,000 responded. From all over the suburban and rural metropolitan area, the returned cut-out cartoons filled box after box. The suggestions and advice ranged from "nigger" this to "nigger" that: "nigger should be under the jail," "nigger

The local newspaper created a comic depiction that solicited not so funny comments from its readers. © Richmond Times Dispatch

ought to be strung up," "nigger better stay with the rest of the niggers!" The hatred and contempt almost bled from some of the replies.

I believe the trial was in July because the jury selection took way longer than the two-day prosecution. It was not an all-Black jury. I believe there was one White woman. At least she looked White. The foreman was a Black man who took pride wearing what was called a kufi hat, a colorful African cap. I took the stand before a jury of my peers, giving clear illumination of my position: I had no idea that Blackie was speed-balling that day. I explained that when an addict admits his problem and wants recovery, he doesn't leave out a problem; he wants help from anything that controls him. My problem was heroin, not cocaine, and that is what I was treated for. The police and attorneys knew that and so did the treatment center at St. John's. The jury understood and believed what I was saying, and they understood the nature of the forces after me.

I was found "not guilty!" Black people at the courthouse celebrated and, most of Black Richmond did as well. In one newspaper's front page photograph, the jury foreman, with his bold kufi hat, was seen offering me a cigarette outside the courtroom. The image must have enraged my detractors.

I stated earlier this was a time five or six years before the O.J Simpson case, and I'll say it again. The point is not to suggest anything other than the similar shock that rolled across Whites after the verdict of a mostly Black jury on a Black defendant. I'm certainly not comparing the charges against O.J. and me but, in a way, what happened on the national stage was witnessed in Richmond years earlier—outrage at the notion Blacks could judge Blacks fairly.

The day after the verdict, I was asked to appear live in front of my home to talk with television anchor, Charles Fishburne, on the evening news. Mr. Fishburne, speaking from the desk back at the television station, said to me, "There are many solid citizens who disagreed with the verdict and believe there is a problem with the system," then he waited for my reply. The implication, of course, was to at once say: A) I was guilty, and B) that the system of a peer jury was dysfunctional when it came to Black people. I wanted to smile a little at what I was hearing, but I replied saying, "The system has always worked fine before with others, apparently. I don't think the problem is the system. I think the problem may be those 'solid citizens' you refer to. Maybe you should question them because I'm not sure how *solid* they are suddenly objecting to one of our bedrock principles."

It was that way for weeks: an indignant, dubious White community raising their voices. To think of the whole volumes of American history that cataloged the wrongs of racist juries—and a largely compliant society—overtly blinded by what they now claimed to see.

During that year, 1988, with my admitted struggle and the known culprit of Vietnam, I waited each day for Barney Ross. Very few knew of Barney Ross, even fewer today, but it was hard to believe his was never alluded to, not once. Who was Barney Ross, you may ask? An attorney? A friend of mine, or a politician? Private Barney Ross was a Marine, and a decorated hero in World War II. He was a celebrated champion boxer in the 1930s who volunteered to serve in the Marines at age 32 and fought in the most harrowing days of Guadalcanal. Ross

Cease Fire! Cease Fire!

There was, occasionally, positive press as well.

saved three fellow Marines and received the Silver Star for heroism. Severely injured, he was put on morphine for several months, and when he returned home, he had developed addiction. For years after his service, Barney Ross was a heroin addict. As a known celebrity, and war hero, the addiction was understood and mostly seen with empathy and concern about his torment—and the well-being of his family. Eventually, with help, he endured a tough recovery through treatment. The Barney Ross story was so compelling, it was made into a fairly successful movie in the late fifties. *Monkey on My Back* told the story of one warrior's burden after war.

I wondered almost every day when the Barney Ross story would come up, when would someone say, "Damn, this kid was in a war, decorated with two purple hearts and the Cross of Gallantry, fighting so we can have the very right to judge him fairly. His use of heroin began there. Let's understand that the origin of his offense was on *our behalf.*" But it never happened. I was never Barney Ross. Chuck Richardson was not a White war hero; to many he was just a Black street addict that did not deserve care, and in fact, deserved less. The Barney Ross narrative was about a hero-in-addiction; mine was simply an immoral heroin addiction.

Alcohol and drug addiction are one of the toughest personal fights any human being will ever face. It is an all-day, everyday battle against your own passions. It is resisting a desire you love the most, on a second-by-second basis, and you don't give in to one of those seconds or you lose. Fighting a struggle under normal conditions is bad enough, but when some power invokes the police department of the city in which you live as a force to help you lose this struggle, your chances are zero.

That power was persistent, a shadow that clung closely but not obviously. The Richmond police were rarely far from me but, as police, they knew how to stay out of sight. On the other hand, I sometimes happened upon them without their notice. I remember on Labor Day of 1988 that there was an event at Byrd Park. Perhaps a thousand people—the vast majority Black—were enjoying themselves with picnics and music by a Richmond DJ known as "Valentine." I saw a couple of officers confronting a group of Black celebrants at the table where Valentine was spinning his plays, and I approached them out of curiosity. The officers were insisting the music was too loud and they were getting complaints. It was mid-afternoon on Labor Day, it was sunny and pleasant, and if many hundreds of people celebrating the holiday couldn't play music in the park, then when the hell could they?

Cease Fire! Cease Fire!

I had lived in the Byrd Park area for years and had heard music much louder many times that didn't warrant police intervention. The crowd was upset, complaining to the officers that they were simply acting at the behest of White residents living several hundred yards away. I agreed that the music was not a nuisance given the time of day and the holiday that it was. I told the police they could not demand the DJ, who was providing a legal performance for the holiday, turn his music down, and suggested they just move on and assist with other holiday enforcements. The officers knew who I was, as did the crowd, and while they hesitated and sighed with a "just doing my job" demeanor, they knew their job also answered to people on the Council like me. They walked back to their cars and left without pushing the issue.

The brothers and sisters were all smiles and high-fives. Such an inconceivable action: a Black man telling the police to basically shut up and move on. Some of the older partiers came to me and expressed how they could remember when that kind of thing could have gotten them an ass-kicking by the police. They said it was beautiful to see Black power displayed in the little ways that made it more genuine. Many encouraged me: "stay strong," and "we support you, Chuck!" It was always helpful to hear words like that, knowing so many others were praying for my demise. Not the least, many in the Richmond police force.

That same evening, around 10:00 pm, I was headed home from the area of Monroe Park. As I drove by the park on Main Street, I noticed the unremarkable appearance of a police unit at the corner of a street. I glanced as I passed and recognized the officer; he had actually been a member of the mounted (on horseback) units. When I looked in my rear-view mirror, I saw him pull out behind me—the usual. I was getting so aggravated at this bullshit. I thought, *I'm staying clean, going to meetings, trying hard to advocate for others and promoting education, and I got to deal with* this shit *day-in and day-out.* He caught up with me and followed closely; not unsafely, but right on my tail. I made a decision. "Okay, you want to play this bullshit! Let's go! Fuck it! Let the games begin!" I said aloud.

I slid down and over in the seat just a little and let the car drift ever slightly within the lane, then back, then again. I knew if I stayed within the lane, there should be no violation, and knowing I had not had anything to drink, I thought I'd see how he'd respond. Boom! Here came the lights!

It was a dark stretch of street, lights only at some corners. I wasn't going to let him stop me in the dark without people around, so I kept going. I passed Plum Street, then Vine. He hit his siren for one second, but I continued up West Main. I knew I couldn't absolutely ignore him, but it was just another two blocks until I would be able to cut through a parking lot and stop in the BP gas station near Meadow Street, which I knew was well lit. We all hit the service station at once: units sped in from the front, back, and sides. He had called backup as if I had run over someone and was fleeing. I rolled down my window and expected to see the officer come up. Instead, "Get out of your vehicle, Mr. Richardson," screeched from his speaker. I opened my door and stood up, staying in place behind it. A half-dozen people had started to watch, and others slowly came out of the convenience store.

The two additional officers practically sprinted at me. "What's going on? I didn't do anything wrong. I was simply coming to a well-lit area." One of them looked in my car, a big dude who seemed to be Middle Eastern, tried to open my passenger door but it was locked.

He said, "There's something in the seat." I had a small vial of cologne laying on the front seat, the kind you would get as a sampler. But *his* eyes saw something else and he hustled around the car. That clown decided he was going in right past me…bullshit!

I blocked him and said, "Hell no! You ain't got no right to go in my car! What the hell is this?!"

He laughed under his breath and pushed me again. Bam! I punched his ass square in the jaw and nose, which drew blood. Both cops grabbed me, and we scuffled. I was kicking and cursing for a second. "Mr. Richardson! …Mr. Richardson!" came from the cop that had tried to pull me initially. I was smart enough to stop resisting. I just hadn't expected they would get physical with me in the light.

And with the crowd of Black folks slowly moving in around us, an escalation was the last thing necessary.

The three cops were all over me, twisting and pulling at me with vengeance as they handcuffed me. The onlookers were mostly silent, a surreal separation from the festivities at Byrd Park earlier. The big officer wiped at his nose to see if it was still bleeding, then leaned into my car and grabbed the small vial in the front seat. "Let's see what we have here…" He grabbed it and put it in a bag.

"It's fucking cologne, Gucci cologne. Damn, y'all have no right to enter my car!" I exclaimed. I was put in the car with the officer I had hit, and we headed downtown. They were excited about the possibility this would bring me down; I could read it on their faces. But on the ride downtown, handcuffed, I spoke lucidly and logically to the officer, explaining why his actions were wrong, and how I was straight, under the influence of nothing but truth and anger! I could tell he was realizing this was going to be problematic.

Back at the station, as I knew I would, I cleared the breathalyzer test. I remember the ease I felt when I saw, and they saw, zero-zero-zero. But they said I would be charged with assault on an officer. I argued that I have a right to resist if I believed there is an unlawful search or arrest, and the officer engaged me first! They ignored me, consulted with others, and described to them what happened. "Plenty of people saw what happened, which is exactly why I wanted to reach an area of light and activity," I told them.

They prepared to release me and said there would be a hearing scheduled, as if I didn't know. "Wait, wait, no, uh! I want a blood test done," I insisted. "It will be in the paper and on TV, and even though I was not drinking, because I swerved a little driving and had that little scuffle, everybody will believe I must have relapsed. Isn't that convenient? No, take me down to MCV [Medical College of Virginia]. I want a test."

The two officers looked at each other, wondering what to do, asking themselves if could I demand this. One went upstairs to their supervisor to check. I was left sitting on a long bench that ran along the set of lockers officers used for personal belongs. It took about ten minutes, a not so simple question: policy-wise or politically. The officer returned, looking as if he had been disciplined by a parent; he sighed and told his partner, "We gotta take him."

I knew I was clean. While I had been for many months, I knew I had to eliminate the suspicion and accusations that would explode throughout Richmond. I gave the officers a smirky, I-told-you-so look.

Amused at their wimpy discontent, I figured I'd fuck with them a little. "You know you have to read me my Miranda Rights again." Another puzzled look was shared. "That's right! This is a separate charge, and you have to read them to me, again." Those fools looked at each other like a couple of kids about to blame each other for losing the keys. "Let's go! Let's do it and get outta here," I said.

To be honest, at the time, I didn't know if that was the case or not. I doubted it, but I just wanted to see them look stupid simply questioning it. They walked over to another cop and asked him; he shrugged his shoulders. One of them came over and sat next to me; "You have the right to remain silent, anything you say…" A big grin was rising from my belly, but I didn't give it away. Ten minutes later, we were at MCV. The fact that I was a councilman carried weight unavailable to countless men who had been in my situation: driving while Black. But driving while Chuck was another level, and I was tired of it by that night. That whole year I was often front-page news, and much to the chagrin of those attacking me, I prevailed. But it rendered such unnecessary aggression and harassment by law enforcement.

One month. One month. Yes, one month is how long it took for the results of my test to come back from the state lab. What were they looking for, Bubonic plague traces, kryptonite? Or a way to say there was something in the nothing they found? It was a month when everybody prognosticated, rumored, wagered, and hoped for one result or the other. The media, once again, gleefully anticipated what hadn't been successful twice in less than a year. Even some of the voices in the Black community, people who had once supported me, expected guilt, and began the subtle, and not so subtle, conversations about the unredeemable sinner. And through each week, I was the only one who knew that nothing from nothing leaves nothing. When the results came back, Black people high-fived and shook their heads in amazement—and appreciation. Of course others, it seemed, needed a drink.

There was still a bridge to cross; another trial for the charge of assaulting an officer. Several judges recused themselves and they had to bring in a judge from Falls Church, Virginia. Finally, seven jurors, all women, four White and three Black, found me "not guilty." The judge, however, told me that I "struck an officer of the law," and he could not allow me to leave without some amends. He decided that while I had not been convicted of an offense, I needed to pay a debt, and required I complete twenty-five hours of community service.

I said to the judge, "Your Honor, I have spent the last ten years in public service…as a Richmond City Councilman. But thank you, Your Honor."

Despite the court's ruling, the police bureau continued to pursue me as though I was still using drugs! I was speaking out against drugs at schools, youth groups, community organizations, and churches. I was leading marches and parades against drug and alcohol. I had become "Mr. Anti-Drug Use" in Central Virginia, but the Richmond Police wanted me to relapse and became obsessed with the idea. The surreal aspect is I did not deserve it after successful treatment. But truth is too often lost in an easy narrative.

For a couple of years, I remained a target simply because they wanted me to be a target. The police utilized tax dollars for months, 24-7, in efforts to influence my relapse. Not to catch me using, because I was clean, working a 12-step program, and going to meetings successfully, but to get that charge of distribution. They were using tax dollars to encourage drug use and cause a relapse! Not to stop the illicit use, but to encourage it. I remained clean and sober despite the police efforts. They would get close friends of mine to offer me drugs, but I refused. They had the help of people I trusted along with the State Police and Henrico County cops and I still said no!

What hurt me most of all, though, were those police personnel who professed to admire and respect people who have served their country. They were chasing me, a decorated Vietnam veteran, an honorably discharged Marine, who had been introduced to the evils of heroin through no careless character of his own but while in service to his country as he partook to endure the unspoken horrors of war. Horrors that many of them could not begin to imagine! It is the truth and should at least be considered in the context of any criticism.

If you have a friend, loved one, or family member whom you suspect might have an abuse problem; if you're tired of hearing them lie, had enough of the deceit, taking money from family members, making excuses that everybody knows are lies, tired of the smell on their body and breath; if they're not that vibrant, loving person you used to know; and if you want to see that person again, go to them and take them into your embrace. Tell them you love them and ask them if you can help them to get back home with you again. You can do this by yourself or you can have many people that love them with you. It's called an intervention, and it works.

Raw, Honest, and In Front of Hurting People

Since I had been a prominent city councilman for over ten years when I was arrested and brought to trial, the news coverage was phenomenal, consuming virtually all daily television, radio and print media relentlessly for some four months. This was ultra-conservative Richmond, Virginia, and an elected official caught in the grips of drug addiction, and yet, getting re-elected was a bomb-shell storyline. Since my recovery was so public, I was perceived as somewhat of an expert in it. People from all over Richmond would call me about their friend, loved one, brother or son, and it could be overwhelming. I would often speak at drug centers, but of the hundreds of desperate and despondent people I encountered, it's impossible to tell how many were actually helped. My first recovery effort lasted over well over five years, and I'm not certain, but part of my relapse was assuming the monumental task of thinking I could help heal people. *That* was an ego trip that only led to an illusion—and my own relapse.

Suffice to say, as I was being asked to speak everywhere, it was a shock to many, Black and White, to see me in person. The perception of a drug addict had been painted to look like a skid-row, down-and-out, dirty-clothes-wearing, unshaven, gutter monger. Many had seen me over the years on television but probably still thought they could discern that drug addict within. To witness this good-looking, immaculately-dressed, well-spoken person was not what many would have ever imagined. For good or bad, it shattered their perception of what they imagined a drug addict would be like, as it should. However, children saw me as just me: a friendly adult telling them about difficult things they should know about some grown-ups and even some teens. They were too young and had no preconceived notions. They just looked to me for whatever good I could do for them.

During one of the many anti-drug talks I gave, I was caught by surprise with a question from a young student at West Hampton Elementary. Ann Jenkins, the principal at West Hampton, had invited me to speak with a class of third graders. Now, you cannot take for granted that because of a groups' age they will be easy to talk with. Indeed, because of their age, kids are honest, straightforward, and unassuming, and the questions they ask can sometimes be devastating. I adjusted my speech from my usual expressive politician vernacular and kept it at a very fundamental level. I tried to exchange information in a way that maintained their interest without making it too convoluted, causing the boredom seven- and eight-year-olds despise. They were unaware of my history as a city leader until that very morning. To them, I was just another adult who was teaching, as it were.

When I had completed my talk, bland and uneventful as it was, I must have convinced them that I had some answers to the problems of drug and alcohol use. They asked questions which were typical, and some that were related to drugs and alcohol as it affected their world. It was fairly light and generic mostly, and I believed I was doing well with this group of third graders. When one little White kid stood up to ask his question, however, I was totally unprepared. He was all of seven, stood up, and looked directly into my eyes with real expectation of finally getting an answer to a problem that he had long suffered, and sadly asked, "Can you come to my house and help my father stop drinking? He hurts us."

I was beyond stunned. My mind raced about what he was saying and what he must have been feeling. I could not move and didn't know what to say as my eye wells filled. I looked over to Principal Jenkins. Though I was in the midst of a reflexive need to run to this boy and hold him in my weeping heart, I caught myself, but was thinking, *Help him! Help him!* So, I quietly recomposed myself, softly approached him, looked down in his eyes, and said, "Yes, yes, you bet we can help you. Mrs. Jenkins and all of us are going to try and help."

The whole young class was still, not one fidget; they were just staring at him and me. I was no good for the rest of that morning, occasionally holding the tears as I remembered his face, his fear, and his courage to ask for help for his dad. I don't know what the principal was able to do for that little boy, or his family, because it gets so delicate of a legal matter and there is only so far the schools can go. I know there are thousands of heartbroken children that cry themselves to sleep each night because of what drugs and alcohol can drive people to do. I knew on that day, though, this boy had driven me to do something for him. That's the worst part of chemical abuse; the children it hurts so deeply!

People are their own best healers if they find a place in themselves to believe it. They are certainly their own destroyers as well. So, I saw him; there he stood, sad-eyed, blonde-headed, the picture of innocence, a precious child who did nothing to earn the misery of his question: "Can you help my father stop drinking, he hurts us." All I could see were visions of this little boy ducking his father's fist as it zoomed passed little him and hit his mother. I could picture the frightened look of bewilderment while his drunk father slurred his words cursing his mother. But most of all, I could picture the little boy, no more than seven, brave enough to stand in front of the whole class and ask for help. It was such unearned suffering, desperate and so innocent. *Help him, he needs hope now, give him hope,* I thought when I broke from my silence and spoke ... "Yes, yes, you bet we can help you..." I was so moved by this little boy that I couldn't forget his dilemma.

Two days later, I followed up with the school to locate the boy's home and father. I was really reluctant, as there were so many risks and complications, but I had to; he wouldn't leave my thoughts. I found the home and sat for a moment before going to the door, thinking "what if's." It was a mild, pleasant late spring day in Richmond, and I thought about the pretense I would use to visit the home of a third grader. They had a well-kept home, yard, and side garage. While I walked to the house, I hoped I could get a sense, at least, of the conditions the family lived under.

His father met me on the front porch, looking like nothing I envisioned him to be: a soft-spoken, polite, and small-framed man. He recognized me but couldn't figure out why I would visit his home of all people. I told him I thought he knew why I was there. He said no, he did not. Why should he have known? I was totally perplexed and didn't know whether I should tell him the truth about what his son had said in school about his drinking.

I started out by talking about me and my drug problem, which he already knew about through the news. I confessed to him several of the ugly things I had done while an active addict, and how badly my wife and children had suffered because of my illness, that I regretted so much not seeking help sooner. I did not say anything at that point about his son, trying to feel the right moment. He was not a big man, so I wasn't concerned he might physically confront me if he got mad about learning what his son had said in class. After sharing more of the things I had done, and my remorse, he softened and said to me, "I know why you're telling me all of these things. You know that I drink and get out of control at times, don't you?"

I said, "No, I don't know what the problem is. I only know that I spoke to your son's class in school the other day and it was the first time a seven-year-old made me cry."

His head fell slowly, and he looked down for a moment, then looked back up and down the street, his eyes belying the pleasant breeze in his face. "What did he say?" he asked.

"He had the raw courage to ask me—in front of the whole class—to help you stop drinking because you hurt them when you drink ... but it's not your fault, it's the alcohol's fault!"

This father didn't know what to say to me and looked away again. He slumped a bit as if he remembered a great weight on his shoulders and started to slowly slide down to sit on the stoop. I put my hand on his shoulder and said, "Hey, man! Do you know how much he loves you to defend you in the face of your drinking and all the pain he's seen?" He began to cry and turned his head to the sky, blinking uncontrollably. I said, "Man, you're almost as bad as I used to be." He was crying, but he laughed. Sitting on his porch stoop, he sighed through his slow tears.

I told him, "It's hard to stop drinking on your own, but if you really want to make that great little boy in your house smile again, I can give you some names of people who can help you." He broke a weak smile and looked back down. I hardly knew this man, had just met him. He had a drinking problem but was a human being, and that makes him the same as thousands who suffer addiction; hurt, needing help and not knowing what to do about it. So they sit down and cry with just about anybody who's willing to listen to them and offer a bit of hope...and maybe some help. I could sense a bit of hostility rising in him when I first disclosed to him what his son had said in school, but it quickly dissolved when he considered the despicable, ugly truths about myself I offered to him. Successful communications are predicated on individual relationships based in raw honesty. He recognized that I would bare my nakedness and it freed him to trust me, and do so likewise.

I told him about a program at Rubicon Treatment Center and that

I could put him in touch with folks there. He nodded yes. We spoke for a little while longer about the power of addiction and also about the power to overcome it. When I left, I could only hope he would get the help I advised. A short time later, the friends at Rubicon let me know he had come in and asked that they let me know. I can't be sure if he ultimately achieved sobriety, but for the sake of him and his family, I hope so. I think about that brave little kid occasionally. He's probably about forty now, and I hope he is well. Honesty is contagious, especially when it is raw, painful, and in front of other hurting people, or even third graders.

CHAPTER 11

Who Was I Fooling

City Council was still my job. As busy as I was helping with substance abuse, I still had the responsibilities of representing the Fifth District. And there were still times that we, too, Council members and citizens as well, acted like third graders. The cost of ignorance and the fear of change was exemplified on an October evening in 1989 when Manny Deese, Richmond's City Manager, introduced the idea of a new method of refuge collection called "the super can."

The super can was a large, heavy-duty, green container that rolled on wheels and was designed to be conveniently raised and emptied into compaction haulers. From the outset, 95% of the citizens were totally opposed to giving up their traditional trash cans that had been used since public refuse collection began. Although there were a few obvious advantages to inaugurate this new can, people were simply averse to change and unaccustomed to anything different. Even the City Council members were reluctant to the change, though primarily that was because an overwhelming majority of the citizens opposed it.

Mr. Deese lobbied strenuously to get the Council to accept this new proposal. When Bob Sarver, Director of Department of Public Works, and his assistant, Irving Bey, came to a Fifth District community meeting to present and explain the proposal to some citizens, the residents practically threw the two gentlemen out of the room without a word. Mrs. Bessie Jones, a Ward leader and community advocate, maintained total confidence of the people. Fortunately for me, she was one of my strongest supporters. With the two men waiting in the large hallway in the former school building, she asked me to explain the proposal to the citizens. Considering the cold reception they had been given, Mr. Sarver and Mr. Bey had planned to leave, but I asked them to wait briefly in the hallway.

I told Mrs. Jones that none of us knew enough about the proposal to make an intelligent decision. I went on to explain that I would request the City Manager to implement the super can on a trial basis. If the results were good, we would go city-wide; if not, we'd abandon the proposal. At any rate, our district would get the credit. Also it would help us get other requests approved from the City Manager in the future, and that he would appreciate Bessie's leadership on this matter. Bessie Jones was an astute political observer and realized immediately what I was saying to her. I recall telling the crowd that people in the City knew who Bessie was, and respected the relationship and knowledge of the district because of her.

They all looked to Bessie, and I told her it was a win-win move! She agreed and I explained to the crowd that a number of R-CAP proposals were up for funding. By the time I was ready to invite the two men back into the classroom, the setting was packed with pleasantly smiling, cordial faces, poised to vote on the matter. When Sarver and Bey returned gingerly back into the room, Mrs. Jones thanked the men for coming to the Fifth District, and she proceeded to call for a vote on the issue without me having to utter a word. Bessie said, "All in favor?"

"Aye!"

"Opposed?"

Silence.

"None, next order of business!"

I escorted the gentlemen from Public Works outside the room, closed the large, heavy wooden door quietly behind the three of us, and walked with them down the long hallway to the outside. Irving Bey was an old buddy and outstanding athlete at VUU with whom

I ran track. He was giggling with an ear-to-ear grin, trying to restrain his laughter. His boss, Mr. Sarver, asked me, "Mr. Richardson, what in the world just happen?"

Cracking a smile at him, I said, "It's a Black thing, Bob, a Black thing!"

Irving broke into a loud laugh and could not stop laughing all the way to his car.

For the upcoming budget session, I introduced a budget amendment for $90,000 to be added for a trial program; it passed nine to zero. The Super Can Proposal was a booming success and the citizens never looked back.

I had not mentioned in the midst those meetings was my conversation with my brother-in-law, Maynard Jackson, then Mayor of Atlanta, to inquire about the super can. They had already had the program in operation in Atlanta for two or three years. Their cans were known as a "Herbie-Curbie." Everybody there opposed it initially, but everyone ended up loving it. That bit of information shared with me from Maynard allowed me to go forth with the knowledge and confidence that, for Bessie Jones and me, it would be a win-win proposition some thirty years ago.

Drawing the Line

Self-respect and dignity are delicate personal qualities to be maintained and protected in life, and particularly in public office. When they are real, people can sense these characteristics, and yet false pride is a worthless quality which often detracts from the individual. I was always willing to take a risk in being the target of laughter and, at times, ridicule. Of course, the circumstance had to be properly arranged and a line drawn.

I had been very successful at improving the area in Richmond known as Carytown, a business district on Cary Street at the western end of the Fifth District. I had won the approval of sidewalk dining, police foot patrols, curb cuts for the disabled, and additional lights, among other successes. These things made Carytown a very popular place in Richmond, drawing new unique businesses, restaurants and entertainment making a pleasant walking experience as well as attracting grocery stores for residents in the area.

The most impactful addition was a large, two-story, free-parking garage. It was a $900,000 project that I worked through the Richmond Metropolitan Authority (RMA). I was always challenging the answers most Council members accepted, pushing harder, and drawing out the "hard-nosed" Marine in me.

All types of events were held in Carytown to raise money, have fun, and promote community spirit. Each year, Carytown merchants held the great "Watermelon Festival," and the tradition continues today. Jay Rostow was the president of the Carytown Association at that time and we maintained a good friendship with mutual interest in the success of Carytown, as well as the success of the annual festival.

Jay approached me in 1990 and respectfully inquired, very nervously, if I would consider being the subject in a "dunking booth" in the Watermelon Festival that year. People would pay money to throw balls at a target that, if struck properly, would result in me falling into a large container of water.

I do not believe that he had any other ulterior motives beyond fun and raising money. However, it is worth mentioning that this was during a period shortly following my second trial where I was found innocent. While the Black community celebrated in this judicial victory, a greater number of White citizens were appalled at the verdict and vented their resentment and opposition to my continued services as a city councilman. Taking all these factors into consideration, I did not want to flatly reject Jay's offer, but I was well aware of the potential fallout (no pun intended) of my being the target of dunking. Both politically and physically, I faced a risk in such a festive environment with drinking and partying, where so many people of different backgrounds had come together. I seldom feared being embarrassed or being the butt of a joke. Any man who cannot laugh at himself misses some of the greatest laughter in life! However, a line must be drawn and done so with tact and diplomacy. I told Jay Rostow that I would always be willing to sacrifice my own humiliation if the cause was significant and the benefit, financial and otherwise, was great enough. So, I stipulated that the decision would be his, provided they would agree to the cause of my choice and that the fee for each ball thrown would be set by me.

Many of the merchants were totally thrilled and excited. They envisioned a large booth, filled with a six-foot tank of water and the esteemed Councill man sitting atop the plank, wearing a suit and tie, ready to be doused by some racist redneck cracker from Powhatan County. It would be an event covered by every media outlet in the Richmond region. The coordinators were anxious to announce the new event. Everyone was aware of my good-natured sense of humor and willingness to enjoy the fun and attention of a good laugh. What they did not know, however, is that even Councilman Richardson drew a line in the sand when it came to self-respect and dignity.

I was fully aware of the kind of persons anxious to symbolically dunk Black Richmond into a pool of humiliation! The genuine resentment, hate, and anger people had expressed to me in thousands of letters and post cards with cruel, despicable epitaphs, certainly kept me cognizant of that. To those innocents like Jay and some of his friends, it may have been all fun and games. However, too many others felt deeply about my political agenda.

The side of the coin that Jay and others had not considered were the number of Black citizens who held me in high regard and would have been deeply embarrassed to see me made a fool, even if it were for fun! I say this at the sufferance of my modesty, but as the author of many pieces of legislation benefiting Black citizens, the exploitation of such an image and reaction to it was serious business. As the author serious pieces of legislation such as the MLK Holiday Bill, a major thirty percent minority set-aside program awarded through *City of Richmond v. J.A. Croson Co.*, and the City of Richmond's Tax Relief for the Elderly and the Disabled program, and the main proponent of the Arthur Ashe statue on Monument Avenue, people important to me would not have understood this act of sheer folly carried out, and celebrated, primarily by White detractors of Black progress. Five days later, in a private meeting between Jay and me, I told him that the proceeds of this booth event would all go to the NAACP, every dime, and that the cost of each ball thrown would be $50.

Without a great discourse between the two us, Jay politely withdrew his offer, and it was never mentioned again. I was somewhat baffled; I thought my stipulations were more than reasonable—to have received such a valuable prize at such a small cost, especially, if one of those White boys could pitch. Ultimately, he refused an offer I could not accept.

Another part of that dignity I tried to hold close was staying clean and dealing with post-traumatic stress disorder (PTSD). I was

Speaking in front of the U.S. Supreme Court fighting for minority participation in city government contracts.

continuing to visit schools and businesses to talk about abuse and recovery as well as keeping focus on my duties as a councilman. The job of any recovering addict is 24-7, regardless of any other duties or distractions, and I fought every day to keep that job. Keeping your thoughts in places stronger than memories or desire is a job mostly for the mind. The memories of the horror in Vietnam, and the desire that was sometimes faint, other times deep, but always there, to feel the heroin. When that desire became difficult to suppress, I would try to remember the horror of withdrawal. Staying busy was important for the control of those things, but the body needed distraction as well.

Many years ago, in the early '70s, I learned the game of golf, and I became a damn good player, too. Golf is an amazing sport; it requires the mental and physical busyness that helped me. I played much more by the late '80s and early '90s to alleviate the stress of fighting my internal enemies. If you have never played golf, you have missed one of the greatest microcosmic versions of life: triumphs, mysteries, profound disappointment, and unpredictable outcomes. Whether it is a chunked chip, unexpected slice, or a lip-out putt, it evokes the very worse and very best that life might produce. A perfectly struck ball represents the essence of perfection, a physical and mental alchemy that is hard to describe. The art of the golf swing is the meshing of the most impossible the mind can comprehend with the greatest the body can execute, and to do it again, and again, and again. It is an experience those who've never felt it could possibly understand, and those who have, could never forget.

You might wonder, how could a man who competed with the FBI, fought in combat against the Viet Cong, challenged the devils of local politics, and survived the terrorization of prison thugs be overwhelmed by a little white ball? I can only conclude that one involved the demons of the outside forces against you, and the other involved fighting the demons within. Instinct, habit, logic, and how you wish things to be are the inner demons, and they go against every rule required to strike a golf ball properly.

When the body executes the perfect strike of the ball, meeting the

Cease Fire! Cease Fire!

sweet spot of the club face, it does not matter who else might witness the act. Only you need to feel the momentary attachment of the ball to the club head, the pure swish of air against the shaft of the club, and the explosive crack of the ball's compression heard only when the club head hits exactly square against the ball at the highest speed of the swing.

The human experience consists of two fundamental components: the mental and the physical. Golf is the only experience where the two must be perfectly aligned to achieve the intended results. For the golf swing to achieve success, the mind must train the muscle to intuitively perform at a speed too high to make any conscious adjustments. At ninety to 100 mph, if the club-head is off-center or not perfectly square, no adjustments are possible once the swing has begun. That's why you will see professional golfers practicing hours on end repeatedly hitting ball after ball. They are "grooving" their swing: doing the same thing over and over again until the perfect swing is automatic and the muscles' actions become the subconscious equivalence of breathing, digestion, or your heartbeat.

Perfection in a golf swing is, for the most part, on accident. The margin of error is so infinitesimally small that it is not a conscious phenomenon. That's why there are so many professionals like Tiger Woods, Phil Michelson, Gary Player, and maybe 200 others who are pros, but no single player always wins. In every other sport, there are variables to a certain extent. In golf, two men of equal skill and ability cannot do anything about the way the ball bounces, or when the wind will come up, or how long and hard it might blow, or in which direction. Still, you are the only participant to blame or credit. In fact, all the other players as well as the spectators are expected to remain quiet, allowing you the full benefit of individual concentration. When all is said and done, it can be so painfully unfair, and conversely, a great stroke of luck. Again, a microcosmic parallel to life is that no matter how good one might become, how the ball will bounce, or the wind will blow, there is always an unrelenting unknown.

Is it fair or unfair? Who's to say? These are the parables that make golf so much like life. So, the game was something I tried to play as often as possible, not only for its ability to consume several hours of enjoyable distraction, but the therapy it provided to help keep a healthy perspective and confidence as the ball of life bounces—win or lose.

One Saturday after a round of golf, I was driving down Cary Street in my dad's old 1966 Rambler he loaned me. Old and slow, it was still dependable after twenty-five years but would hesitate at times. Within just a few moments, I saw an intense fight on the sidewalk between a man and woman. The glass window of the shop next to them was broken and I could see blood on the man. I pulled over immediately and tried to separate them as a small crowd gathered, seemingly wanting to just watch the fight and not intervene. It was obvious that the two had been drinking heavily and my efforts to separate them was not what I pictured when I pulled over. Within a few seconds, I had blood on me, and my white golf shirt and pants were catching the slings of that drunken tussle. I continued to yell at both and pushed them apart as a few more people stood and watched their councilman literally try to resolve a problem in his district.

As the couple separated but continued to yell and reach for each other, I noticed a Richmond Police unit coming down Cary and I felt the situation was about to be controlled. I looked at the officer—and he saw me—as he slowly drove by and turned onto Vine Street a short distance away. I assumed he didn't want to block traffic on Cary, so he was pulling to the side street where he was going to stop. He did, for a second, and then continued down Vine. I was shocked and could hear some in the crowd in disbelief as well. I managed to get the help of others to keep that couple separated and to call an ambulance if necessary. Then I immediately jumped back in my car to go after the policeman. Talk about "Car 54, where are you?!"

As I drove up Vine Street I slowed at each intersection to look both ways, trying to spot him. I was slow to pull away as well, as that old Rambler sputtered and smoked a little when I hit the gas hard as I was trying to catch up. I was cursing to a point—I don't know if it was more at the cop or the car. It was like Zorro trying to ride a donkey. I saw him one block later and sped, intermittently, after him, blowing my horn and flashing my lights. He continued but eventually pulled over at Allen Street. I had basically chased down and pulled a cop.

As I got out and quickly walked to his door, he rolled his window down. I started cursing him and asked what the fuck was he thinking; he saw the crowd and the scuffling, the broken window. He's got a badge and a gun—and he saw me! He sat at his window looking, in a way, half-sad, and then slowly got out. He was a White officer, a bit older, maybe fiftyish and wore eyeglasses that looked heavy on his face. He was calm as we walked to the back of the car and leaned against it, and then he began to apologize and explain. He was a nice officer and looked me sincerely in the eye.

"Look, Mr. Richardson, let me explain. I saw you there...and well, frankly, thought it best I not stop. It's not that I believed you or anyone were in any danger. I saw the couple had been separated and you in the middle, and I knew you were a greater calming presence than I would have been in that situation. When I turned the corner and looked in the mirror, it was clear to me you had it under control. You have a great deal of respect in this district and I simply believed it was handled better, in this instance, if I went on. If I had approached, it very easily might have sparked something unnecessary."

I might have thought, as with many officers, *this guy is bullshitting me,* but I could read a calm sincerity through his dense eyewear. We actually sat down on the curb and talked for a while. I remember some of it was about Magic Johnson and Larry Bird; imagine that! Afterwards, I thought about it, and he was right. I did have it under control; the couple had been separated and nobody had been hurt, just a minor, but bloody, cut from glass. I had reacted from a reference of animosity toward police, in general—with good reason—and overreacted to him leaving. It was a part of that compulsive nature in me. Just as I had stopped to break up the fight, I had also sped off after him.

I took away a couple of things from that experience with the officer: I was seen, even by some police, as a type of hero among most Blacks, politically if not physically. In the context of a need to influence and soothe friction between Blacks, I had an advantage over most police. Second, there are some discerning, well-motivated cops; not all are like many I had encountered the previous decade or so, those whose judgment did not carry justice, much less my best interest in mind. And third, and more importantly, I knew I had better find out how to get blood stains out from my only good golf apparel!

In June of 1994, when five incumbent members of the Richmond City Council were swept out of office, I was the only member remaining with sufficient experience, institutional knowledge, and a relationship with Corporate Richmond to lead the City with any degree of confidence. We were on a precipice of competing forces, where different individuals vied for influence behind the scenes. Bernice Travers, Neverett Eggleston, Bessie Jones, and a number of other neighborhood leaders worked together with the Richmond Crusade for Voters to energize the voting ranks. Doug Wilder, Louis Salomonsky, T. Justin Moore, III, and Clarence Townes had the ear of Black grass-roots organizations, despite our periodic differences.

Bernice and Neverett wanted me to be mayor, and Clarence had convinced the corporate boys that there was no other choice. They had T-shirts printed up: "It's Chuck's Time! Chuck for Mayor!" The others were newcomers and staunch adversaries. And the growing expectation among each of them was to nominate my name in July. What a few suspected strongly, but no one knew for certain, was that I had returned to drug use.

As I had returned to a full-blown addiction to heroin, I could not, would not, possibly attempt to commit myself to a self-destructive suicide mission of attempting to fulfill the task of Mayor: getting up every morning, going to early breakfast meetings, making speeches, being neat and clean all the time. I could not risk the disappointment of accepting something I realized would end in disaster and embarrassment for many. I had placed my family, friends, loved ones, political supporters and the City in the untenable circumstances of coming to rely upon someone who, himself, had to acknowledge his

The final campaign poster of my era.

own unreliability. It was a rare and awesome sense of helplessness and humiliation. But I had to acknowledge the reality of my circumstances since it would have been a virtual impossibility to go through withdrawal on my own and get clean by July.

And yet, with all that, the votes were there to make me mayor. I knew I couldn't let it happen and had to tell those I trusted. Louis,

Doug Wilder and a few others, to my surprise, must have discussed the situation because they all were aware of my relapse and suggested professional in-patient treatment. Doug Wilder was quite disappointed with me during this time. A few of his close friends and political allies still believed in my capabilities and loyalties, however, and were willing to take a risk helping me. However, any public word of my return to drug use would have destroyed any consideration of being elected. I don't know who persuaded whom, or who paid what, or who might have been against it, but two days later a check was cut for a plane ticket for me to Los Angeles, California.

I entered a hospital for a treatment "unknown" but paid for in full. When I asked about the source of the money, I was told it was from a "rainy day fund": all done by somebody who cared enough, believing I was the best option for mayor at the time. I entered the facility under the name of "Charles 'Chuck' Tanner" and cannot recall more depressing, dark, lonely, agonizing days and nights than those two weeks in June. I remember the bizarre view one evening, standing with many at a fence looking over the L.A. expressway where a string of police cars followed a white Ford Bronco ever so slowly: O.J. Simpson on his journey to nowhere. None of us realized it was O.J. we were watching though, and only learned about it on the news later. My withdrawal was horrific, including three nights of excruciating pain, nightmares, hallucinations, and depression.

I missed my daughter's high school graduation, inexplicably to most. It reminds me of how much our families and loved ones suffer from the results of our behavior as alcoholics and addicts. Drug addiction is complicated and difficult for people to understand. Sometimes people give up on you too soon. It is impossible to know when the treatment will take, but no matter how many other people give up on you, if you don't give up on yourself there's a fighting chance!

To those I will not name with certainty, you know who you are, who took the time to care, who had the "rainy day fund": never think for a minute that my gratitude and indebtedness is taken for granted, all done secretly in order that I be made well enough to become the

Mayor of Richmond. I only regret that I was unable to prove my worth in that instance.

When I returned, I was too late to be viable, and Leonidas B. Young, II, would become Mayor of Richmond. Immediately I returned to the work I knew, and like a fish after bait, I returned to the drug I knew—heroin! There was no excuse—NO excuse! But when you are using, it doesn't matter; the world seems fine. Joel W. Harris, Mayor Young's chief assistant, asked if I could help with committee assignments and other advice for the new councilmembers. Given I was fully experienced with the institutional machinations of the City Hall, it was reasonable that I was needed. He asked me to meet everyone at the Mayor's office one morning to brainstorm with him and the others.

It was a warm morning when I went to the City Hall and I felt the comfort of power, the knowledge that I was indispensable. I walked to the Mayor's office and was directed straight in. It was quite the surprise: standing there was the Mayor; Clarence Townes; City Manager Robert Bobb; my attorney, Michael Morchower; Phyllis; my mother; my dad; and other important people in my life. It was an intervention. I didn't resist; I just dropped my head. Those of us in a position to exercise the love and compassion for someone suffering from the infirmity of addiction or alcoholism should do so without compunction or remorse. They did it for me, and I had to show resolve, honest resolve, to beat the addiction.

I held a press conference at the City Hall, telling everyone I would make a statement but would not take questions. I stated that I was dealing with a journey that I had first encountered many years ago and it now needed to be attended again, but I would not talk about the nature of the journey, and I would be out of touch for a few weeks. Despite the burst of questions, fighting my natural urge to respond, I answered none and left the room.

Of course, the wolves would not leave it at that. They scattered all about, heading to the exits to catch my departure whenever I left, to pounce in louder, more intense pursuits of me. Fortunately my friend, Robert Bobb, came to me once they left. He looked at me empathetically, told me to let him know when I was ready to leave, and he'd help me get past the press. About twenty minutes later, Bobb led me through the back of his office to a stairway exit. We practically tip-toed down the stairs, slowing at each floor as we passed the door to listen for voices. It was another version of the game I had played for years: cat and mouse. Playful for the cat, fearful for the mouse. When we made it to the bottom, Bobb peeked out the door to the employee parking deck and then walked out alone to be sure. We quickly walked to his car and then drove out unnoticed.

Bobb drove me directly to the Westbrook Clinic, now Charter Westbrook Behavior Health Systems, Inc., on the northside of town. It was only four or five days after I checked in when it became clear that insurance was going to be an issue. Then, with the City's help, I ultimately checked into the Willow Oaks Residential Treatment Center in Carterville, Virginia. My thirty days there were similar to other treatments I'd been through: tough. At Willow Oaks, however, there was a difference: two people I met there, both addicts, would have a bigger impact on me than I would imagine.

Jim Barrett, a White dude like any White dude, with sharp features around forty-five years old, had had an abuse problem a long time, but he was still trying to kick it. We got along pretty well regarding things not related to politics; he lived somewhere in Henrico County about which I was familiar. The other was Tammy Taylor, a young, very attractive White girl who was new to the rehab ritual. Tammy was maybe twenty-four or twenty-five. As she slowly became clean, it became obvious she was gorgeous. So, I became a better friend with the additional drive of lust pushing me after her.

I was the first to finish the program and headed back to Richmond, agreeing with them to stay in touch when they were out in another week later or so. As I came home and jumped back into work, I felt a refreshed and clean comfort. I was back to dealing, of course, with the crazy press I had dodged with Bobb weeks earlier, giggling to myself about that escape. Later as summer approached, I continued to push for the Arthur Ashe Monument to be placed on Monument Avenue. It was getting push back on both sides, but me being me, I was fine taking on both sides. I had begun the push for at least one monument to a Civil Rights hero on Monument Avenue. In 1991, seeing the Soviet Union collapse and the angry citizens tear down Stalin statues, it got me thinking that Richmond should be a continuum of acknowledgements, not simply a place of glorified Confederate military. A little more than a year later, Arthur Ashe died, and Doug Wilder suggested his monument be added to Monument Avenue. I was determined to see the tribute to him put there.

Meanwhile, I remained in limited touch with Jim and Tammy and gave support to them to stay clean, something we all knew would be an ongoing fight after we left Willow Oaks. Jim relapsed quickly and started shoplifting, recklessly, to make the cash he needed daily. I knew Tammy was at great risk as well—she liked crack, and that shit don't play with anybody! I was smart enough through the years to stay out that game, a fool's gamble akin to playing Russian roulette with only one empty chamber. I did my best to steer her straight but, never having done crack, I could not totally understand or relate to her fight. But the thing that helped was the fact she was so damn beautiful after she got clean. I was determined to help her stay so. She went back to her home, Norfolk, clean and hopeful, and worked to maintain herself and her health.

Ring, ring, ring—an innocent telephone call came in from another constituent in need of assistance and, when I was at home, no one answered the phone but me because if it was a citizen's complaint, and they can be difficult. But it was no ordinary citizen, and it was beyond difficult. It was long distance.

"Chuck, please, Chuck, you gotta come get me!" It was Tammy Taylor in full-blown addiction. She was desperate and had relapsed because of money. "I'm freaking, I'm fucking freaking, Chuck. Can you come and get me?!" She was in shock, paranoid, and out of control, crying desperately and pleading with me to come and get her.

"Tammy, I can't come tonight. I am in the middle of something!"

"Oh shit, Chuck! You gotta save me! I relapsed and was trying to score with these two brothers who beat me and then raped me and took my money! And that goddamn Kevin don't understand shit and let me down. You gotta help me. He don't understand shit. Chuck, please help me!"

"Tammy, I'll come tomorrow, but I can't come tonight," I said.

"Oh shit! I'll die by then!"

"No, you won't. Just hold on! Where will you be?"

"Chuck, I'm freaking out! Save me, I'm freaking out, Chuck, please!!" She was having a panic attack and my head was spinning. She was back on that shit, and if I went after her, it would put my ass in a really dangerous place. I believed I could do it. I could resist the dope, even if I couldn't resist her fine ass—that was the issue.

The next afternoon, I went to my man, Fred Pryor, my best friend and the owner of CMC limousine business for whom Tammy and I had worked . Tammy had worked for him for a while and was a real go-getter. But she had her problems, and he was aware of them. Fred would do anything in the world for me; we were like brothers—even closer. He said, "Tammy is a good girl, smart and reliable…when she is clean."

I said, "Fred, she needs help and I'm going to get her."

His response was, "Chuck, you know how hard of a job it is to save an addict!"

"Fred, I'm clean! I ain't using," I said.

"Yeah…now," he said. I asked Fred for $200 and a car. He shook his head and sighed like a despondent junkie himself. "Look!" he said. "I'll give you *five* hundred dollars… if you stay!" Fred said it knowing he was not going to be out $500 because he knew I would be out of town: Norfolk. He knew the pull that White girl had on me, that White girls seem to have on most Black men. It is one of those inconvenient subjects that we Black men laugh and jest about towards one another, comically bragging or teasing ourselves about such conquests.

But what is the truth about this dynamic? What is it about the thought of having a White woman that Black men always talk about—only with outrageous laughter and bravado? How much of an influence *do* White women have over us as sexual objects? Never have I heard a group of Black men *seriously* discuss the effects of 250 years of subservience to a desirable object that was forbidden to us beyond any realm of possibility. What was the effect in chaining Black men up like beasts as beautiful White females walked constantly in their presence, and yet forbid their desires as even thoughts? Is it possible that after 250 years, there might have been some genetic repercussions that cannot be scientifically measurable? I doubt it, but still, should I be ashamed of thinking aloud about indulging in what could be actual science, a silly attempt to psychoanalyze the Black man's relationship with "forbidden fruit"? Is it because after 250 years of forbidden fruit it would be a natural reaction to want it? Could it be mere curiosity? Could it be revenge, anger, or perhaps any number of reactions to a trained historical behavioral condition? Is it a notion that we Black men, whether consciously or subconsciously, will have our "pound of flesh," so to say, from a willing, lustful daughter of the Daughters of the South, as a means of visiting the sins of the fathers upon the heads of the sons?

A Black man's desire towards something he has been forbidden to have should be no less understandable than a Black woman's resentment for such a desire. Due to that sensitive nature, we seem absolutely reluctant to discuss it, to unearth any psychological basis for the attitudes, behavior, or ideas of Black men regarding intimacy with White females in America. On the other hand, since we have already expended the latter half of the last century laughing about it, maybe it deserves serious perspective. Whatever the reason, it should be anything *except* shame and embarrassment, and simply a reality. When we acknowledge that it was the extreme constraints, coupled with the temptation and exposure that created controlled conditions of psychological desire with no outlet for release, we can better understand the laughter and irony, the pain and pleasure, and we might, amusingly, consider history an aphrodisiac.

This was no laughing matter for Fred; we both knew, sadly, what I wanted. And Fred knew for certain, if I didn't, the consequences of going after that White woman could be almost as bad as a slave with "masser's" wife! We didn't argue. Fred also knew me well enough to know it was my call, so he gave me the money and a big pretty Cadillac to drive, and an even bigger question to answer: you sure you want this? I headed to Norfolk the next day.

I hit Interstate 64 East to Norfolk with a balance of confidence and fear, with faith in question, thinking: *should I, no, could I do this? Could I get her clean again, could I stay clean with her?* I started to talk to myself as soon as I left the City: "You gotta go back man. Yeah! She's fine but don't go!" Norfolk was about an hour and a half away, and after about thirty minutes, I knew I had to stop and return, telling myself to stop bullshitting, and turn around. I kept seeing her in my mind's eye: *"Please, Chuck, I'm freakin' out. Save me, Chuck, save me!"*

It was 9:08 pm, and I was speeding down Interstate 64 wondering whether Tammy had survived the last twenty-four hours. My mind was racing even faster over my friend's $500 admonition to remain in Richmond. Fred loved me and I realized his instincts were on target. I began an agonizing debate with myself when I crossed over the Martin Luther King Junior Memorial Bridge leaving the City. And when I left Mechanicsville on I-64, I said to myself, "Chuck, this will be a life-changing decision beyond the ordinary." I could keep the course of my life by turning around and going back home, or fuck my life up over a White woman, trying to convince myself she was just another addict like the others I struggled for this month.

I had several exits that turned off that interstate to Richmond. Any one of them would only require a split-second action to exit. The first one was coming up in about one mile. "Are you going to take it? It's Bottoms Bridge in one-half mile and you can get off, turn left, go less than a quarter of a mile and go right back to Richmond," I told myself.

But it came up too quickly, and I chose too slowly. *Well*, I thought, *I still have Croakers, Talleysville, Barhamsville, Norge, Toano, and West Point to turn around—plenty of opportunity to beat some sense into myself.* I just zoomed past Barhamsville without even a consideration. I became tense, though, arguing out loud with myself:

Am I thinking properly or bullshitting myself? Is this about saving another addict or that age-old story about the Black man with the White woman? Come on Chuck, get your shit together! Look! Don't run that bullshit down on me about White women—I'm Black! I know who I am! I have had all the kinds of colors, types, and beauties that ever existed so I'm not running to Norfolk after no pussy. Let's get that shit straight; not Black, White, green, or orange, this is a drug addict in trouble! Yeah, punk, but what if she was not gorgeous and what if you were not in a position to possibly have sex with her? Would your enthusiastic commitment to rescue her from this dreaded addiction have your foot on the accelerator at eighty—passing the exit signs so fast not even considering what a relapse might do to your future? Slow this vehicle down, my brother! Look at this thing realistically, Chuck! Can I get Tammy into treatment without risking my own return to drug use? And, moreover, am I really doing this to help another addict or is sexual attraction more of a motivating factor than I am willing to admit?

I began to ease up on the gas as the two-headed debate began to take hold in my mind. I tried to gain the calm, balanced, rational tone of the atmosphere in the plush new Cadillac Fred had provided me. The velvet interior, the quiet ambience of George Benson's "Nature Boy" playing in the background with Gucci cologne permeating the air, as I sat in high-fashion clothing, enjoying pleasantries as a result of a clean way of living, drug-free. It was an appearance belying the impoverished state of my discipline and focus. A life not encumbered by the weight of illegal substances, all of which this trip would be risking. So, my mind, like the car's speed, shuttled back to a reasonable pace. And still, exits were passed to the cuts on the Benson tape: "Give Me the Night," "I'm In the Mood for Love," among others, reminding me of the nights of pleasure and ethereal heights of my heroin fueled enchantments…until I realized my speed was back to 80. The Croaker exit was gone, and I had passed Toano. The last turn-around exit—West Point—was only four miles ahead.

Would it be straight ahead or return to home? Then two miles, then one mile ahead, I still had not decided. Confident Chuck was still in a foolish debate mode about this life-changing event with the remaining exit on the horizon! One half-mile ahead. Finally, I came to my senses; this could not work, time to turn around, but when I tried to take my foot off the accelerator, my dick stretched down and pushed it back with abandon. All the lights on the instrument panels went haywire, flashing while the music when dead silent. My arms attempted to turn the steering wheel, but some power froze them, locking my torso in a freak contortion. I felt an intense heat permeate my body and I could not feel the road moving beneath me! West Point exit—Zooom!!! Norfolk, Virginia, here I come! Once again in America, it is a Negro man and a Caucasian woman—the feigned story of the resistance struggle of the Black man and White women.

It is inevitable, a comical ending as told by a brother to avert the serious nature of his deed ... Zooom! It was over. The game was over...White girl: 1, Chuck: 0.

I brought Tammy back and I actually, at least, kept myself straight around her. But she relapsed hard and it was clear she had to get help. I got her back up to Willow Oaks for her second treatment. When she completed the thirty days, she decided to move to Richmond where I would help her stay clean and, hopefully, get her job and a place to live. I was able to help her with both and she stayed clean and stayed beautiful. We began a torrid relationship.

But Tammy had another problem. An old boyfriend, Kevin, the drug-using cop from Norfolk, was basically stalking her, following her to Richmond. It was a bizarre confluence: a stunningly beautiful and smart young woman, a police officer from another city, and a councilman in a triangle of secret lives. Kevin found out everything about me, Tammy, and Jim Barrett. So, I guess he thought, *I'll call his wife.* He found out how to reach Phyllis and told her that I was staying with his girlfriend at the Massad House Hotel. Phyllis came to the hotel to confront us in person. Tammy and I were in the room when a knock came at the door.

"Tammy, do not answer the door, don't," I said.

Then a voice on the outside said, "It's flowers, you must sign for them."

Tammy, so anxious to see who would send her flowers, moved before I could say, "don't...open..." Tammy flung the door open, and suddenly, with both hands, Phyllis grabbed Tammy by the hair and slammed her wall to wall until I could subdue her.

"Hold on, hold on," I yelled. "There's nothing going on, Phyllis! Hold it, hold it!" I had to hold Phyllis with both hands. Thank God I was fully clothed in suit and tie, hair in place, with the appearance of innocence. Breathing deeply, Phyllis didn't say a word; she just stood looking at Tammy as her chest rose and settled and she gradually calmed down. I don't remember all of what I said but catching us fully clothed made all the difference in the world. I told her that Tammy was in Richmond before she would go back to Willow Oak Drug Treatment, and I was just helping her get the room; that's all it was. Tammy was at the bedroom door, behind it, far away from Phyllis, looking like a little frightened puppy.

Despite my best effort to keep Tammy from using drugs, she just wasn't ready and made her own way back to the Richmond drug culture. I, however, remained clean while Kevin, clean or not, continued to pursue Tammy and me.

One night, Kevin waited near my home to confront me near Byrd Park. I had arranged for Tammy to live near Byrd Park, and that night, Tammy was with me in my vehicle going down North Boulevard. When we got near the tennis courts at the Columbus statue, Tammy yelled out, "There goes that motherfucker!"

"Who, that goddamn Kevin?!" I asked. "You best stop and talk this shit out..."

Tammy yelled, "Hell no, Chuck! Run!" I was on empty, not even gas fumes, but I hit the pedal and we took off past my house on this all-out race to nowhere.

I told her, "Tammy, let's just stop."

She hollered, "No, Chuck! I don't want to see that nigga'." Although Kevin was White, that's how Tammy talked around me, especially when she was anxious or intense. We continued speeding through and around the residential streets of Carytown, the stadium area, the Carillon, and Randolph Street, trying to lose him through the tight neighborhood. It was a chase to a finish line I couldn't find! I told her, "Fuck it, Tammy! The chase is over. I'm stopping."

She said, "No, no, no," while she twisted herself back and forth looking behind us, then forward repeatedly with eyes the size of walnuts!

I decided to stop where I might be safest: the BP station at Meadow and Cary Streets, about four blocks away, which was like a home base for me. When I sped north on Meadow, the car left the ground at the hump to the overpass, and I felt my ass lift off the seat for second before we hit the street again with a loud scrape. At Meadow and Cary, I slid through the light into the BP lot and stopped next to the front door. Tammy and I were breathing hard, and when we looked around, only seconds after we stopped, right there next to us, was that goddamned Kevin.

I said, "Hey, Baby! You can handle him. He ain't go do shit with all these people around. Just talk to him!" She got out and he got out; it looked like he tried to touch her, but I couldn't see too clearly. Kevin was tall, about six foot two inches tall and built, but he was almost in tears trying to convince her to go with him.

"No! I don't want to be with you!" Tammy said. Kevin, who was a cop but not the unnecessarily violent type, only watched in confused anger. She got back in my car and we drove away while Kevin remained at the BP while Black folk came and went by him. It was a damn shame, all that chase and anxiety for such anti-climactic bullshit. I told her to talk to him the first moment we saw him, but we had to be chased so she could say, "I don't want to be with you."

Kevin continued to come to Richmond even after Tammy had found a job and settled in an apartment on Parham Road. When he found us there one night, Tammy called the Henrico County Police on him. As Kevin and Tammy argued, I noticed that one of the Henrico officers showing up was Black. He came over and asked me, "What do you want us to do?" He was basically deferring the situation to me. I told them I was a friend of theirs and would not take a position, so they looked at Tammy and Kevin and just decided to leave. I did that for him even considering what he had done to me two weeks earlier with Phyllis.

Meanwhile, other law enforcement was determined not to defer *anything* about me! Since early 1994, just before I went to L.A. for treatment, there was an orchestrated effort by Richmond, Henrico, and Chesterfield to entrap me, not for only using, but as a dealer. Efforts of police to push someone to relapse may seem counter-intuitive, but not only was it so, it demanded an amount of man-hours and money that would shock you. Given their surveillance of me, they knew I was clean, but it did not stop them from hoping otherwise.

During the period after I left Willow Oaks, they somehow met up with Jim Barrett. Jim had been arrested for shoplifting a second time and it may have been his "third strike," as they say. He might have approached the police to help them trap me in exchange for some deal in his case. I can't be sure, but who knows! At any rate, they had apparently been planning to use Jim as a means of trapping me, even though I was still clean! One day in the late fall of '94, Jim invited Tammy and me to come over and catch up on things. It was a setup, a sting operation with full support: cameras, state police, SWAT team, and backup, all ready to spring into action once I took the bait. The bait, however, was crack cocaine. The Henrico Police prosecutors did not want to charge me with simple possession; they wanted me on a distribution charge. But for whatever reason, they had not procured heroin—even with all that money they were giving Jim to get it—they had to go with the crack.

Tammy could not resist the idea; she pushed me hard to try it. "Chuck, come on baby, just a little, baby," she said all sad-eyed.

I said, "Sure Tammy, sure. That's like if I asked you for just a little pussy, just let me put the head in…you know damn well that's some bullshit!" I would not relent. I was not doing that fucking crack! I was clean and started telling Jim how good I felt in the 12-step program.

I changed the subject and moved it to something I was passionate about: Arthur Ashe. I must have gone on for twenty minutes giving, if I may say so, a helluva argument on the virtues of why his monument should be on Monument Avenue. I'm certain those cameras had to be rolling, and if that recording is still in the police files, it would be a beautiful record for that time. But Jim was not moved by forceful condemnation of the slave owners on Monument Avenue.

I suddenly had an eerie sense about things and decided I would leave. I had already made a business appointment for that afternoon at 4:00 pm and was ready to go anyway. Tammy, though, remained, apparently to do the crack, or maybe she and Jim had other plans. I didn't even give so much as a hint or suggestion during the whole time the cops were waiting to jump that I might even consider using the crack.

I left and headed to my appointment at the Holiday Inn on Boulevard with, of course, an agent in tow. He followed me to the restaurant where I met my acquaintance. He sat in the booth directly across from us in an almost empty place. My meeting was strictly about a legal proposition, but even if it wasn't, he was wasting time and money: tax money. He sat there knowing I knew he knew I knew he was following me. This, however, was not the issue; there was an aggressive nature in the need to trap me that likely hinged on bigger issues. My long-standing fight to challenge Monument Avenue's "horseback heroes" statues was making new headway. With a big chance that a Black hero, a superstar in tennis and humanitarian causes, might break the lost cause, the score in this game would not be "love."

By November of 1994, I was again fighting back. That year, Richmond was going through a horrific murder epidemic. It was so bad that the U.S. Postal Service stopped mail delivery in one area, and much of it was believed to be drug related. This didn't help with any sympathies toward me, but I was focused; I had to be. I was always involved with the Richmond Crusade for Voters, and had, for all intents and purposes, led the group. It was an election season, and an endorsement from the Crusade was very important to any candidate.

In that role, I felt additional purpose as I fought to stay clean.

I recall one particular time Doug Wilder needed that endorsement, which meant he needed me. I can't remember if it was his race for U.S. President, or U.S. Senator, but it was his need for the Crusade endorsement that stirred a bitter memory about my friend,. Black political and religious leaders in Richmond and beyond were tremendously influenced by the Crusade, so it was imperative he get their support. He had met with Richard and Bessie Jones, the Fifth District ward leaders, and believed he could convince them to gain the endorsement of the Crusade for his race. But Doug knew nothing was certain unless he had my support in any matter with the Crusade. When he asked to meet me for breakfast at the Bull and Bear restaurant to talk, I knew what he wanted. Doug could be very savvy but also predictable because of his ambition. I said, "Sure, we can meet, 7:30 am, but just for coffee…not breakfast. I don't have time to eat."

The night before, I thought about what he might say, and what kind of twist on things he would urge me to see. Doug could be pretty manipulative, as any good politician can be, but there was also a slightly cynical streak in him. While I had planned to support him, I wanted to remind him—of himself. I remembered how he treated Henry Marsh during Roy West's selection as mayor, calling him for a meeting, making him wait an hour, only to ultimately not show up. And I thought of how he left my side on the Arthur Ashe Monument fight. But Doug was a fighter, and he had supported me in my first run in '77. He and I were close in those early years, playing golf, having lunch every couple of weeks. I saw him as a type of 'big brother." But something he had done in those same years really surprised me, hurt me, and it taught me something about my friend.

I believe it was in 1982 when a Chesterfield County policeman tried to sue me. I supposedly defamed him in a dispute over a ticket he had given me claiming I called him an absolute liar in the newspaper. He said it impugned his character and caused distress. The suit was thrown out of court in less than five minutes. Doug Wilder, as a friend, offered a new, young lawyer from his firm come to represent me in court. An able young attorney named Roger Gregory, who is now on the Virginia Supreme Court, spent maybe a half hour with me in addition to the ten minutes in court.

Fast forward a couple of years, and Phyllis and I needed to refinance our home to gain some much-needed cash for difficult times. Doug, again as a friend, said he would handle the closing for us. The night before, as Phyllis and I looked over the paperwork, we saw a $5,000 charge for legal fees. I called Doug and he said he would see us in the morning, and we would clear it up. He didn't show up at the closing. We had to sign the papers to avoid foreclosure, and the check we received, which we had expected—and planned for—was practically nothing after losing the $5,000. Phyllis was outraged and blamed me. She cried and cried at the thought of not being able to make ends meet.

When I called Doug, he said the fee was for his services, the bulk of which was for the help with the ten-minute court hearing two years earlier. In two years, he had never asked for or mentioned any charges for that *entire* time. We never got the money back—or any portion. He wrote a letter to me a week later saying, "I can't imagine what reason you think I *wouldn't* charge you." I thought to myself, *What about friendship, man?!* Phyllis was so distraught and angered that we considered filing an ethics complaint with the Bar Association. But I let it go.

Now, fast-forward some years later back to his run for office, and the help he needed from me with the Crusade for Voters. We met that morning for coffee and Doug was all smiles, effusively describing my power with the Crusade; I could see it pained him to do it, but he had to make sure I would help him. I was coy, reluctant to automatically show my intention to be there for him. I told him I didn't hold that kind of power over the Crusade. I was only a councilman.

"I don't know, I'll let you know," I said.

He went on for several minutes, lauding my influence, urging I should go back and insist forcefully that they quickly endorse him. "Just be firm, show strength…get a little mad."

I got up and walked to the large window, thinking about what he had done for me, or should I say, *to me*. The sun was almost blinding, and I turned back and looked at his squinting eyes. "Doug," I said, "I don't get mad…"

The look on his face, with the sun showing everything he was thinking, let me know he knew what I was saying, and he knew why I said it. I don't remember which race it was—so many years ago—but he dropped out before the Crusade made any endorsements. I do remember that much. Whether or not it was related to my indifferent response about support, I can't say. Nor can I say I got even. And though we have remained friends for years, there has always been a sore spot in our history. I suppose it's like the saying goes, "There are no permanent enemies in politics, only permanent interest."

CHAPTER 12

The Long Cause: Monument Avenue

―

Only a day or two after my election in March 1977, I received a call from a reporter with the *Atlanta Constitution* newspaper who asked me almost immediately: "Mr. Richardson, are you all going to tear down the Confederate monuments?" The obvious underlying acknowledgement in the question was that Black people were offended by those structures and wanted them, at the very least, removed. That was over forty years ago. How is it that in 2020 that that underlying recognized truth remained simply rhetorical to so many Whites? One of our great presidents said, "All we have to fear is fear itself." I have come to believe that one of, if not the ultimate of, those fears is that of truth. Whether as the ostrich puts its head in a hole, or we keep ours in the clouds, we know truth can be intimidating.

Nearly twenty-five years ago, fifteen years after I first began the effort, I wrote a letter to the editor of the *Richmond News Leader* about Monument Avenue, which was printed along with comments from supporters of the monuments in rebuttal. At the time, in a moment of weakness, I was willing to allow the Confederate monuments to remain if a few Civil Rights heroes would be honored on that same avenue. I had not, at the time, determined who but I submitted the concept. Ultimately this lead to the placement of the Arthur Ashe monument that I had to almost push through a few single-handedly years later.

One opponent, John M. McCaffrey, replied to the editor in a rather weak response that: "What emerges with Richardson's 'number of statues' for Monument Avenue is one more step in the current zealous movement to demean a proud and honorable part of Southern White and American history, and ultimately to eradicate Southern White culture. It is high time we quit being genteel Southerners and started emulating the men commemorated on Monument Avenue by hitting back and hitting back hard!"

Even though that was in the early '90s, that sentiment, with Donald J. Trump and his supporters empowering it, has an even more fervent animosity today. The pride in which they indulge such a giant blind spot in their culture and history, wishing to emulate their heroes on horseback, is very sad. Stop being "genteel Southerners"? Wow! Two hundred-fifty years of polite, courteous, discreet, decorous slavery; look away, Dixieland. No, Mr. McCaffrey. We don't wish to totally eradicate your culture, only that Jupiter-sized blind spot you keep in it. A blind spot that remains because of your fear. Truth, Mr. McCaffrey, will set *you* free. And for the sake of our American culture, let go of that lost cause. What if, Mr. McCaffrey, the shoe was on the other foot? What if the boot was on your neck? What if an unspeakable, inhumane, and murderous cause was against *you?*

Prior to that letter to the *News Leader,* the subject of Monument Avenue was something the Black members of Council had always thought about but rarely, if ever, spoke about publicly. We would talk about the possibility, or impossibility, and the forces that would come to bear. I had mentioned the issue many times privately since the early '80s, and now, I thought as MLK said, "The time is always right to do right." Andrew J. Brent, or A.J., the lawyer for the *News Leader,* once said, "Those monuments will be moved over my dead body!" I remember sitting there that warm July morning waiting for those White men to come into the room and practicing what I would say to them about why the Jefferson Davis statue should come down, and why perhaps a Black Civil Rights leader could be added to the avenue. None of the other Black City Council members had agreed to meet to talk with them. They said we had bigger fish to fry.

Speaking of A.J. Brent, Claudette McDaniel once said rather jokingly, but half serious as well, about the nature of the issue: "He's mean, Chuck. He knows guys in Philly; he can get a contract on your ass and—poof!" Her big round eyes widened, and her hands flashed open with those long, elaborately painted fingernails. Then she broke into a big smile and her large breasts started bobbing up and down while she roared with laughter. "One day you'll be just gone! Ha, ha, ha."

I understood her tease toward me, but Andrew Brent was a mean "cracker." He was malicious and carried a demeanor that made Claudette's joke not so funny. My Black and White friends warned me. Tazewell Carrington—a millionaire tobacco landowner with more money than God—once told me, "Chuckie Boy, you have to be reasonable, son." He really liked me, and would always help when I was in need, but he was concerned and worried about me. He said I should, "Get off this foolish grown notion 'bout them statues."

Shallow Excuses for Symbols of Oppression

How long will supposedly intelligent people cling to the vestiges of evil and continue to glorify the symbols of people who fought desperately to uphold the institution of slavery? How long will good men, under the pretext of selective history and heritage, conceal the real symbolic meaning of the Monument Avenue statues in Richmond, and all around the South? How long will decent, Christian White men and women, in inimical fashion, force their brothers and sisters of color to be humiliated and demeaned each time they pass these monuments to White supremacy? And how long do our White brothers and sisters expect their Black brothers and sisters to remain indifferent to these insults?

I pose to them this question: how many times would you pass the soaring stone image of Jefferson Davis, the avowed White supremacist, and remain docile and quiet as you know in your mind, clearly, the sins for which his doctrine was responsible? How long could you tolerate, in your mind's eye, slave children, barely three or four, sold to the highest bidder, never seen again by their mothers? Or twelve-year-old girls pulled from sleep, routinely, to have their virginity brutalized for the master's pleasure? It is hard to imagine these things: your White brothers working from sunrise to sunset to simply live and eat, your brothers lynched two-three-four at a time without trial, or, monstrously thrown into boiling hot vats of oil. Hard to imagine—horrific to realize. How long would you remain unsullied and act as if it did not crush your dignity and wholeness as a man or woman?

The Monument Avenue statues symbolize, and glorify, real men who fought to preserve that way of life, those kinds of acts. Would you then proclaim: "Don't change our history?" Would you then appeal to state's rights or some other asinine excuse to avoid the truth? Truth is not disputable; truth has no context; truth is the same for you as it is for me. How can truth be denied so callously for the sake of some misguided pride? It is true that Robert E. Lee used his best military tactics to prevent the North from intervening in the slave trade, and had he been successful, slavery would not have ended. Each state, in its declaration of secession, was clear that slavery was their predominant concern and motivation, that Black people were meant to serve White people. It is in black and white, read it!

The truth is these things are what define Monument Avenue. Robert E. Lee was to Jefferson Davis what Grant was to Lincoln, or Eisenhower to Truman. Anyone who would question where Lee's loyalties were need only refer to the Constitution of the Confederate States of America (CSA). In that Constitution, to which Lee pledged his oath of allegiance, it states very clearly that: "The Constitution of the CSA will mirror the Constitution of the Union in all regards except the portion pertaining to Negroes; wherein we declare they are subservient to White people, and whose purpose is, and always will be, to serve."

To accept that the symbols of such a belief should be praised, glorified, and placed on public display to be honored is barely conceivable. To continue to praise and uphold the symbol of Lee and his subordinates on Monument Avenue makes hypocrites of citizens who consider themselves true patriots. Patriotic Americans do not honor traitors who took up arms against their country in defense of an inhumane cause.

America has since become recognized as the greatest democracy on earth, but that period of history continues to serve as the one great blemish that stains our history. That stain is recognized by the entire free world because slavery is—and was—wrong. But regrettably, this City and State's leadership has failed to accept what the rest of the world already knows. We will never justify what was done in the past and we cannot change our mistakes. However, we must justify what we do—or don't do—today!

Acknowledging that something in the past was wrong but, at the same time, upholding the symbols that represents that wrong is itself unconscionable. The position taken is so often steeped in arrogance and haughtiness as well. Over time, even the most ardent supporters of the statues will come to recognize the void of moral standing, unless they are White supremacists. Otherwise, the evaluation of truth and logic will eventually dictate the removal of those statues.

I recall the experience in Vietnam when two Marines, one Black, the other White, argued over the small Confederate flag the White Marine wore on his helmet. It was only after his Black friend was killed the next day that the White boy from South Carolina, regret the stupid offense he displayed toward his fellow Marine, his Black friend, and ripped the flag from his helmet. I think back on those days and realize how little things have changed. But how much can change if we don't give up? It is true, we don't listen to each other enough and that only if someone dies or some horrific event takes place, are we then willing to stop thinking about ourselves long enough to hear what someone else is trying to explain to us!

What "Big Red," the poor White redneck from South Carolina, learned that day on the combat fields of Vietnam is what many White people in America (especially in the South) have not yet stopped to take the time to consider. I refuse to accept the notion that White people are so cruel or insensitive that they will disregard the feelings of Black people so readily and not consider the effects of these symbols or their meaning—to their fellow Americans. I am convinced they are more unaware than viciously indifferent to Black people. That is certainly not to say some are not straight-up asshole racists, but I believe most do not have a full grasp of the implication of wearing the rebel flag or defending the monuments.

The golf professional, Bubba Watson, who purchased the red "Road Runner" car used on the "Dukes of Hazzard" television show, seriously and innocently admired the vehicle with its Confederate flag painted on top of it. Once he fully understood what that symbol conveyed, he had the flag painted over immediately. There are many bigoted, uninformed people in America, but the lion's share of them are good people who will eventually do the right thing like Big Red and Bubba Watson. There is no middle ground because there is no gray area!

Today, I continue with the quest to remove the monuments. In 2018, I wrote to the commission tasked with the question, and this is a portion of it.

Part of my Letter to the Monument Avenue Commission / 2018

I have been involved in the Monument Avenue statue controversy since 1979, attending meetings, panel discussions, private sessions and some of the most intense debating groups. I have, essentially, been involved from the start. Early on in his position, I admonished Mayor Stoney not to convene further public hearings pursuant to the resolution of this matter, given that all the public hearings since 1984 have resulted in no beneficial progress. To ignore this inherent tension can only result in more of the same racial discontent we have witnessed thus far. I have attempted only to offer my institutional knowledge as a backdrop and a way of assisting the Mayor to resolve this problem; however, my efforts have proven unsuccessful, my suggestions have fallen on deaf ears. The Mayor has not acknowledged my letters, phone calls, or visits to his office. In no way do I intend to disregard protocol or to do harm to his reputation; my only concern is the City and a way out of this seemingly unresolvable impasse.

Since 1984, I have attended seven or eight hearings, hearing the proponents only offer a subjective viewpoint that contributed nothing at all towards the intended goal of resolving differences. Whether your Commission conducts one or 1,000 more public hearings, whether in large or small groups, the sentiments would all be the same, and you would be no closer to an answer than when you first began.

In 1981, a group of intelligent, fair-minded Black and White ministers, attorneys, businessmen, and elected officials came together in an earnest effort to address the problem. Unfortunately, they could not arrive at an accord regarding this question for one reason; namely, that the White proponents of the Confederate statues were unwilling to acknowledge that the men symbolized by the statues had fought to defend a cause that was wrong or evil. They were not willing to condemn their idolized heroes. The group was caught in a conundrum: how do you separate men from an evil cause for which they fought...or could you? The meeting of dignified persons evolved into an argument, then a shouting match, and ended as all the other public hearings had ended, including the one this commission held this last summer at the Museum...an unexpected disappointment.

Mr. Clarence Townes, Jr., and Reverend Miles Jones both argued to the group in 1984 that public sentiment should not be a factor in the retention or removal of the statues because it was a moral issue not subject to political persuasion or public opinion. I would be inclined to agree strongly with their argument and regret that they are not still around to make it themselves. The issue for the Commission will be to determine the truth regarding the purpose, motivation, and meaning of erecting those statues and render that unto the Mayor.

The Mayor's Commission will likely recommend ultimately that Monument Avenue be an Avenue of an American doctrine or a street dedicated to a divided nation as Davis believed. If the Commission fails to speak truth to power and does the same thing that every other group before them has done, then this fight will go on until one day our children or their children will finally speak that truth—that slavery was wrong, White supremacy was wrong, and the men who defended it were wrong. To continue to hold up these statues for praise in public places is wrong, and to tell the Mayor anything else would be wrong!

Our City's school board and Council members are incessantly at odds over the paralyzing short falls in financial expenditures. But, an equally perplexing dilemma, that we have neglected to address over the years has been the miseducation of our children beyond the parameters of the classroom setting. As a Commission, your impact upon the future education of our children looms large with tremendous effects on their impressionable minds. Education must not be perceived only as the transmission of cognitive skills within the classroom, but also those experiences on the streets and avenues, in the signs they read, in the songs they sing --- and in the statues that they see, learn and hear about --- that shape their vision of the society in which they exist.

What contradictions are we teaching when we espouse the values of freedom, justice, and equality inside the classroom, but maintain statues of men who fought to deny the freedom, justice, and equality of Black people on our streets? How do we teach children in classrooms that they are equal in the eyes of God and men when we leave before them sixty-foot statues that glorify the opposite? How do you educate children about the dignity and equality of all people, when the entire history of Monument Avenue is the glorification of the enslavement of people for over 250 years? And how do you teach within classrooms that Black Lives Matter when the symbols that punctuate Monument Avenue from Belmont to Lombardy enshrine the memories of these men who would have kept millions of Black lives shackled and chained?

Like the honorable men of the Richmond Renaissance "conundrum" some 35 years ago, the question remains as difficult, perplexing, and painful as before, but it is a simple question couched in truth. Those good men could not bring themselves to condemn Lee, Jackson, or Stuart. They could not separate the generals from the ill-conceived cause for which they fought. ... But one day, these edifices will be gone; as certain as Winter will follow Fall and Spring will bring rain, they will be gone. They will be gone because their cause was wrong and it never should have been glorified, but it is taking time for the ideals to be advanced. "Time makes ancient good uncouth." Soon, our children will look back and think how uncouth we were to praise symbols that glorified a system of human bondage that treated their fellow men as chattel.

The issues at the root of the Monument Avenue symbols is not simply what people think about the statues today, but rather what did the people who erected these statues have in mind in 1890, 1909, and 1926 at the time they were dedicated?

Find the answers to these questions and you will have done this city a just service of truth. Look to the archives of history, and from those documents, speeches, and dedication ceremonies, you will disclose to us today what their hearts really felt. If the Commission does a good job at disclosure of historical truth, the good people of this city will do the rest. It will not be political; it will not be expedient, but, at long last, it will be the proper thing to do.

Arthur Ashe

The battle for the Ashe Monument was, no pun intended, monumental. I had been a fiery proponent of a Black person on

Monument Avenue for years. When Arthur Ashe died, Doug Wilder suggested the monument to Ashe be placed on Monument Avenue. Doug, who was Governor when he said that, had his eyes on a U.S. Senate seat by early 1994, and, unfortunately folded under the White, and Black, backlash against the idea. Meanwhile, my proposal before the City Council gained support by having Arthur's name attached as the specific civil rights symbol to which my proposal had earlier referred. But, even then, the opposition to it being on Monument Avenue followed. I met, secretly, with the business sector and said that I would withdraw my proposal to take down the Jefferson Davis statue if they would support the Arthur Ashe statue. They agreed, but the vote was not unanimous. And needless to say it would have been a bitter pill to cease my efforts to remove Jefferson Davis. Some of the businessmen and Mayor Leonidas Young's assistant, Joel Harris, broke off and created a group to support the Arthur Ashe statue being placed downtown.

I continued to push for Monument Avenue even when my Black friends told me, "Chuck, you have gone far enough with this Monument Avenue issue. Let someone else carry that cause." Bessie Jones, my primary community organizer, told me one morning on the phone, "Chuck, let this Monument Avenue thing go. You are starting to lose support." Even Ray Boone, the editor of the *Free Press,* whom many saw as "Mr. Black," said he didn't want Arthur up there "with them losers." When Ray told me I was brainwashed, I said to him, "Yeah, my brain is washed, washed of the thought that those Confederacy monuments will always be there—yours is not!"

As the controversy ensued, the opposition grew stronger over the Ashe statue being placed on Monument Avenue. Different groups proposed alternative sites for various reasons. I called Douglas Wilder and asked him to make a statement of support to reiterate his position. "I've said what I will, and I'm done with it. Arthur would not have desired this rancor and bitterness. I will say no more. I'm through with it!" was his response. I was so disappointed! Just when I needed his voice the most, he said the least.

It was the recollection of that July morning waiting in the Renaissance office in dreadful suspense of facing those powerful White men that I knew the destiny of a Black statue was a Monument Avenue imperative, as the prelude to the removal of the heroes of a lost cause.

What many could not see was that the principal rationale for those against Mr. Ashe being on Monument Avenue was race related. What people failed to realize was that the opponents did not want the Ashe statue to break the sovereignty of Confederate ground and what it stood for. They were missing the larger point. I remember one council meeting in June 1995 when we invited the public to speak and the room overflowed with opinions from Blacks and Whites. The debate was somewhat symbolized in an exchange I had with an opponent of the idea. He was, if I may say, a pretty stereotypical redneck in those days, and a bona fide believer in the South's lost cause. R. Wayne Byrd, the head of the Danville, Virginia, chapter of the Heritage Preservation Association made the trip to Richmond to defend what he called "hallowed ground."

Byrd said if we wanted a Black on Monument Avenue, it should be for the slaves that fought with the rebels to keep themselves slaves in Dixie. Yes, you read it right. This clown wanted to honor slaves that were willing to die to stay a slave. I would have to believe that if such a monument would exist it would rise well above Jackson and Lee because of how heroic it would be to see that a man could loveth his brutal master so much that he would lay down his life to stay his slave. Byrd's reference of heroism was bizarre. But as that fictional great son of Alabama, Forrest Gump, said, "Stupid is as stupid does."

I said to him, "Arthur didn't ride a horse, he didn't shoot a gun, but he was hero." Byrd said placing the monument there would offend the "sensibilities of Richmond's Confederate-Americans." He then, in a very resentful Southern drawl, invited me down to Danville to hear from their points of view. I grinned and looked around at the Blacks who were grinning at each other and shifting in their seats, and said with a gentle chuckle, "No, thank you."

He continued to describe the lofty nature of the Avenue, and that having Ashe there would "just make it different." I asked him what would be different, and he said, "It would just be different, you know…"

I said, "No, no I don't, what is different?" He remained silent for a few seconds and I asked again, "What, what-would-be-different. What-is-different?" He still remained silent, as did the room, and he avoided any eye contact with me. I just stared at him, waiting for an answer patiently, allowing him time to squirm and feel the pressure his idiocy and racism was reaping at that moment. He knew, I knew, the whole room knew what the hell "it's just different" meant. I insisted on asking again, "What's different?" He couldn't even come up with some bullshit like he had not been dead long enough, or we should consider someone else. R. Wayne Byrd couldn't find the right lie, so his silence spoke the truth.

Then—like a good Negro—a young new councilman named Anthony Jones jumped in: "Mr. Richardson, are you going to interrogate every speaker?!"

I couldn't believe that Negro would try to give that redneck a break and deny the Black people in the room a moment to see an obvious racist squirm. I wanted him to squirm, coming all the way here to argue about the "sensibilities" of Richmond's Confederate-Americans without any regard for African Americans and their history with those confederate feelings. I wanted to send that clown scurrying back down to Danville just as his idol, Jefferson Davis, cowardly ran to the new, and last, short-lived capital of the Confederacy in April 1865. Maybe *Mr. Jones* was curious about what the White folks down there might have to say about the issue. Certainly, their hospitality would be like his, the same—only different.

It was an intense summer around the issue; even the international press came to do stories about the uniquely American dichotomy. And less than a month later, the City Council, in a packed marathon meeting, heard again from many, including Arthur's brother. After then councilman Tim Kaine spoke in favor of the project, the Council voted unanimously to place the Arthur Ashe monument where I was determined to see it: on Monument Avenue. Then, in less than two months, before all the final Planning Commission approvals were complete, I had the press' attention again, for reasons that were hardly heroic.

And Now, An N-word from Our Sponsor

With so much debated about the Confederate monuments, it once again speaks to the nature of that argument when considering the perplexity of another. Let me explain, my nigga. Yes, I said it, the word that has become, in White society, so special you could say. A couple years ago, a White associate of mine, rather incredulously, asked; "Why do you use the N-word so frequently, but, let me even think about saying it and all hell breaks out!" It was glaring how he actually believed that if he shouldn't say it, I shouldn't say it. This opinion, or mentality I'm sure, is very prevalent among those who defend the Confederate monuments. They would argue that, yes, the N-word carries a hateful and ugly past, that we must not give it any space any time in mixed company. Yet, the very people who birthed, nurtured, promulgated, and defined an aspect of history replete with its use and sentiment, sit revered and honored with grand monuments. And admirers have no quarrel with that.

Most of those men on Monument Avenue are in full regalia, every medal and badge, every demonstration of their heroic experiences worn from hat to boot and steed as well. Perhaps my White brothers can relate to that when they hear a Black person say "nigga'"—just consider it a badge, a testament to their battles. A badge that a White person cannot wear or claim—period. Black people were referred to as nigger with every strike of the whip, called nigger as they were lynched, heard nigger as they tried to hold on to a child being torn away, or even bore the illegitimate child of the man calling her "nigger wench." We heard it for 300 years, as it was inescapable, from the most mundane usage to the most horrific. Likely, very often, it was probably the last word many heard.

Black people can say "nigga'" because Black people heard "nigga'!" It was, along with screams and tears and prayer and song, the soundtrack of our history. That battle, our history, warrants a badge for those whose heritage earned it. So, don't say a word when we wear it. Let me be clear, though. I am not advocating the use of the word. I am simply saying when it comes to its use by Blacks, it is to be determined by Blacks. The others should simply shut the fuck up (STFU).

I know that there are many Black people who have sincere disdain for the word and find offense no matter who says it, and I can understand it. The word carries a history that cannot be ignored, and it is that history that is conflated with its use today. Again, I am not promoting the use of the word. Its use is a very complex and emotional issue in our community. Many believe the word should be struck from any vernacular; however, the word has, in a somewhat ironic way, helped us as well. We took the word and appropriated its use to de-fang its venom, using it as a kind of comical barb toward each other, most often only around our friends. Over the twentieth century, Blacks turned it around, intentionally, rendering it as just another piece of boisterous slang, or even endearment at times. But as White folk have done for over a hundred years with almost all Black culture, from art to comedy to jargon to athletics—and most significantly, music— they took it for themselves, again.

And here came the problem: hip-hop rappers have used the word gratuitously, and often with much more animosity, in their music today. So, with White boys hearing it almost everywhere "hip" music was blasted, it easily flew from their mouths as well; just singing the song...with a nice added kick of getting away with something. Society has to grapple with that: accepting offensive speech in marketable music, yet absolute intolerance of the word in free conversation—the contextualization of the use and by whom. In the case of this word,

I don't believe there is any context where White people should use it, whether in song or debate. The "conversation" should be had among Blacks about its use going forward, and I welcome that debate.

Ironically, the use of the word among young White boys today is probably greater than ever, but I'm inclined to believe most of the time it is not used for the same purpose their lineage did so. More likely, it is often because, as usual, they're just trying to be Black. Nigga', please…

CHAPTER 13

Now It's History

By the late spring of 1995, I had a real juggling act on my hands. The cops had been patiently trying to catch me, even attending AA and NA meetings posing as fellow addicts. They must have been idiots to think the group didn't know what was happening. Despite my best efforts to keep Tammy from using drugs, she just wasn't ready and made her way back to the Richmond drug culture. She returned to the Meadow Street area and was using crack, the worst drug in the world from my viewpoint: psychologically, the most powerful mood-altering substance on the streets! I never touched crack, and although I was fearless with most things in life, I was a sissy when it came to crack. It made men and women into craven whores, doing anything to anyone to get it.

Tammy stayed on the run from me because she knew I would get her back into treatment. The word had reached the streets that Tammy was Chuck Richardson's girl, so my connections would help me find her—and I did. After I was told about a house on Parkwood Avenue, I went in, and it was like a family of addicts. Everyone was doing crack. A girl told me, "Wait a minute, Mr. Chuck," and she scurried up the stairway into the darkness. Two minutes later the girl came back down. "She comin', I said we'll hide you from da police—but not Chuck Richardson."

Tammy was ashamed and too high to talk. I looked at her and tried to imagine a once so beautiful woman, now in the midst of hideous self-destruction. I asked her, "Where in the hell did you get money to buy crack?" Tammy, in a slow, weak, shameful gesture, turned her hand upside down, closing all but her index finger, which she slowly, almost reluctantly, aimed at me. She looked so awful, terrified, and unable to say anything, though it was clear what was happening. It was so tragic, and I could hardly say a word myself. A modern version of beauty and the beast... crack.

I can't say what the tipping point was but, to make a long story short, I relapsed that summer, and maybe that trip to Norfolk was bearing its fruit. I had managed to avoid Jim Barrett much of that summer, still feeling cautious about him, but I was not totally suspicious of him. Tammy and Kevin were still playing hide and seek, and I was in and out of that ring as well. Jim had reached out a couple of times asking me and Tammy to come by; he knew Tammy was using and thought we might get together again. It finally happened one day in mid-September. We decided we would hang out and do a small piece together, the three of us. When I got there, Kevin was outside leaving. He looked at me and said, "Chuck, you don't want to be in there." I figured he was trying to keep me away from Tammy, but in hindsight, he was warning me. Being a cop, he had his ways of keeping an eye on Tammy, and me and Jim for that matter, and probably knew all about Jim being the bait for the task force. I went in not thinking any more of it and met with Jim and Tammy.

We sat at the kitchen table and bullshitted a little. Then, Jim reached in his pocket and pulled out a small piece, worth around fifty dollars, and put it on the table as Tammy fidgeted in anticipation. I reached to grab it and felt a deep heat from the inside out roll over me, and then the presence of another person as my eyes fixed on the small foil wrapper. I hesitated just an instant, thinking it was stupid on my part not to have recognized Jim's persistence to "hang out" with him as odd. Right as my hand grabbed it I looked up and there stood the police right behind Jim. In a few moments, the kitchen flooded with officers, SWAT team members, and detectives as Jim stood and snuck out his own kitchen without a word. I realized I had been set up, by someone I thought was my buddy. This was not going to be one of my normal days.

"Okay, Chuck, don't move," were the first words I heard. Plenty more was said but my mind went into one of those moments I had in Vietnam, a block out of reality, even though what was happening was profoundly clear. The heat radiating from my core was flooding my brain and my balls, but I looked at each of them as if I was reading their thoughts. They cuffed me and Tammy and, I suppose, read us our rights, then led me out while surrounded. Even when I think of Jim Barrett today, I must wonder how he feels about himself, knowing that I had helped him when he and his girlfriend couldn't pay the rent and her little boy was hungry; how I drove all the way across town to feed them. And I learned of his earlier failed attempt to bust me with the crack several weeks later in jail. It didn't matter to him as he slid like a quiet snake from that kitchen.

It was over twenty-five years after that Marine asked me what I was afraid of: "You probably be dead in three weeks anyway as an M60 machine-gunner." I was not afraid that night as I was taken into custody; just mad and resentful at how law enforcement from three jurisdictions conspired to pull me back into heroin, almost as callously as federal lawmakers had pushed me into that insidious war, and heroin, in 1969.

They led me to one of the cars that had zipped in around the home on Bridges Avenue. As we started the ride to the jail, I remained silent, still upset, and angry with myself—but also with them! It was clear to me they felt a sense of accomplishment, like a hunter that had bagged a big one. Glaring out the window, ignoring their vanity, I slowly felt a bit startled. I noticed that our route was not the planned ride to the jail on Parham Road. I thought about what was happening, imagining what might welcome me at the destination. We pulled into an underground parking deck in a business complex on Malvern Street. It was an ominous scenario, and I felt a threat like something on television: an empty, dimly lit, parking deck underground with cold concrete, cinderblock walls, and a low ceiling concealing a nefarious deed. They remained quiet and still. When we stopped, I was preparing myself for almost anything as they glanced at each other as if asking, with their eyes: *you ready?*

They took me to the elevators, and we went up to some office spaces where I was led to a back room. It was rather unsettling with just a couple of chairs and a small desk. They told me to sit and be patient. After maybe a minute, the door opened and in walks Toby Vick, the chief prosecutor in Henrico County, like a kid in a candy store. He slowly slid the other chair in front of my shackled feet and leaned back. "You got any statement you want to make?" he said, leaning further back tilting the chair slightly.

"Isn't this the time you offer me a deal, something to get the big fish not just a street-level addict?"

He looked amused and slowly spoke back. "We got what we want." He rocked slightly and looked down his nose at me like he was playing Perry Mason, pompous and certain of himself. "No bigger dealers, huh? But I guess, I mean, what could be bigger than Chuck," I responded. He repeated himself, "We got what we want," and at that exact moment, he lost his balance in the chair and almost fell but caught himself. He tried to be cool about it and said the words again as if nothing happened, even though he went from Perry Mason to Deputy Barney Fife (on "The Andy Griffith Show") even more comically. It shifted the authority in the room in an uncanny way, embarrassing him and his boys, like tripping while walking to accept your diploma.

It was a brief moment that allowed me a second of respite in the middle of my rage, but they didn't notice because I was *authentically* cool. Vick got what he wanted, not the big heroin supplier or Mafia boss, but a political nuisance that had to go.

The morning following my arrest, and the police departments' long, diligent effort to have me take the bait and nab me, a map of my entire route was in the newspapers, including the house with heroin where the dealer and others lived—but the police never even so much as questioned the residents. The people of that residence visited me in jail four months later and laughed about the police being so stupid. The police were not being stupid; they were not focused on drugs. They felt their job that evening was a political responsibility, not so much to stem the proliferation of drugs as to silence a strong political voice.

Why else would the arresting officers interrogate Tammy about the Arthur Ashe Statue on Monument Avenue while Chuck Richardson was fighting so hard for it? Take a good hard look at my push for a Black symbol on Monument Avenue and the timeframe of the police investigation. All the dates, news stories, and timeframes are traceable. Sadly, there were citizens, Black and White, who chose to believe that all of this was about getting one addict off the streets of Richmond, and conveniently, one audacious councilman from office: two birds with one stone.

The next morning, with help from Mike Morchower, I was released on bond. I went directly from the Henrico County Jail to "Nine-Nineteen," which at that time was a rehabilitation center at 919 West Grace Street. The scene outside after I got there was a circus, with the media hopping around each other and trying to get a picture or an interview with anybody that would say something. The privacy and nature of such a place was strictly protected, however, inside and out. So, television cameramen and reporters set themselves up at the corners, in parking lots, wherever they could position themselves for their live broadcasts. Men and women constantly jogged back and forth with pen and pad in hand.

That morning, there was also commotion inside Nine-Nineteen as clients wondered what all the craziness was about. I was in a relatively small office space with three desks and three administrators, including the director, and I could hear the polite whispers outside the office. "Chuck Richardson, who? Chuck Richardson ..." The protocols are very strict: no visitors, no private phone calls, everyone is known by their actual first name, and I was referred to only as "Henry" as I registered myself to be admitted. Reporters would call and try to get

Chuck Richardson with Monte Richardson

Entering a second court battle with my attorney, "Magic Mike" Morchower. © *Richmond Times Dispatch*

Leaving a hearing with my ever-positive mother, Ruth. © *Richmond Times Dispatch*

information, but they got nothing, no denial, no confirmation, nothing.

Within a just a few minutes, the office phone rang again, and a lady named Mrs. Hollins answered it. She looked at me and listened, then said, "It's for you, Henry."

I took the phone, and the voice was my wife, Phyllis. She was utterly shaken, tearful, and confused, pleading with me for answers. "Rich, what is this, please…" Phyllis had been out of town in Washington visiting her sister, Betty, so she didn't expect me to be home, but she did pick up the morning newspaper. Plastered across the front pages was "Rich."

"What is happening, Rich? Tell me this is a bad dream. What's going on, why? Why, Rich?" She wasn't surprised about the arrest at all; she even expected it sooner or later but … a young twenty-four-year-old White girl was in those papers as well: Tammy Taylor. The stories relished in the poor, young little White girl that had been wooed by the unscrupulous drug addicted Councill man.

Tammy proclaimed her love for me. "He promised me the moon," she was quoted as saying. "I love him, immensely."

Phyllis cried in my ear and pleaded with me to explain, to assure her it was wrong. I was standing there with three women looking at me, hearing everything I said, barely more than an arm's length from me. The little room left no room for intimacy to say to Phyllis what I needed to. I could sense those ladies felt badly that they could not allow me a moment of privacy, but it was out of the question. I've had many poignant moments in this life: sad, exhilarating, horrifying, and mystifying. But those few moments on the phone with her that day stand profoundly alone. My heart broke as I listened, unable to ease her pain. It was simply a pitiful situation I had created, and I could only listen to Phyllis cry.

It was big news: it made *The New York Times*! The stories in the local press were pretty much what you'd expect: "Chuck Richardson Charged with Heroin Distribution!"

I remained at Nine-Nineteen for over two months until my hearing on December 8th, the same date in 1968 that I reported to my draft induction. I was sentenced to ten years in jail, with nine years suspended. The media continued its obsession with all manner of narratives about me: Black Richmond, City Councilman, drug abuse, and opinions from everybody and their mothers. The *Times Dispatch* put out an editorial that read, "Richardson should talk," and they urged for a grand jury to extract the names and places that were already known unofficially. And what do you know? The Commonwealth Attorney obliged.

The intent was to have me turn on the people about which they were already fully aware. After fifteen months, 24-7 surveillance, they had it all: top to bottom. They didn't need the answers they had: they needed Chuck! It would be the emasculation of Black Richmond, a champion turned chump in the face of the real power—White power—nothing but that. It would go like this: they'd pull me before the Jury—and the next day, there would be six or seven arrests, all because of me. They'd say it was because I "talked." There was no fucking way I was going talk to that Grand Jury; it was a cynical plot that stiffened my Black ass. A day or so after they announced it, my garage behind my house was blown up, causing a big fire and lots of damage but, fortunately, no injuries or damage to my home. The anticipation around my appearance for that Jury was as heavy as the "Thrilla in Manila."

A grand jury was called and all of Richmond waited with bated breath to see Chuck "roll." It was a tumultuous moment in Richmond, basically pitting Black against White. On one side, a pathetic, arrogant Black drug dealer. On the other, a hero of their causes fighting an illness, entrapped to shut him down. After some time, the jury was in place and the day was at hand; would Chuck talk? I remember that morning, still angry at the way a war veteran was being treated, as if he had not been through the valley of the shadow of death but was also now being delivered into a fashion of evil. I knew what this was about, and it was outrageous to consider capitulation. Meanwhile, the actual dealer, Jim Barrett, was a "free bird"—they did not care to change.

Cease Fire! Cease Fire!

Grand Jury

Waiting in the holding cell was another lesson in humility. Six to eight men, all Black, were crammed into a dingy ten foot by twelve foot crucible. The area, for our convenience, had a sink and toilet complete with the stench of urine. Ironically, the other men there behaved as though this was a way of life for them, almost unfazed. Their attention was only drawn to anything that looked female, which would trigger animalistic cat calls and whistles each time a woman entered the other side of the bars in this tight holding area.

Even though court officers normally release leg irons before the accused enters the court room, I felt an odd sense of relief when they came to shackle my hands and feet, a strange empowerment. I was first brought up from downstairs by Toby Vick and Virginia State Prosecutor Bob Trano, and was outraged at what these guys were doing: setting me up as some display of a triumphant catch for law and justice, and its power to break those in its snare. I argued with Vick while we entered a very small transfer area, where one door is locked before the door on the other side is opened. I told him it was a damn shame they were going to give Jim Barratt, a two-time felon, virtually no time while I, a simple user, was looking at many months, if not years had I not given them names they already had. "You know every spot I've been the last year or more. Y'all know damn well this ain't about information you already have!"

It was a tight area, barely four feet by six feet, and I was literally rubbing against Vick while I confronted him about such bullshit. I said, "Look, give me your word it won't get to the media and..."

"Chuck, we can't make any promises, so forget it."

I said, "You take me for goddamn fool, don't you? You have all you need to act against the people you supposedly need me to name. And then three days after I talk, you make arrests, and guess who squealed to the court all over the news? I'm not saying shit to that grand jury!"

I know Vick must have been counting the milliseconds until that other door opened because I was righteously indignant in his face. Then the door was unlocked, and the humiliation returned. I walked down the corridor and watched the familiar faces of news reporters to whom I had once given spirited, articulate, and proud interviews. Although they had all been barred from the courthouse hallway, heads and eyes turned and searched from windows of the doorway.

Journalists Michael P. Williams, Allen Cooper, Jane Olsen, and a few others looked curiously bland as I passed, surrounded by deputies, and shackled like a vicious mass murderer. I thought to myself: *what an overreaction for somebody guilty of just an addiction.* I rarely, if ever, even stepped on an ant. As a lover of nature, I consciously do no harm to small creatures whether they are wasps, bees, or even ants. And while I may have been forced to take human life in Vietnam, the thought of harming someone, other than in self-defense, was unthinkable. Yet, here I was being marched along by two state police agents, an assortment of deputy sheriffs, and Juris Doctors of the court: Toby Vick and Bob Trano, all of whom were escorting me with such proud serious resolve as if I were Baby Face Nelson, Legs Diamond or Pretty Boy Floyd headed to "the chair." It was the biggest bunch of ceremonial law enforcement bullshit you'd ever want to see.

I was led into a large, eighteen-foot-ceilinged room that had a light gray decor with pictures of dead Civil War generals—rebels, of course—hanging around the walls. As I walked baby-steps over to the stand where I was to testify, I could feel the gaze of those racist warriors, though dead for a hundred years. The living eyes in the room seemed from that era and mentality as well, watching me as though I were some strange, dangerous creature for whom these distinguished citizens had the task of determining the appropriateness of its existence. I was clad in a maroon prison jumpsuit with one zipper form neck to crotch and a denim overjacket, still human.

When I reached the podium's seat, my handcuffs were removed. I believed that, except for the need of raising a hand to swear in, they would have preferred my hands to remain cuffed. I felt a vague eeriness about the whole courtroom, as though I had lived this long before, a "déjà vu" if you will. Perhaps some time back in the Jim Crow Era when "niggers" didn't have a chance at legal justice. As I looked down the long line of seated jurors on the other side of the courtroom banister, a "lynching feeling" came over my soul. All but one of them was White, a mean-looking White! I thought to myself: *this is Richmond, the city I love, where half the population is African American. How am I seeing this? White people, old White people, Colonial Heights-looking White people, not at all my peers. This was not a random selection from my city!*

An old lady sat looking at me with full contempt, sporting a ten-inch-high, stiff white hairdo with a blue tint. Wearing a loud pink top, she was ugly, and I mean "God forgive me" type of ugly. Her makeup was caked on unevenly and her face appeared to have encountered a waffle iron—like the kind my momma used for pancakes. Before there was anything to write, she was upright with a pencil and pad waiting and eager to record any marks against me. One old man, who sat at the far end, did not appear to be alive. His bald head had drooped forward, and his bottom lip protruded beyond his chin with a slight drool starting to escape his lip.

All the White jurors possessed varying degrees of redneck, but they were distinctly redneck. There was a lady who resembled the character Aunt Bea from "The Andy Griffith Show": her large round eyes peered suspiciously over the round, gold rimmed glasses attached to a chain. However, she didn't carry any warm quality of Aunt Bea from television. The women jurors looked like a list of who's who from the Daughters of the Confederacy. The clothing of the men, who wore blue or white bow ties along with long sleeve flannel shirts, alerted me that the home team was in trouble. Beyond the comically slanted makeup of these grand jurors, the entire setup seemed to be so contrived. Bob Trano, the prosecutor, was not from Richmond, but from Henrico; the police were not from the State nor the City; the court was Manchester, not John Marshall; and the presiding judge was certifiably the most racist in Richmond, James Wilkerson himself. Not Judge Randy Johnson, or Judge James Spence, but James—Jimmy—"Jim Crow" Wilkerson.

As I glanced across the faces in that courtroom and the portraits on the wall, it occurred to me that this courtroom situation was not about drugs at all. This was an exercise for certainly political, if not racial, retribution. "You goin' t'jail, boy!" Ever since I was a little boy, I can remember White folks sayin' this.

"You better get outta this neighborhood or you goin' t'jail, boy."

"You better leave this store or you goin' t'jail, boy."

I remember a policeman telling me in 1963, "You talk back to me and you goin' t'jail, boy." I was trying to explain to him that I had to walk up Thrash Lane through an all-White neighborhood to go to school, Henrico High School, which had no Blacks until that year. He couldn't understand why I was walking on that street and had no interest in a single word from me. Just, "get outta this area or you 'goin t'jail, boy."

I felt that same resentment when Judge Wilkerson warned me of six more months jail time if I didn't answer Mr. Vick's question. The only unspoken word was "boy," but I could still hear it echoing at the end of his admonition; "BOEYE, answer the question or you goin t'jail ... you understand that, boy?" *Nothing has really changed,* I thought. The pain and suffering of chains and slavery were so damaging that they seemed to have etched a genetic fear in the soul of Black men. A fear White people have played beyond the chains. As Douglas A. Blackmon described in his book, *Slavery by Another Name,* the justice system continued to provide White America with the means to threaten Black men with a return to bondage, chains, and servitude, only by another name.

The best kept secret in Richmond politics was the Regional Crime Task Force, complete with its own grand jury. There were no Richmond police officers and no Richmond prosecutors. In fact, our Commonwealth Attorney was not even aware of this group's existence. It was a case of inter-jurisdictional meddling: Henrico, Hanover, and

Chesterfield County law enforcement operatives had gathered to pass judgement on a Richmond crime... and the politics were so thick that the judge placed a seal of secrecy on all the proceedings.

Sitting there with my hands free, grasping and understanding the power that held me, I felt like the character Kunta Kinte of the mini-series, *Roots*. Though full of pride and with all the past momentum of courage and glory, I now found myself powerless and vulnerable. As much as I wanted my freedom and could gain it by acting like some Stepin Fetchit, chicken shit, Uncle Tom, I could not resist this one moment to put everything important to me on the line and say, "White folks, kiss my Black ass!" And so, I did...though quietly and with words respectful of the court. I told them, "Do what you want with me, but I find no response to Mr. Vick or any of his questions." I was firm and resolute, but polite, submitting that I would not provide the court answers to his questions, period.

Mr. Vick was at once perturbed and embarrassed. This was to be his moment of glory, his chance to humiliate and reduce this uppity nigger into something less, something submissive, obedient, and inferior. And I would have been humiliated had this whole thing been only about a drug inquisition, but it wasn't. When I refused to speak, one lady seated to my far right, sat up, stiffened her back, dropped her chin, and looked over her glasses at Judge Wilkerson, asking with her eyes, "Are you going to tolerate such insolence from this nigger?!"

My back was to the judge so I could not see if he caught her eyes, but he seemed, a bit pleasantly, surprised. He responded as though his fondest wish had been delivered unexpectedly before him, and he was prepared to graciously take the opportunity at hand. He grumbled in his distinguished tone and then directed the prosecutor to ask the question two more times—because a person must be asked three times before being charged with contempt. Twice more, Mr. Vick asked the question; twice more, I refused to answer.

Judge Wilkerson asked my lawyers, James E. Sheffield and Michael Morchower, if they had spoken clearly with me and if I understood what I was doing. Sheffield somewhat sighed as he looked at the judge and said, "Your honor, Mr. Richardson is a former City Councilman of nineteen years, and is usually well aware of his circumstances."

Wilkerson cocked his head down, looking at me, "Well, Mr. Richardson of nineteen years, I can hold you in jail as long as I decide if you don't talk. Are you aware of that?" he said.

"Yes, I am, sir, but this entire proceeding is futile. You already have the answers to any question you can ask me! Mr. Vick knows this, as well as the investigators who have followed and surveilled me 24-7 for over a year." I told him, "Anything I would say would only benefit Mr. Vick politically. It would not mean a thing to the drug use in this city.

"The real culprits of Richmond's drug problem are millionaires—not a user like me. People who live in neighborhoods like yours, Your Honor, not mine. You may even play golf with them, go to church, or maybe do business with them. They deal in huge volumes ..."

The judge interrupted, "Mr. Richardson, you will stop right there! You will not presume to know any of my personal friends, and you will cease your comments or take the stand this moment. Mr. Sheffield, control your client ... *and his mouth!*" The judge then asked the deputy to be sure the courtroom doors were closed tight.

Morchower and Sheffield probably wanted to choke me; they had admonished me about my words. "Chuck, this isn't a debate, it isn't council. He's the judge ... now cool it." I know they were saying what I should hear, but damn! I just looked around that courtroom at all the symbols and images of men whose crimes were in trading far worse than drugs.

My attorneys asked for a brief recess to speak with me and the prosecutors in private. The five, maybe six, attorneys and I went back to a small conference room where they all tried to persuade me to talk. One by one, they implored, demanded, cajoled, and pleaded with me to see their perspectives while every eye looked directly at me, enforcing the voices I heard. I heard each one and looked back at them, all in suits and ties, clean-shaven, projecting some facade of authority while I sat in a prison jump suit—chained.

All but one had spoken: Mr. "Big Shot," Toby Vick, sitting directly next to me on my left. Vick sighed for a second with the lost patience of an adult who had to come into the room to handle some little brat pulling the girls' hair. He sat there a second like he was going play Perry Mason again or some shit, and said, "Look, Chuck! You know you to have to talk. Stop playing these games, you have to tell us what we need."

I leaned in slightly, looked right at him and said, "I don't have to tell you a goddamned thing, you redneck motherfucker!" The instant that last syllable left my mouth, the oxygen left the room. As if a mild earthquake had struck, every chair seemed to jerk away from the table with each lawyer holding on as a dozen chair legs screeched an inch across the wood floor, every eye unflinching like they were watching a horror flick. Vick turned a shade of red so intense I'll never forget it. He didn't say anything. He just stood up, and walked out. The others followed, and my guys, Morchower and Sheffield, were silent as well as we went back to the courtroom. Vick then confirmed to the judge I was not answering the questions.

I then took the initiative to offer a statement of apology to the jury by saying, "I, in no way, intended to disrespect the court, but like each of you, I must consider the things most important to me beyond my own will of well-being." I went on to explain that the out-of-control publicity of this supposedly secret grand jury hearing had placed my family at peril, and added that "I will do what probably each of you would."

With a surprising response, Judge Wilkerson, in a rare moment of apparent humanity, stated, "I understand your position regarding the media on this matter, and I am quite disturbed about it myself. I further place this grand jury under the seal of secrecy and will charge with contempt anyone I find in violation."

Next, indeed, was my contempt:

Contempt of Court

Judge: Mr. Richardson, do you understand the question?

Me: Yes.

Judge: Do you further understand that your refusal to answer the question constitutes the crime of contempt? Your refusal is an arrogant display of selfishness, Mr. Richardson and you will regret it, I assure you.

Me: Yes, sir.

Judge: You think that, because of who you are, you don't have to abide by the same laws that every other citizen does. And that is to act within and abide by all the laws that govern this Commonwealth.

Me: Your Honor, I think I am acting within the law and it provides me, as a citizen, in the amendment under freedom of speech, the protection against incrimination.

Judge: You have been given immunity, Mr. Richardson. You cannot be held in criminal charges for any information that you might reveal. Now why don't you cooperate?

Me: Your Honor, it might place me in a more productive position with the court—if I thought anything I say would make a difference—but it won't. You have granted me protection against court action, but that's not the protection I seek, and you cannot provide me the protection I need. You don't have that range of power.

The judge was almost surprised to realize his power was, in this case, limited. He was insulted that his powers didn't reach into the neighborhoods, communities, and back alley locations he never knew existed, or knew anyone who existed.

Judge: Mr. Richardson, you are being held in contempt of court as of this date. Any time being served on your criminal record will stop until you decide to talk to the Grand Jury. Mr. Richardson, the key to your door cell is in your hands. You may walk when you decide to talk.

Me: Thank you, Your Honor. You do have a way with words, Judge Wilkerson.

Judge: Well then, what are you going to do, Mr. Councilman?

I wondered to myself, why in the hell did he patronize me with that "Councilman" shit? He's trying to get me out of here? This shit must be weighing heavily on his ass. I looked up to the judge and I formed a smile.

Me: Your Honor, the key to my door cell is not in my hand. It never has been, and it never will be as long as the Constitutional right to freedom of speech includes the right not to speak. As long as a man has the right to protect his family, he should in any way he deems appropriate. The key to the safety of my home is the key I hold. You, your court, nor Mr. Vick can have it. My walk will be with the deputies back to my jail cell. I will be there as long as I deem it necessary, but it will not be through the grand jury. I have decided that much, Your Honor.

I then politely requested the court if, before the judge-imposed sentencing, I could have the opportunity to discuss this matter with my wife and family. He took my request and then ordered me back into cuffs and shackles. I had no intention of testifying before that grand jury. If the hearing was indeed about drugs, though it was clearly not, my decision would have been far more difficult.

Their own vigor to prosecute me had now changed the very question regarding my incarceration: Should Richardson be in jail for drug use? Can we still intimidate "uppity niggers" into submission with the threat of jail time?

Toby Vick approached the witness stand and asked me if I wanted police protection. It was insulting to hear this asshole posture for the grand jury with his sympathetic bullshit. I politely responded, "No, thank you." To think that the cops had had me under surveillance since May of 1994, around the clock, and then claim to not know of my drug contacts was a law enforcement abomination. What in the hell were they spending money on?! Now, right before the Grand Jury's eyes, they were asking me if I wanted police protection? If their protection was anything like their surveillance, I was better off without it! And with that, I was soon led back to confinement.

Through reading law manuals I recognized that a defendant could only be held in jail as long as it could be a coercive force. My only hope was to convince these people that incarceration would not make me talk. My every act and every word were designed to let them know that keeping me in jail had lost its coercive force and, maybe, would begin to force the question outside my cell.

The jail conditions were certainly, and predictably, miserable. However, I knew that I had to make them think that it didn't bother me at all. When my lawyers or family went back to talk to other people, I needed the word to get to the judge that jail, for me, was a piece of cake. That was the only way that he would believe it was having no coercive effect. But, in reality, it was getting to me: the dirty, filthy conditions, lack of air conditioning, dark and dank cells, no sunlight, bad food, terrible medical treatment, and the little things, like having to use the bathroom in public.

At the New Kent Jail Farm, the toilet was at the front end of the barracks with only a half-top stall, permitting you to see the entire eighty-man barracks from behind a half door—and they could see you! Hell yeah, I wanted to get out, but the judge needed to think I was indifferent, that it was no big deal—that it was just short of a stroll in the park. Plus, "contempt," in all honesty, is the most appropriate reason for anyone who has a problem with our system of justice to be in jail. It is an honorable deed to remain behind bars because your government is wrong, and in this instance, my government was wrong. Judge Wilkerson wanted young Black men to see how they would be treated if they do not do what "Mr. Charlie" says…"when you are disrespectful, talk back, or in general disagreement; in 'contempt' of the court, this is what you'll get!"

It is too painful to consider the degree of loss in productivity and contribution the Black community has suffered, not even withstanding the human toll. Without the full understanding and true witness of the prison system, we will continue to fail our brothers and ourselves. Prison is a place in which the cruelness and unfairness of life is taught, and where lessons for the outside are bought at such a heavy price. As Black people, we all must feel these pains together as the structure of the system is devised to address us all until we of good will, who are well-intentioned, whose plates are filled and pockets are full, know the hopelessness, injustices, inequities, and cruel treatment that our brothers experience on a day-to-day basis. Americans are so utterly unaware of the level of suffering in our prisons. It is sad to imagine that we don't care. We like to tell ourselves that anyone in prison is deserving of any punishment or suffering they receive, cruel or unusual; once that door is shut, so are our minds regarding them. And that's pretty convenient for those profiting across the entire spectrum of the penal system.

The way in which we respond to people's behavior has so much to do with our perception of them, generally. As individuals and groups, we allow the gross miscarriages of justice because of the way a person looks. Both our resentment and favor are overly influenced by our perceptions! Sentencing disparities demonstrate that darker-complexioned African Americans are subject to harsher judgments in court. I am convinced that court judges and prosecuting attorneys give heavier sentences to those defendants whom they, by virtue of their complexion, perceive as more intimidating. Although the statement sounds absurd, I am convinced it is, nevertheless, a fact! In examining my interviews of inmates, I started to recognize that not only were Blacks given longer sentences than Whites, but also that the darker-complexioned Blacks were, receiving yet longer sentences.

Initially, I glossed over the possibility that this practice might be a real pattern. However, after returning to pages and pages of written interviews, and comparing them with the physical description of the interviewee, I was astonished and taken aback. As James Baldwin wrote in his book, *The Fire Next Time,* "To be a Negro in America, and conscious, is to be in a constant state of rage." The rage stems from the absence of an outlet for the anger against unwarranted injustices. Depending on the circumstances, subjective perceptions may or may not be harmful in the interpersonal encounters of everyday life. However, when the subjective perception is used to discriminate against a group in the distribution of justice, something dangerous and cynical is affecting judicial behavior. This reality is a damning indictment in our system and should not be taken lightly!

While incarcerated, I was shipped to eight different holding locations. They all had a disproportionally higher number of Black faces. Even Arlington County, Virginia, where the population was eighty-one percent White, their jail population was eighty-three percent Black! Henrico County, Chesterfield County, Deep Meadow, and New Kent Jail Farm all have the same patterns of color. And in the City of Richmond, where our city's population is approximately forty-six to forty-eight percent White, less than seven percent of the inmates down there were White. How do you get these disparities? Of the over two million incarcerated in the U.S., more than half are Black, even though we make up only twelve percent of the population. The rate of Blacks serving in the Federal and state prisons is six times that of Whites.

What we call the justice system is, in reality, a legal system. Laws are manipulated, abrogated, exaggerated, dissipated, and misappropriated—in other words, exploited to maximize the detention of Black men. Most of us do not see this discrepancy in daily court proceedings, but we need only look at our news media to see the way Blacks are considered in our social dynamic.

For example, the large number of young Black men and women

who experience rape, assault or murder every day seems to escape media attention. However, if one pretty White girl is kidnapped, the story makes the front pages of the news across the country, and the media solicits everyone's help to find them and bring the guilty persons to justice. Nothing is clearer in the criminal justice system than the fact that no other crime, no matter how brutal or sadistic, how evil in its intent, will bring the death penalty with more certainty than a Black man killing a White woman—a documented fact! The observation is even true regarding kidnapped children. Post the picture of a little White girl or boy, and a markedly different response will occur both in time and intensity than to the reaction to a Black child. When young children witness these different responses played out in their daily experiences, they are often tempted to devalue their own lives.

When I was in high school, students could not tell, at first sight, that I was African American. They were confounded, confused, disappointed, and some were even angry with themselves for liking a person like me. They had been taught it was wrong, only because of what they had been told about Black people, not based on the actual experiences they had had with me. The bright or reasonably intelligent teens would contemplate the experience and possibly learn, but those with limited capacity, or empathy, usually better known as rednecks, would immediately react as though they had made some monumental mistake by treating me fairly.

The most ironic and saddest aspect of this picture is that Black people occupy some of the positions responsible for this outrageous discrepancy in numbers. It starts with that individual patrol officer on the street who treats a Black citizen different from a White citizen. Like it or not, it is true. It is a shame how the self-hate indoctrination heaped upon the African American during slavery and beyond continues to haunt us and cause us to commit despicable acts of resentment against our own kind. The conditioning is so deep, some among us who are guilty do not even realize when we are doing it. It is not right, and Black people who have not awakened to its inappropriate nature need to wake up!

While incarcerated, I witnessed Black deputies who took pride in abusing Black inmates just to impress their White superiors or peers! This is akin to the ignorance of the old "house nigger" behavior to acquire White acceptance—still done today. I'm not saying that because you are a deputy at a jail you are a "house nigger." I'm assuming that you are not. But, importantly, beyond your behavior, you have an obligation not to tolerate it when you observe it in someone else. That's my point. Sometimes, we can be our own worst enemies, and for what reason? Jealousy, envy, personal insecurity, lack of achievement? The reasons are unlimited, and we must stop it. Each Black citizen of this country has a moral obligation and duty to fully recognize behavior conflicting with our collective enlightened interest.

While in the Richmond City Jail, I was able to attain a position as a school tier instructor, helping inmates reach their ability to receive their G.E.D. In my new position, I instituted several changes. Rather than the normal classes on dinosaurs and plate tectonics, I initiated classes on job applications, writing resumes, how to give a job interview, filing income tax forms, setting up checking accounts, and other classes pursuant to everyday survival skills. Without hesitation or reluctance, I was openly critical of the jail's curriculum and how it was being utilized to harbor and protect White inmates while at the same time depriving Black men of securing a G.E.D.

I sent a letter to the sheriff of the jail, Sherriff Michelle Mitchell, suggesting that I be allowed to help with implementing a curriculum for inmates that was more practical for them. I explained that I could use my experiences to assist her in developing better programs of parity and fairness to all the inmates. It also would have enabled me to better utilize my time as an inmate of the jail. There were nights when, as much as I may have attempted to conceal my struggles with PTSD, it was difficult and made worse with useless days. The sheriff never once responded to my concerns. It could have been a win-win situation. In any event, her disregard for my efforts to improve the school tier was an opportunity lost, due to inexperience as a sheriff as well as her fear of being innovative and trusting. Unfortunately, it was a perfect example of how failure occurs because of what my brother-in-law Maynard called the SND—the "Scared Negro Disease": when African Americans in positions of power are too frightened to act on something to make a difference, and don't, because of fear. Apparently Michelle was just too inexperienced to handle that position. She could have trusted my efforts but was afraid to believe in me, another Black, who had demonstrated a record of commitment to our community.

Her ultimate response came to me one morning following breakfast. There were several deputies who continued to respect and hold me in high regard at the jail. One of these deputies came to me and, in a reluctant and shameful manner, instructed me to pack up my gear, and said that I was leaving. I had no idea what was about to occur, but I could tell it was not good. Mrs. Mitchell had decided to transfer me out of the Richmond Jail to the Arlington County local corrections facility. It was a cruel and unnecessary effort to prevent any further disruption by getting me out of her jail.

It was 100 miles from home and constituted several inconveniences that added to the already painful experience of incarceration. As a result, it made visitation of friends and families more difficult. It complicated any efforts to communicate with the press and newspaper. I was removed from the protected environment of people who knew me. The only positive aspect of this move to Arlington was that it was a no-smoking facility. Even though it was extremely nerve-shattering, not smoking did help me. Although there was this one time … being caught with a book of matches in my belongings.

I had been transferred from Arlington to Richmond for court hearings, and at the Richmond Jail, smoking was permitted, and I did so. After the three-day stay in Richmond, the oversight of my search when I left did not disclose the presence of the matches until I arrived at my return to Arlington. I explained that Richmond was a "smoking facility" and—was told that was "IRRELEVANT!!" Sixteen days of miserable, painful, solitude can make good men bad and bad men evil! I never was able to understand the logic behind measures extricating good from the hearts of men by forcing them to face hours, end on end, day after day, with no purpose. The anguish of the dark walls, unable to distinguish day from night, not knowing weekdays from weekends, losing all sense of time and perspective. The mind is in an interminable search of balance or equilibrium.

The confinement had definite negative effects on my life, some that did not surface until much time had passed. It is a particularly cruel treatment in some facilities where for twenty-three hours there is total silence. There is nothing to read, no human communication: only a slot through which to be fed, limited lighting, and a very small area in which to exist. There is no real purpose for such treatment, and I spent sixteen days under those conditions in the Arlington system. There are no purposes of a rehabilitative nature, penitence, reform, or reason for improvement of the human conditions that might call for such practices. There may be circumstances when an inmate might need to be isolated from others for the purposes of safety; however, confining individuals as a punitive means of mental cruelty is extremely harsh and worse than some of my most horrific days in Vietnam. Minutes, literally minutes, could feel infinite, slow, like quiet perceptions of death more painful than the gallows of hell itself.

Specifically, it traumatizes one's emotions and left me in a temporary state of mental illnesses for short periods of time. When I think that men and women have served literally decades in solitary confinement, not for the crime they were in jail for, but at the discretion of a warden, it is as disgusting as almost anything I can imagine. How Robert King, Albert Woodfox, and Herman Wallace, inmates at the Louisiana State Penitentiary known as the Angola Three, spent thirty and forty years in a nine by six-foot cell for twenty-three hours a day is beyond my grasp. God forgive us.

CHAPTER 14

Fortitude

The course of my confinement and the people I encountered were at times an amazing revelation. Some of the brothers were really articulate, well-read, and they would reflect on the system from a perspective only gained by time in it. And as they say in this country, "Time is money." It has become apparent over the last few decades that the time spent by hundreds of thousands of Black men in the penal system was by design, but their time equated to somebody else's money. The prison system has become a boon for private businesses like CoreCivic, formerly called the Corrections Corporation of America, who actually lobby for tougher criminal penalties to create greater numbers of prisoners and the need for more private prisons, funded with our taxes. This system is predicated upon contracts to support the industrial correctional complex. Contracts for jail construction, food services, uniforms, canteen supplies, automobiles, medical services, and thousands of other requirements and personnel to operate and support—and perpetuate—the demand for them.

There has to be a structural reform, and we, the Black community, must drive the social conscience as we did in the '60s, to reform this insidious, punitive arm of racism.

One my time in the system had passed the one-year mark, I was developing a calcified resolve to endure the day-by-day struggles.

Mike Morchower, nonetheless, was becoming more concerned about the impact incarceration was beginning to have on me. He was aware of an incident where I became involved in an altercation where an inmate walked up from behind and knocked me out cold with a broom handle. I only recall waking up and remembering nothing at all, nothing about anything. Jim Sheffield, my other attorney, was almost in tears one day as he looked around at the jail conditions and said to me, "Chuck, you've got to stop and go to the grand jury. You can't keep this up, Chuck." Jim was a kind, caring, and very emotional man. I put my arm around him and assured him I could take it, that it was not that bad and that he just had to hold on, too—just hold on.

My supporters were faithful and committed to our cause. My wife was heroic, remaining very poised in her public statements, truly noble, and dignified. Friends, like Marty Jewell, Reverend Bradley, Eva Woods, and many others orchestrated public opinion rallies that were effective and made a tremendous difference. Bernice Travers was an expert, strategic organizer and kept the pressures on. T-shirts and buttons would be seen around town saying, "Free Chuck!" People

Fighting for my freedom my wife Phyllis is speaking with a supporter on the Old Manchester courthouse steps with my son and daughter, 1997.

Cease Fire! Cease Fire!

would look up every time there was a rally and ask the question, "Is he still in jail?!" It was becoming more of the conversation around Richmond, even among Whites, that Chuck Richardson does not deserve this. And each time, the public refrain would become increasingly more embarrassing to the judge. I wrote letters in jail and sent them out to be read at the rallies, expressing my gratitude and trust in them, and my determination. The letters served to rally my fortitude as well. I had nothing but time...so to speak.

I wanted young Black men to see than none of us should just "go along to get along." The struggle of Black people has been made doubly difficult because not enough people stood and disagreed when they should have, because they were afraid or did not recognize that the only thing you have exclusive control over is your mind! Your money, car, house, even your freedom can be taken from you, but you have to *give* your mind away! I still had control over the one thing I always had, the one thing that they feared the most, and the one thing for which I was actually jailed—my mouth! I wanted to maintain control, at least, over that, if nothing else.

I didn't know how long that would be, but I found out that Judge Wilkerson's wife had said something to him about how bad it looked in the public's eye for him to keep me in jail. I knew it could be only a matter of time. Once your wife starts to "pillow talk" about a court case, the judge's judgement has a second thought. Morchower, my trusted attorney, had a personal relationship with Judge Wilkerson and his wife. He had shared this with me on previous occasions, although he had never gone into detail regarding how close they were. But I could discern from the description of their dinners together that Morchower was akin to an adopted son. He was proud of the close relationship but could not share with me things in great detail.

But one day at the City jail, he slipped. He mentioned that Mrs. Wilkerson had openly complained at dinner that the judge was being regularly criticized for holding me in contempt for so long, particularly since he had stopped my time for the initial charges, and I was no longer getting credit for the time I was serving. He shared she felt that it appeared too harsh and extremely unfair and the public sentiments were turning in my favor, even among some of my detractors. Even they feared that the judge would miscalculate public opinion and maneuver himself into a position of resentful disfavor.

It was announced on Thursday, October 11, 1997, that I would be released on Sunday the 14th. That Sunday, Fred Pryor came out and picked me up at Deep Meadow Detention Center—in a limousine. There was a big reception brought together at Second Baptist Church on Idlewood Avenue, open to all, and more than 300 people showed up: old folk, young folk, Black, brown, and White folk, poor and privileged. Even alumni clients from Nine-Nineteen showed up for me. It was such a mixture of emotions created: pride of endurance, love of my family, appreciation for the supporters who, as I've said before, showed me that for all I've done wrong, I've done enough right.

The new start was invigorating. Being confident I could stay

After two years, my release from prison welcomed with a kiss from Phyllis, 1997 (Photographed by Kirby Carmichael).

Cease Fire! Cease Fire!

The same day I was released from prison and welcomed back into the community at Second Baptist Church, 1997 (Photographed by Kirby Curmichael).

clean after two years, with a broad range of people supporting me, and emerging back into society, excited me. I was an icon of Black politics in Richmond. While often there were sneers or cutting eyes, the great majority of my encounters were positive and praised my record and courage on the Council. However, the job market for such an icon was not exactly beating the path. I worked for several years with Fred at CMC Limousines, mostly as a manager but occasionally driving. When I did drive it was almost always a surprise for the clients, creating conversation, which is normally something minimal as a driver; it was Chuck this, or Chuck that, and "What do think of him, Chuck?"

Once I picked up a client at the airport and he was amused to see me, not to mention that I was picking up his bags laying at his feet. He tilted his head and said, "Well, isn't this something." He was an older White man and tried to be nice while obviously recognizing me. I believe he was a prominent banker in Richmond and, as I loaded his bags, I felt a bizarre feeling of nobodiness. From the halls of power to subservient footman, yet I carried his bags with the same dignity I carried my legislation. The nobodiness feeling was fleeting because I perceived myself as his equal—and he knew it. He knew I was accepting the hand I was dealt; no self-pity, no nobodiness ... still Chuck Richardson.

In the car, he casually asked me, "What's it like, the 'fall from grace,' picking up bags?" I smiled and refused to let him believe I was any less than I was twenty years earlier, and he knew as a matter of wits that he'd better tread lightly.

I said, "It's the hand I've been dealt, and I deal with it. I hope that seeing me in this role is tempered by seeing the Black man who is honored on Monument Avenue today, and by the thirty percent set-aside Blacks now enjoy in City contracts." He knew well the point I was making and politely changed the subject. I remained generally quiet the rest of the ride, reflecting on the reality of my place, my fall from grace. No man, no matter how confident or enlightened, can be untouched by the forfeit of such eminence.

Right or wrong, the consequences of drug addiction are life-lasting. If families are lucky, they can weather the disastrous effects; if not, lives are ruined, and friendships are quickly lost. The cost of drug or alcohol dependence will even take you from society. As with myself, the incarceration of thousands upon thousands of drug offenders leaves them almost valueless in the world to which they return. The struggle to first survive the addiction and then the incarceration only to be dropped in a world that will, in most instances, have an automatic, insidious denial of your worth: job opportunities, housing, jury service, various occupational licenses, and other things that shackle even hope.

In early 2001, along with Maynard Jackson, I founded the National Organization of Rehabilitated Offenders (NORO). It was my desire to reach out to those I viewed as rehabilitated offenders, not "convicted felons." Our goal is to provide information and direction to help them maneuver the labyrinth of barriers and restrictions to their efforts to regain meaningful, productive places in society. In this country, we have a core viewpoint that says, "when the debt is paid, the ledger balance says paid in full; nothing else due." And for rehabilitated offenders to continue to carry the yoke of an unpaid debt is not right. Even those who have, in earnest, made attempts to change their lives, establishing a set of values such as hard work, honesty, staying clean, must confront and overcome—daily—the stigma of "convicted felon." But when you constantly have doors closed on you, you become a non-entity, and that sense of nobodiness sets in and attacks your spirit. Then, after a while, time after time when the psyche says, *no, no, no,* you give up.

Maynard and I felt one of the most fundamental acknowledgements of citizenship in this country is the ability to express oneself freely. What more important expression in a democracy than your vote? And by that virtue, hold office? As a councilman for almost twenty years, I might have a deeper appreciation and sensitivity for that right to vote. I suspect I am more fervent about it because I was so much involved in urging others to vote, and know the debt that I've paid to retain the right.

Maynard and I appeared before Congress to push for the reforms needed to return the vote to millions of rehabilitated offenders. The effect of those lost voices in our democracy is not lost on the Republican leadership that already do everything they can to suppress and complicate the voting of minorities. Today, many more states, including Virginia, are recognizing the clear ledger of those who have paid their debt and are returning their rights to vote and hold office. Because of the awareness of groups like NORO, the hopes and aspirations of many thousands are given new potential. Not only the vote, but also the diminishing stigma of a convicted felon, and the social changes that are starting to see people as rehabilitated offenders rather than as ex-cons.

Chuck Richardson with Monte Richardson

Rightful Pain

While employed with CMC Limousine, I came home one evening with a pain in my side. Hoping that it would eventually go away, I laid down on the couch in my den. Unfortunately, it grew worse until it became unbearable. At that time my daughter, Nikki was still living with us. As I lay groaning in agony, she walked by and looked down at me with indifference and disgust. The pain grew even worse and I slid off the couch onto the floor. When Nikki passed again, I looked up and told her how badly I hurt, but she only looked down at me rather smugly and asked me if I had returned to using drugs. Even though the question hurt me, her conclusion was totally rational and quite understandable, given that she had witnessed me go through drug withdrawal before.

The pain was similar, but I had been drug-free for almost five years; moreover, I lacked the typical symptoms: perspiration, vomiting, dripping nasals, nothing at all. Because Nikki could not discern the slight distinction in my behavior, she genuinely believed that I was experiencing the aches of withdrawal. I had been clean for years, but my family had been through years of seeing the "bomb" come out of nowhere, the sudden realization that "dad was using again."

When I asked my daughter to help me, this young woman, usually so characteristically thoughtful and compassionate, only walked away from me and went into the living room where Phyllis was sitting. I heard my daughter and wife talking quietly, although I could not clearly hear what was being said. The pain was worsening, and I called out to Phyllis, "Gimme a hand! I need help." When Nikki returned instead, I told her that I was very serious, and that I would appreciate it if she would take me to the emergency room at Retreat Hospital. In response, she just casually placed her hands on her hips, gave me a motherly pose, and asked if I was sure that I had not been using drugs again. The question enraged me, but I could not respond; I was hurting so badly that I could hardly talk. Nikki walked away so I called out to her mother in the front room again.

I became convinced that both believed that I was going through withdrawal. Phyllis would not respond and also treated me indifferently. Her non-verbal body language communicated the attitude, "I'm not going to help. It serves you right." The pain was at a critical point and I did not have the strength to argue or beg either of them to take me to the hospital.

I dragged myself to the car and drove myself to Retreat Circle. I had to lie down in the seat of the car to rest after arriving at the hospital but eventually I was able to get out of the car. I staggered like a drunk and stopped at the doorsteps of the hospital before I entered, hoping that some passerby would help me as I lay there, at night, in my suit on the curb. After several minutes with no assistance, I pulled my way through the hospital door, but the front desk was dark, and few people were around. As I attempted to look for the receiving area, I fell to the floor at the base of a water fountain, curled up in a knot, and just laid there. I literally could not move.

Two White female nurses ran over and leaned down to help me. I recall the first kind words that I had heard in almost two hours, "What's wrong, honey?" One nurse attempted to help me, but I couldn't even talk. Then, a White male, dressed in all white attire, came over and leaned down. As he and the nurses pulled me into the light, I then heard him say, "Oh, that's Chuck Richardson ..." and he just stood up and looked back down at me. He obviously was familiar with who I was. He looked at me for a moment, turned, and walked away. The nurses continued to assist me onto a gurney and rolled me into a treatment area. Following a quick evaluation, in which they asked me a few questions, they administered an I.V. solution. The excruciating pain had been persisting now for over two hours and I thought I would pass out. After a short while, following some x-rays, the agony, thankfully, began to subside.

A half-hour later, a physician came in and advised me that I had passed a gallstone. Gallstone! *Lord, I'll be damned*, I thought.

I quickly understood why twenty years earlier my father-in-law, Dr. Ford T. Johnson, a tower of strength, had been brought to his knees in pain by a gallstone. Dr. Johnson was a former star football player at Florida A&M University. His incident was the first time I had ever heard of a "gallstone," but I never had understood what could have brought down such a larger, strong man like him...until that night at Stuart Circle Hospital. I found out exactly why!

Hurt by my wife and daughter's response to my pain, my first inclination was to verbally rip them apart with an excoriating lecture to cast guilt. When I further considered things during my return drive home, I realized that their behavior was the exclusive fault of all my previous actions. I was the one who did the drugs and exposed them to the ordeal and pain of withdrawal. I was the one who ultimately gave them reasons to suspect drug use on my part. So, the behavior of both my wife and daughter that night—and my subsequent suffering—was the price paid for the pain and humiliation brought on by my own actions during my years of drug use. Even though I had been clean and sober for almost five years, I was the only one who could have known that fact with certainty. How could they have known it was a gallstone when the only thing that they had ever seen that resembled my behavior was withdrawal pain?

I changed my mind. Instead of cursing them when I arrived home, I told them that I just had a bad case of indigestion and I managed to fart in front of them. I then said, "Oh, damn...gas, strong prescription they gave me!" We laughed, and I never told them anything differently.

Over the years, I have discovered that being happy is that state of existence we all pursue, sometimes blindly. However, many unnecessary and preventable things get in the way of achieving that happiness. Sometimes, it is the energy we waste trying to be right! We want to be happy, but our ego wants to be right. Even when right might not bring happiness, we intuitively have that unquenchable desire to be praised for our insight, knowledge, and wisdom by being right.

I don't always catch the passion of my ego in time. Too often, I allow it to rule me rather than me ruling it. I also have paid for this failure in those days and hours when I felt grief and remorse for having run my mouth in devastating vengeance and anger. To control the impulse to strike out at people in the name of being right is difficult and sometimes almost impossible. Most of us are on a constant journey of attempting to be right throughout life. The need is strong and powerful because each time, it affirms our relevance and need to be. Conversely, when we are not right, we fear the perception by others that we are less than, or that we are reduced in stature and relevance. If you are the kind of person who wants to be right all the time, and yet you never consider the impact of your attitude on the feelings of others, especially those you love, then you are blind to the importance of other people in your life.

When my daughter stood above me with the arrogance and haughtiness of a spiteful dictator, certain that I had returned to the use of drugs, my only burning desire, at that moment, was to prove her wrong. Not only did I want to prove her wrong, but I also wanted to watch her suffer the painful humiliation of being wrong. My daughter, on the other hand, would have suffered deeply and endured hours of misery for something she did not intend to do. She made an error in judgment with no malicious intent: human error. What would I have achieved in my dramatic demonstration to be right? Nothing! I suspect that by 2002 or 2003, my wife and my daughter would have reached their limits and patience with me. I had taken my family through more ordeals for which no man should have expected one bit of forgiveness. Luckily, I had not returned to drugs; that trial was never had. For this reason, I decided, in my drive home from the hospital, that they deserved an excuse.

All these perceptions should be secondary to the goal of being happy and making others you love happy as well. The ultimate goal in life, whether we realize it or not, is to feel good, eliminate dissonance, and to, hopefully, enjoy the comforts of good health. Sometimes, these ends are mutually exclusive; we cannot decide whether the best feeling is being right or being happy. So, the question becomes, do you want to be happy or do you want to be right? Had I returned home and shoved guilt down their throats to make them feel wrong, just so that I could be right, all of us would have walked around for the next three or four days holding hostile attitudes and feeling unhappy. Life is too short to deprive ourselves and the people we love of as many happy moments as possible.

So, I laughed and farted, relieved in many ways, and happy. I think I was right about how I handled that.

My son, Chuckie (Karl), dear wife Phyllis, me, and daughter Nikki (Nichole).

Dirty Red

The ultimate betrayal of drugs is what they will do towards the destruction of long-term, twenty-plus year friendships. When someone you have trusted like a brother, given money, allowed to sleep in your home, vouched for employment, and given him clothes off your back— someone you've known since childhood and would never believe they'd deliver you into the hands of the police, does just that, the sinister reality of crack is realized. When the habit of crack cocaine has you, the lure of police money, or any money for that matter, to procure the drug, renders no act an issue of compunction.

The devastation and trouble my "friend" brought into my life almost eight years after my release from prison, ten years after I was clean and sober, was unbelievable. This individual had continued to use drugs, so we no longer had a social relationship as before, but when he and I did indulge, ten to fifteen years before, he knew all the concealed places I kept things when we used. In the early 2000s, he would occasionally visit my son who rented the basement unit of my home. My son, Karl, whom we call "Chuckie," had secretly grown some marijuana plants in the basement. I suppose that was the lone reason for his drop-by. This pathetic clown, my old friend, Ronald "Red" Coleman, had once even been a tenant and stayed in the very space—for free—that my son now occupied. I should have suspected something, but I had agreed to stay out of the basement and give him space as he was now in his 30s. Our relationship was tentative, so I attempted to salvage our ability to function without conflict. He kept his girlfriend there in close quarters and her need for privacy was an additional reason to ensure that I not just break in on them. When my son began to grow marijuana plants in the basement, he would dare not let me know because he knew, instinctively, I would have gone ballistic!

During this time, Red was in a critical struggle with crack cocaine. Crack addicts will do, close to literally, anything to get the hit they need. If you turned in a drug dealer to the Richmond Police, you would receive reward money. Red, distressed and in need of money to get a hit, went to the police, and told them about the marijuana plants. But in addition to the marijuana plants, that "nigga'" told the police about a place he remembered from twelve years earlier where I had hidden my "works": utensils, syringe, cookers, and ties. They were in an old bathtub shower entrance, behind the wall where you would access plumbing, and I had long since erased any vestige of memory about those things possibly being there.

When the police arrived, having no idea why they had come, I was more than cooperative, and escorted them to his downstairs apartment entrance as they requested. The police, in their ever-grandstanding posture when it came to me, brought the news media in tow—and the cavalry no less: fifteen or more law enforcement personnel. Chuckie was not home, so I offered to let them into his place. I went for my keys, but they said no; they had to use the battering ram with two officers. Going through an unlocked door was not heroic enough; it needed to be "breached"—they had TV cameras to serve, there for "news-food." It was all so dramatic and overdone, such an unnecessary spectacle. All I could do was shake my head and think, *God dammnnn ... Damn.*

When I saw the plants, I was shocked! I couldn't believe my eyes. Following the discovery of the plants, they advised me that they would have to search my home—the entire house. I was personally offended; the implication was unadulterated. I replied, "The whole house! Jesus, c'mon!" but I made no other protest because it had been ten years since I had last used illegal drugs, and I had nothing to hide. They proceeded directly to the bathroom location; no shell game—they knew exactly which dome to lift.

They returned with an old, cloudy plastic bag that had a couple old syringes and paraphernalia, which I knew might be possible they'd find given twenty years of use in this house. The officer in charge could obviously tell by the condition of the package that they were old, dysfunctional, and had nothing to do with any possible current drug use. We discussed the matter momentarily and he was uncertain about pressing charges. I told him, "Look, using on-and-off for over twenty years, hell—you might find other such items, but I've discarded everything to my knowledge. I'll take a drug test right now, on the spot!"

He walked away and spoke with his superiors on the phone. He finally came back saying they decided to press charges because, even though the paraphernalia were obviously old and dysfunctional, they were found in my possession. They said that was sufficient enough to bring a charge but they would not subject me to a drug test. I suppose with so many officers around, it would look bad not to, but it was such bullshit because they knew it would hurt their case if my test came back clean.

Unfortunately, as had been the incessant case for over twenty years, I realized that this had nothing at all to do with justice, fairness, the fight against drugs, good honest police work or anything else other than the same game. The whole exercise with the seventeen officers, nine police vehicles, television, and newspaper camera crews—and police ramrod equipment—was the same game. Toting a search warrant that was illegal and a fifteen-minute discussion with his superiors before deciding they would bring charges, a derelict police force that had no qualms with supplying cash to a crack addict to stage the seizure of their old nemesis, and the political embarrassment just to bring a new charge on Chuck Richardson was their game, when really this was about crackhead that needed money—at the expense of a friend's freedom.

At the subsequent trial, my amazing attorney, "Magic Mike" Morchower, laid out, beautifully, the weak and contrived case against me. The jury was empathetic and convinced it did not meet any measure of guilt on my part. I was acquitted.

Meanwhile, Chuckie was convicted and spent several months in prison while he never revealed his partner in the scheme. His partner was his friend and his boss, Michael T. Barber, at the Carytown Burger and Fries restaurant. Chuckie said Barber had a real substance abuse problem. When he almost lost the restaurant, he was saved by Chuckie's "tough love" toward him and reigned in his business negligence several times. I had remembered seeing Barber visit Chuckie in the basement at times but thought they were just getting together to smoke, nothing more.

After the trial, Chuckie told me all about it. Barber had been the actual facilitator of the whole venture: acquiring the seeds from Amsterdam, the financing for special halogen lights, a ventilator system, carbon dioxide tank, seabird guano for fertilizer, and a book!

But Chuckie felt saying something in court would not only be a turn on his friend, but possibly on his co-workers who stood to lose their jobs if Barber was found out. "Dad, I was just the farm-hand in all that. I thought maybe it would help me to pitch in a little more to you and mom, too…I'm sorry."

Politics is a nasty game, and so, too, can be the friendship game. Motivation and intent can make for big surprises; the "turn" on you. Red never spoke to me again; I don't even know if he's alive. I can't forgive him, but I know crack was his master. Chuckie's friend was a false friend, venal and driven. He stabbed in the back someone who had been faithful for years, not the least the year when my old friend, Red, turned on me.

Politics: Fighting the Landfill

Today's political landscape is more craven and polemic than anything I've seen, as I can hardly believe my eyes or ears. What Donald Trump—with his sycophant, spineless, hypocritical Republican enablers— have rendered in this country is a bizarre, surreal shit-pile on the right. That the president of the United States incessantly obstructed justice, violated the emoluments clause, ignored the constitution, protected and defended Vladimir Putin against his own intelligence services, shook down other countries for his personal gain, put migrant children in cages, had no issue with violent White supremacists, and the list goes on and on and—oh my God, lies like an old damn rug—while all of it seen as just quaint by his obsequious supporters, is beyond any realm of conscionable acceptance. The culture of lawlessness pervaded the traditional party of law and order. With little hope of any self-corrective measures occurring, are we incapable of dealing with such an absolute threat to our Democracy?

It's been said that America "could only be destroyed from within." Or was that, "make America great again"?

What really got me steaming was when Trump met in Helsinki, watching him defend Putin. When I was in Vietnam you know, the place Trump lied his way out of five times, like the hero he is—we captured a North Vietnamese Lieutenant Colonel. In the firefight, I was almost hit. A bullet hit the large rock I was behind. A chip of stone caught my ear and I bled pretty bad; it was close. When he surrendered, he was carrying a Russian Luger, clear evidence of Russia's support to our enemy. I know the Cold War is over, but just as then, and in 1962, and today, they have nuclear weapons aimed at us. I felt an anger much beyond the usual Trump idiocy and malice; it was the smirk on Putin's face like the gangster that grins when a frightened witness won't testify. Something wasn't right and we all knew it.

The sad, tragic reality of minority rule using its power to ensure the implementation of like-minded, appointed-for-a-lifetime judges, gerrymandered districts and voter suppression, and yet finding no dispute with the nakedly corrupt asshole emperor, was nauseating. The patently egregious overrepresentation in House and Senate of an almost tribal minority should shake the fibers of reasonable minds because tribes very often reason while fixated on intolerant narratives. In recent years, I found myself writing almost weekly about Trump's outrage du jour. Whether about sports hero and civil rights symbol Colin Kaepernick, the 2017 Charlottesville riot, the children at the border, his saying "shithole countries," his taxes, or the parade of crooks and cronies in and out of his incompetent Cabinet and campaign that, again, really didn't matter to Republicans, it came to a point of pointless. To go from the articulate, measured, classy, competent, moral family man whose only alleged fault—by Trump, of course—was being born in Kenya, to this pathetically unfit con man, dictator "wanna-be," spoke to something far deeper that has always been just beneath the surface in America. Something that, regrettably, has been a part of our DNA that we have battled for almost 200 years: race. For a remaining third or more of our country to accept the vile, arrogant, snide, incessantly lying personage that is Donald Trump can only be attributed to a tribal defense of a narrative under assault.

Many Republicans have, for decades, voted against their best interest with the Republican party. They believed the GOP stood for their social and religious concerns, even though the party was totally in corporate pockets. Race has been the tool of that party since the "Southern Strategy." The dog whistle used by them to keep that constituency has, with Trump, become a melodic lure from the shrewd demagogue Pied Piper. What most of his supporters read in the "Make America Great Again" slogan is "make me great again." The new culture of Trump, where rule of law no longer bears consistent meaning, created conditions where the President could openly repudiate long-standing law. And sadly, we see it seeping insidiously into the Republican body politic. I have not been in politics in over twenty years now, and when I think of my downfall from the illness of addiction—not corruption or betrayal of my city—it shakes a chord in me I can't ignore. The arrogant or subtle betrayal of those you represent is the real abdication of trust.

A part of that culture has left us inadequately concerned, and, therefore, uninformed about events historical and contemporaneous. It is not so much the incivility or blatant lying of Trumpism, but the disinterest in important roles of government in its wake. It has left too many of us with a dispirited approach of "so what"?

In the later part of 2018, Richmond City Councilman Parker Agelasto moved from his residence in the Fifth District to his new home, curiously, not in the Fifth District. By law, this disqualified him from continuing to serve on the Council. Clearly defined in the Virginia State Code, the law stipulates, "When removed from said district, the seat shall be deemed vacated." Agelasto had, by that definition of law, resigned his seat. But absolutely no one uttered a word! The other members of the Richmond City Council showed little to no respect for that law. Not one of the other eight members acted to acknowledge the vacancy that he had created. I was terribly indignant about the events and found it crazy that this was happening—especially given the historical significance of the district system in Richmond.

It is particularly sad that none of the Black members of the Council recognized the impact Mr. Agelasto's relocation had on the single-member district law created by the 1965 Voting Rights Act, which ensured African American candidates would have greater access to be elected to local office. Before that act, it was difficult, if not impossible, for Black candidates to become elected to local office on an at-large, city-wide basis. The U.S. Supreme Court reprimanded Richmond to conduct its election under the district system in 1977. In that first election, of which I was a proud part, it was well understood that two specific qualifications to run for City Council had to be met: that fifteen signatures of qualified voters within the respective district had to be presented and notarized, and that there would be no equivocation whatsoever regarding relocation outside of the district boundary.

For the Richmond City Council, its City Attorney, and its City Registrar to all stand mute in face of this law is pathetic commentary. The City Attorney found "no reference" to the residency law in the City Charter as his reason to defend Mr. Agelastos's position. But that Charter was drawn up in 1739, with, oddly, no reference made to automobiles or radio stations. The advice the City Council received was moronic; to say that you must live in the district to get elected, but it is not clear you must remain! Moreover, the newly elected Commonwealth Attorney, Colette McEachin, would not act on this profoundly important issue. It was a type of Trumpian denial to the matter.

It is utterly unsettling, and ironic, that Black people would accept something that clearly carries a tone that echoes the very things Trump's Justice Department was pushing. As a citizen of the Fifth District, and a nineteen-year veteran of City Council, I had to do as a citizen what I had done endlessly as a councilman—speak up!—and I filed a suit.

I should say I have no personal dislike for Mr. Agelasto, and only goodwill to him and his family. Indeed, I believed him to be a good representative of our district; however, this issue was about laws and common sense. His assertion that leaving the district was to provide an adequate home for his growing family is farcical. I am convinced his move was to serve his political objectives every bit as much as his family's. Mark my words—as of the time of publication, he will soon run for the House Delegate seat in which he now resides. And it greatly disappoints me to see his display of nonchalant arrogance about such a serious precedent.

I submitted the lawsuit in January 2019 and a hearing was set for mid-April. In the next ninety or so days, it became apparent how popular Mr. Agelasto was in the Fifth District. Many people simply had no quarrel with his overt violation, believing where he wished to live was an extraneous component. It was not what I expected: a careless apathy. And although the City itself failed to properly address Mr. Agelasto's error, complicating a simple matter—*he* knew I was right—and in April announced he would vacate his Council seat in November 2019. The reluctant powers were required to call a special election to fill the remaining year of his term. Suddenly, there was a new question: Who should run? I had no intention, no real consideration of replacing Mr. Agelasto when I realized what he had done. It was a matter of principle and law, not—as he had done—a move to advance any personal political power.

Others immediately jumped at the opportunity his action, and mine, had rendered. Many of my friends thought it was only natural I make the endeavor to seek once again a position of "Accountable Representation," to defend the rights of my Fifth District. I was a tiny bit dubious of the praise and promises of many of my friends. It was almost unthinkable that I could sustain the level of energy needed for a campaign, and though it was as if a key had been put in the ignition with the anticipation of new propulsion in my life, I declined. My focus was strictly on the petition to the court and I spent much of my time gathering and structuring my case.

After over two months of waiting, the judge announced he would postpone my hearing—until July! It was outrageous! Clearly, the judge, Reilly Marchant, felt no urgency to the issue, probably no merit, and had no concern for my question.

That night, I was so furious, I dropped to the floor … and started to do pushups. I decided I was going to run and the first thing I had to do was to prepare was the body. It was daunting; not only was I ascending to the ripe age of seventy-two, but the district I had represented, with the unwavering loyalty of constituents for years, had changed. The work I had done for "The Fifth" had borne fruit in many parts, creating more affluent, business-friendly, vibrant, youthful areas—and White. Did these people know me, know of me? It was a difficult reflection in very many ways. I wondered, and worried, if it would trigger a difficult resurgence of my PTSD. Would I have to deal with the heart-breaking and sleepless nights, reliving the horror of children dying before my eyes, some, as they looked into my eyes? And the campaign would be in full swing in August, the fiftieth anniversary of my most horrible memories of Vietnam.

I was scared just contemplating the possibility of a type of twilight zone situation trying to get through the days—and nights—of the grind required. I did not announce my intention until mid-June, but hit the ground running, so to speak. I was not able to walk the countless blocks and deliver the countless knocks as I had forty years earlier, but I pushed the Marine in me to fight for the right things. Initially, much of the attention around me was about my past: the "former felon" running for office. But I think it also provided what, especially for many younger residents, was forgotten or unknown aspects of my past on the Council and in Vietnam.

The matter of my lawsuit was set for early July. On the day of the hearing, I appeared and inquired about timing and which room. The clerk informed me, rather embarrassingly, that the judge had gone on vacation! It was beyond any credence, any coherent explanation conceivable—what the fuck! "He forgot to let you know," she said. If it hadn't been so outrageous it would have been funny, but such is the bravado of "Trump World." The next date set was August 8th, and I hoped that, too, wasn't "Fake News."

At long last, on August 8th, I entered the petition seeking a declaratory judgment. And once more, the judge displayed his obvious contempt for my suit; he declared that I had no standing, no right to even ask the system for judgement simply because I lived in the district. The judge further noted that "no taxpayer" had justification to bring such action against a councilperson who moved outside of the district! I was shocked back into a past of unbelievable experiences: combat tragedies, heroin depths, police, and federal surveillance, astonished at the judge's decision.

The judge realized Mr. Agelasto had violated the law, but rather than acknowledge his guilt, he stated that just living in the district and being a taxpayer gave me no special right to question the legitimacy of the councilman who represented me. I could not believe my ears. I had been deprived by the court to question the very person I had chosen to represent my interest—about my interest! The answer was known and well understood, even if unspoken, but that judge deprived citizens of the right to even ask the question.

In another time, another stage of my life, that judge would have felt the wrath of an angry Marine. However, today, I have come to the age of painful acceptance, but goddamn it! Nina Simone, the legendary musical artist and community activist, penned a song called "Mississippi, Goddam." It was about rage and no way to expiate it from the soul, so you suffer with acceptance. Ms. Simone may well as have called it "Mississippi, Cease Fire!"

What on God's earth has this government come to? When my fellow Richmonders someday learn the ramifications of Judge Reilly Marchant's decision, they will understand the significance of this case. But I do reserve the right to express myself in the strongest of language. Goddam that court! There are one or two, tacit city councilpersons currently under suspicion of not living in their districts. Should any disgruntled citizen decide to pursue this issue now, there is little they can do, short of complaining. That is an absolute judicial abomination! Still, my soul sits well with Mr. Agelasto. He made a mistake and should be forgiven. And although the judicial system failed to properly address his error, he at least tried, in afterthought, to do the right thing.

At any rate, my campaign for office went on, and I tried to convey the value of my experiences and institutional knowledge of Richmond government. I never flinched from any issue and was always cognizant of the components needed for successful fruition of my responses. But I would continue to make sure my constituents were aware of the simple, important issue of residency. There were more than a few forums where I put the question to all the candidates, and unfortunately, the responses were almost indignant as if a waste of time to talk about that. Even the citizens attending sometimes objected, particularly in the mostly White precincts. At one particular forum at Patrick Henry Elementary School, I was dismayed at how light-hearted the citizens of Woodland Heights took law-breaking into account. I can understand their disagreement with the law and their desire to change it. But, to laugh, jeer, and vilify me for standing up for the law is not the America I sacrificed a year in Vietnam for. They take it for a joke because they do not fully understand the deeper ramifications of their actions.

Most candidates that evening went along with the temperament of the community that occupies the opposite side of the James River directly across from my neighborhood, and I recognized the pandering that is often ubiquitous in political campaigns. I am pleased, however, to note that there are exceptions such as Jer'Mykeal McCoy, who appears to be more culturally founded and might provide hope for Black people in this regard. I was though, rather ashamed of two of my Black opponents, Ms. Robin Mines and Ms. Mamie Taylor, both of whom defended Parker Agelasto's move outside of his district and his continued receipt of a City paycheck. Their naïve and rather ignorant comments reflected a lack of understanding regarding the historical struggle of the voting district system, and the negative impact of their support for Mr. Agelasto's move.

The very law that provided for the concept of their candidacy, the law that was the impetus for so much social, political, and economic change across Black America, was seen by them as an irrelevant relic, as if to kick the head of the shoulders they stood upon. Ms. Taylor, who just happens to be married to my first cousin, seemed the type who would acquiesce to things without adequate consideration to simply garner on-the-spot approval. It saddens me to think about it. It is a very slippery slope we heedlessly travel when we ignore the laws, regardless of our thoughts about them. It is said we are a nation of laws, but the only thing worse than the malfeasance of biased judges is the indifference of citizens who are affected.

One of the consistent refrains from Trump enablers is "elections have consequences." Given the incredible gerrymandering and vote suppression, which gave us the most corrupt and callous administration in our history, I think all of us, especially those seeking office, should pay better attention… and do our homework!

Ultimately, my quest to return and serve was not achieved, and I congratulate the winner, Ms. Stephanie Lynch, and wish her well in her new civic position. I believe her to be able and honest.

As I approach the close to these chapters of my fifteen minutes, it seems that the justice I have always sought after so fervently, even now, escapes me. I am normally optimistic about the prospects of a better tomorrow and the hopes for things to come in general. I made it through the daily antics of racial insults and painful epithets of racist jokes heaped upon me while attending an all-White Henrico High School. I always maintained the hope that I would return safely home from Vietnam despite the odds of only nineteen seconds of survival in a heavy firefight as an M60 Marine machine gunner. And, although I managed to maneuver myself into an underdog's position in each of my council contests, I always thought I would wrestle the victory home somehow. Even during my darkest hours of incarceration, loneliness, and despair, I never lost my hope of an optimistic outcome. Through it all, I held strong to the belief that somehow victory would come to those who believed in the one, single and simple mantra: "Do unto others as you would have them to do unto you."

In 2017, when I attended a high school reunion, I saw across the room a very elderly man seated at a table. I wasn't sure if I knew him and assumed he was probably a teacher from decades ago. When I was closer to him, he stood and looked at me as if familiar and I recognized who it was: John Brown, a history teacher from the '60s and '70s at Henrico. But I remembered him precisely as the football coach who, in 1964, gave me stern direction when I expressed a desire to play on the team. Brown, who had coached my older brother the year earlier as the first Black player on the team, said to me, "As long as you say 'sir' at the end of every sentence you speak to a White man, you'll be okay." I turned away when he said that, knowing as athletic as I was, football would not be my game. It was simply another of the endless events Black people, from the young to the old, endured for being Black. It wasn't as overt and offensive as coach Lowery had been a year earlier in the Driver's Ed class when he mocked the death of a Black person in an auto accident, but the kind of thing that millions of Blacks have experienced in their lifetimes. The things that left generations with an understated form of PTSD itself.

John Brown stood and shook my hand and I saw a kindhearted pain in his eyes, a type of remorse and guilt only his eyes could vent. I think he knew I remembered, and I think he remembered even more. That old White man in his early nineties, with glassy eyes, was apologizing to me with them. I saw it and felt it. We talked and smiled, and he asked about my younger brother, Monte, who would become a star on his team in the seventies. We both acted with empathy and respect toward each other. And when his heavy eyes moved to release water, it made me think that he thought, *it took too long.* John Brown was not the White hero by the same name who raided Harpers Ferry for arms to free slaves, but he had at least gained a freeing perspective in his old age, which I hope and believe will be found eventually by all people—of all races.

In 2019, I lost my fight with the courts to protect the integrity of voter value and lost my attempt to return to the public service of those voters, but I remain committed to speaking for those same people I fought for many years ago. This is a time when we cannot afford to take our eyes off the prize. The threat of the Trump movement is dangerous, ironically, for his supporters as much as anyone. Money, technology—and our complacency—will find us just as the frog in cool, comfortable water on the stove. We must have honest, brave, intelligent fighters to save the doomed analogous frog from becoming slowly boiled—to cease the fire beneath it! We must find in our communities and nation a moment of "cease fire!" To cease fire on immigrant children, cease fire on the relentless incarceration and brutalization of Black men, the pathetic economic disparities. To cease fire on each other with such absurd gun laws. In other words, to cease the fire of hatred and ignorance.

What Matters Now

As I reach the ending phase of this story, our nation finds itself in crisis. The obvious calamity that was sitting in the White House recklessly neglected to respond to a worldwide pandemic, and took us to the brink of unheard-of disaster. In 2016, like "letting the dog drive," we thought we'd amuse ourselves with the spectacle of a reality television president. "How bad could it be?" we asked ourselves, thinking of our great technical and economic prowess. After all, we have self-driving cars and self-serving lies, why not trust that the dog could do it? Now, as if we didn't know the magnitude of the office, and the dangers of absolutely craven ass-kissing lapdogs, we witnessed the very many suffer for the spoils of the few.

The year 2020 certainly portended a profound reassessment for America we must address if we are to survive, much less thrive, in the 21st Century. Even though Trump has left the White House, we must still reassess how we handle truth, how we handle reality. We cannot delude ourselves with narratives that are manifestly corrupt. Perhaps the pandemic, and the resulting hardship and death, has been the cold, hard shake we needed to see "real" reality. How could we have such obscene wealth and abundance, yet lack fundamental values to provide for an emergency like this? How can we rationalize a system that can provide billions and billions and billions of dollars to a single person but leaves a hospital—for children—to ask for nineteen dollars a month from the salary of a teacher? Things like adequate wages, adequate education—and a healthcare system with plans and supplies for such a pandemic—are deemed optional for the Wall Street mentality. And with a selfish, arrogant, xenophobic leader of the country, it is one reality television show we would not believe to be worth watching…too stupid to believe.

They say the eye is a more willing student than the ear because history might be written, portrayed, or told, but the eye learns uniquely. Overwhelmed hospitals and healthcare workers struggled to save the stricken, panicked people hoarding toilet paper and Lysol, empty streets that only lacked tumbleweeds for effect, then … something else. With all the death and suffering, in a weird, sad juxtaposition, we saw murder. It was by no means anything new or surprising, but with consecutive displays culminating in one of the most despicable sights our eyes would see, in 2020 we were made 'woke." The proverbial "straw on the camel's back."

George Floyd was not a terrorist or serial killer, not a bank robber or even a car thief, but he was every Black man in this country since 1619. Floyd was the victim of a slow, torturous death at the hands, or knee, of a calm, deliberate executioner. A White police officer killed Mr. Floyd with such a casual nature it defies belief. He wasn't controlling traffic—he was killing a man—without a worry. It seemed he believed the law, or society, or his union, or … his president had his back. For eight minutes and forty-nine seconds, we saw, in real time, history's bubble burst.

White America had an epiphany: **Black Lives Matter.**

George Floyd was, in a sense, crucified for America's sins. He may one day be seen as the sacrifice it took to save America. It has been a price paid by countless Black people over our history, nothing new to us, but it was the straw that broke our backs—and the image that enlightened others. Two other deaths had recently been in the news. Ahmaud Abery, a young Black man jogging, was basically chased down and murdered by three wanna-be law enforcement. Breonna Taylor was shot eight times, as she slept, by police with a flawed "no-knock" warrant. But the cell phone record of George Floyd's killing was acutely harrowing. Those kinds of deaths have been occurring with every bit the frequency for a hundred years and before, but something was different this time. We were keenly sensitive about Covid-19, and when Floyd's killer, officer Derek Chauvin, rubbed salt in the wound, this time even most Whites felt the cruel distress.

Suddenly, all over America, hundreds of thousands took to the streets despite the pandemic, at times with destructive rage demanding changes. The racist justice system and police reform was the primary issue but understanding the role race has had in the DNA of this country was being confronted. The symbols and monuments of that DNA were being recognized, finally, for what they are: defenders of the belief that Black lives *never* mattered outside the need for them to serve Whites…eagerly. If we are to be genuine about the legacy of that belief, we must connect the dots from Jefferson Davis to the KKK, from Woodrow Wilson to Donald Trump, from James Earl Ray to Derek Chauvin; we must stay woke. We, as leaders and citizens — plain good people, Black and White—have to be cognizant of those who might make Derek Chauvin look like Deepak Chopra. They exist in the ranks of every institution and state. And unfortunately, they may not respond with the incompetence and obstinance as their leaders with this pandemic, but with a kamikaze intent to revive the "lost cause" and the war it rendered.

The hard-right Trumpian, virtually fascist, turn the Republican party has embraced reflects a desperate base that views the browning of America as an ominous, existential crisis, and to some, an actual threat to their very lives. And whether Trump runs in a future election or not, we know that with his initial election, the cat was let out the bag, and we should expect the dots to keep connecting.

Modern Republicans and their media battalions serve every excuse to themselves to pretend the dots do not connect. They claim there is no suppression, no inequity in police response or treatment of Blacks in America—only radical leftists trying to destroy their heritage. But I will say one thing: if it walks like a duck, quacks like a duck, smells like a duck—and his name is Donald!—it's a goddamned duck. We have seen the aftermath of abject horror of a racist buffoon careening our future off the road as if the dog was driving and we were all handcuffed. And in the spring of 2021, we are aghast at the reality the dog has left. On January six, we almost lost something: Hope. The siege and sedition attempted at the capitol was the shot across the bow that hit us between the eyes.

Although as costly and daunting as this crisis has been, it may have an unlikely silver lining. With the pandemic, we have seen how necessary a national healthcare system is, and we see how fragile the average American's financial status is—while the system finds a way for the billionaires to acquire yet more. But beyond that, many Whites, hopefully most, are finally seeing—dare I say admitting - the truth that undergirds the path that led us here: race … 'twas race that brought us Donald Trump.

In the early '80s, I initiated a holiday in Richmond to honor Dr. Martin Luther King Jr., two years before it became a national holiday. At the same time, I tried to work behind the scenes with White businessmen and other Black elected officials to address the Confederate statues on Monument Avenue. At that time, any attempt to remove or otherwise effect the context of those traitors, sitting high above the citizens of Richmond, was literally comical. Around 1984-85, before I became a polarizing figure for many Whites, I had good relationships with several White businesspeople. I would work with anybody if it were in Richmond's best interest, Black or White. I particularly remember one friend who was high in the Republican party of Richmond, a real "Reaganite." Jerry Waters was a political and business consultant who was not averse to compromise with a young Black politician, and he would help behind the scenes for me, even in futile attempts to bring folks into the conversation about Monument Avenue. Our politics were, of course, at odds. But we could agree to disagree and work with each other rationally, for the good of not some, but all. He could bend a little for me and I could for him.

There was a favor Jerry asked me once while we had lunch. He talked about the old home of Robert E. Lee on Franklin Street, today known as the Stewart-Lee House, and asked if I was familiar with the restaurant that was in its basement. As a tourist attraction, it opened to a patio and garden that stretched to the alley that ran between Seventh and Eighth streets. Jerry told me how that yard, 120 years earlier, was the home of Traveler, Lee's fabled horse. The yard had once held stables and hay, and the various horse tact used for travel—or battle. Jerry suggested a favor.

"What do you think the chances are you could get this alley named for Traveler?" I thought it was joke for a minute; alleys were rarely named, but it was not unheard of. The restaurant itself was named "Travelers" but that was the prerogative of the owners.

I thought about it for a minute: would naming it be an affirmation of the Confederacy? Or could it depend on how you saw the horse itself? I know many would say they could care less that the Confederates loved Traveler, and, therefore, we hate him.

However, Traveler was no more a racist slave owner than the slave that cared for him. In fact, I would be surprised if the slave caretaker didn't have a better relationship with that horse than General Lee did. Traveler, I believed then—and now—is poignantly symbolic of those who were the human-chattel Lee fought to maintain. On the backs of Blacks, the South rode its prosperity, and on the back of Traveler, it rode into war. It was not a quick decision, but I thought, *Why not acknowledge that horse?* And it was not just because Jerry asked me to, but because it was a creature forced into absolute service and danger for a master not of his choice.

In a sense, Traveler was just another slave; let's also remember him in that sense. Considering it was a small act that could bring a dividend to my quest—the big picture of Monument Avenue, and knowing with Jerry, favors went both ways, I agreed. I had the City law department draw up for the consent agenda a directive to name it "Traveler's Alley."

I remained diligent about removing the men from Monument Avenue into the '90s, but my colleagues believed it was the wrong time or a waste of time. The issue of Monument Avenue was my issue, including the Arthur Ashe Monument. And even years after I left City Hall, I continued the quest to remove, at the very least, Jefferson Davis. Alas, deaf ears occupied the powers that could change Richmond, and nothing changed. It would take the kick of the horse, if you will, to rid his back of Robert E. Lee, Stonewall Jackson, J.E.B Stewart and Jefferson Davis. It is Traveler's time.

In early June 2020, when the people of Richmond rose up and literally took that monument in their own hands, I felt a mixture of pride and unease. "The arc of the moral universe is long, but it bends toward justice," Dr. Martin Luther King, Jr., said. But the mentality of Jefferson Davis is still out there with its legacy, a legacy of brutality and civil war—and domestic terror. As much as right is on our side, persuasion should be the course before force. We are right—and they know it. Although, unfortunately, finding Republicans like Jerry Waters is much too rare, if found at all, today.

If the COVID virus pandemic has any positive impact on our country, it may be that people, particularly the young, are moved to cut through the bullshit. We have to do what is necessary to defeat it and save lives, and I pray for success. There is saying that "when America catches a cold, Black and brown people get the flu," and sure enough, they suffer disproportionate death and hardship with COVID-19. The blooming acknowledgement of what is coming to be known as "racial capitalism" has been the unspoken backbone of our story. Whether with health, housing, jobs, investment, schools, policing, incarceration, environmental toxicity, human services, you name it, the homicidal knee on our neck has been there. Pretending to ourselves to be blind of that fact allowed the dog to drive the car. Hopefully, the majority of America is "woke," ready to seize control of the car, to own up to its historical record, atone for it, and move forward. It is our only real hope and I pray for it.

The eight siblings, left to right: Ruth, Robert, Charles, Valerie, Rick, Chuck, Vicki, and Monte, seated.

I feel fortunate that my position and work was not in vain. Henry W. "Chuck" Richardson had a long and impactful arc in Richmond, which, I believe, bent toward justice. Though my life has been an open book over the last forty years, I'm certain that very few know what the "W" stands for in my name. Henry 'Wallace' was FDR's Vice-President during World War II. Wallace was a liberal progressive and civil rights advocate—much too supportive of African Americans. In the election of 1944, the Democratic party conspired and replaced Wallace for a more malleable Harry Truman as Vice-President to Roosevelt. It was an audacious move that would portend the impact of Southern White anger as the party's support of the "working man" included the Negro. And within twenty years, the Republicans used that cold and decisive American dynamic to flip the playing field, eventually nurturing that anger to yield a "Trump" card to attack the smallest remnants of Henry Wallace.

The Henry Wallace of Richmond in the '80s and early '90s was a target as well, not because of the demons of addiction he fought, but for the fight that was in him for the working man—and Black people. My father, Charles H. Richardson, was a working man, a Negro in 1948 that named his son for someone who fought for him! The fight continues. "Chuck" is just a nickname ... Councilman Chuck!

I'm sure many will think if I hadn't allowed myself to fall into the deep demise of drug use, breaking the law—though involuntarily—I wouldn't have to simply reflect today; that maybe had I been able to continue my fight through politics, I could have been there today to leap into action for the causes I believe so important.

I would be the first to acknowledge that drugs are bad, wrong, and will destroy your life. It was the one thing that was the most deterrent for a successful and thriving political career for me. I did not choose to become an addict, and I had no choice but to fight it. In 1994, there were 21,000 addicts in the Richmond Standard Metropolitan Statistical Area (SMSA). As just a former Vietnam veteran with

My children, grandchildren and great-grands with Poppa, 2019. From left behind me are: Zion, Karl Jr, Nichole, Nirvana, Kelsey, Karl, Stafford II, Katarina, Stafford, and Richardson. © Richmond Times Dispatch

a heroin addiction, and not a politician, I might have avoided the courts for years as many others have done. I would have been just another one of them: an addict allowed to indulge—until I killed myself. Considering that, maybe for all the controversial positions, beat-down arguments, disruptive confrontations, the good I did for the poor and needy, for the fight for what is right—for all my victories in political battles—maybe, maybe it was politics that *saved me!* Maybe one day, who knows, there might be another headline:

"Zorro Returns!"

About the Author

Chuck Richardson is a talented writer, artist, and speaker; however, he is best known as a true public servant to the residents of the City of Richmond where he served nineteen years on City Council. After returning from the Vietnam War with two Purple Hearts, he was elected among the historic first Black majority (5–4) Richmond City Council in 1977, and continues to be an outspoken voice of logic, justice, and humanity. He is the current president and co-founder of National Organization for Rehabilitated Offenders (NORO) assisting felons in the restoration of their rights.

In his spare time, he enjoys serving as a mentor to current or aspiring elected officials, playing golf, writing, sculpting, and, most importantly, spending time with his friends and family. He has seven siblings, two children, six grandchildren, three great-grandchildren, and his Pomeranian. He was married for thirty-six years to his middle-school sweetheart, Phyllis Johnson Richardson, who departed in 2006.

Mr. Richardson still lives in the West End of Richmond, Virginia, in the very same district that he served for nearly twenty years on the street named "Chuck Richardson Avenue."